ECONOMIC AND MANAGEMENT APPLICATIONS IN THE GLOBAL ECONOMY

ECONOMIC AND MANAGEMENT APPLICATIONS IN THE GLOBAL ECONOMY

Susiku Akapelwa

To order additional copies of this book, contact:
Xlibris Corporation
1-888-795-4274
www.Xlibris.com
Orders@Xlibris.com
77525

CONTENTS

PART 1: THE U.S. ENVIRONTMENT

PART 2: EMMERGING & "BRIC" NATIONS

PART 3: THE INTERNATIONAL ENVIRONMENT

PART 4: FINANCIAL ANALYSIS, ETHICS & ORGANIZATIONAL BEHAVIOR

Dedication

This book is dedicated to my dearest daughter Susiann with my heartfelt love. I am indebted and grateful to my parents & siblings. I extend many thanks and blessings to my extended family. You are all my key inspirational sources.

Memoriam

To my grandparents Mr. Akapelwa Simataa Ozease, Mrs. Muyunda Etambuyu Akapelwa, Mr. Ngula. My uncle, Dr. Kawana Akapelwa. My sisters', Ms. Nobula Akapelwa & Ms. Kekelwa Akapelwa. Ms. Christy Reynolds, a dear friend & loving mother. And last but not least, to all the departed loved ones. We carry the torch forward on your behalf.

Acknowledgements

I would like to extend special thanks to my publishing team, especially Dana Villarte and Jasmine Hedocil, for their patience, support, and teamwork demonstrated. To all readers, this humble work I dedicate.

Yours Truly,
Susiku Akapelwa

PREFACE

Economic and Management Applications in many respects is an offspring of my other book "International Management", indeed many readers familiar with the text will notice a few familiar themes echoed & reasserted in this book. The bulk of this book however draws on the broader macro-economic policy issues cognizant of the 2007-2009 global economic down-turns. The text also devotes considerable scrutiny to regulatory & statutory law. No man is an island in today's far reaching global economy. We live in an environment that is so interconnected in all facets. Business entities are no longer confined to local municipalities, regions or national boundaries, but rather are structured to operate on a global framework. The world is becoming more intertwined with diminishing economic boundaries and increasing transparent corridors of commerce. While the geographic boundaries may be clearly marked, the economic, cultural & business arena is fluid and wide open. Today's "New Global Economy" is a confluence of geographic, political, religion, cultural and economic forces. Intellectual capital is now spread across the globe, in today's environment technology & commerce are not constrained within borders but rather are very mobile and accessible.

ORGANIZATIONAL STRUCTURE

Part one of the text look's at the economic environment in the United States. In this section I offer an insight into the struggling U.S. economy between 2007 & 2009. I also draw attention to the mortgage and lending industry. The section also addresses labor relations. Part two transitions to Emerging nations & "BRIC" nations. The latter segment of part two largely looks at the Zambian transition from the Humanism ideology to the free market economic aspirations. Key economic indicators are looked at in this section as well. Part three is a bridge to the international environment drawing on international law principles and the overall international economy environment. The final segment encompasses general business practices and principles in a wider instructive & analytical scope.

CHAPTER I

THE U.S. ECONOMIC RECESSION

The overwhelming emphasis in this chapter is devoted to the underlying and fundamental issues driving the 2007-2009 U.S. economic down turn. Interpretation of whether an economy is in recession or not is often subjective, murky and in many respects is typically argued for or against under political persuasions. The core characteristics of a recession are transparent and usually uniform as they are supported by raw data, statistics and economic indicators which typically follow well established historic patterns & trends. Recessions are typically categorized by the traditional definition which entails two consecutive quarters of declining GDP. This is by no means the only measure, the National Bureau of Economic Research (NBER) for instance measures recessions as "a significant decline in economic activity spread across the economy" (see appendix 1). By this measure, the NBER had the U.S. economy entering into a recession in April 2007 and anticipated the recession lasting 14 months. If this prediction stands, it would make this one of the longest recessions dating back to the Great Depression of the 1930s. Invariably, the notion of whether an economy is in a recession or not is academic, the more significant issue is that we can all agree and see that the U.S. economy is in dire straits, reeling and bleeding. The U.S. is in the midst of a full blown three prong recession in my estimation. Phase one began early 2007 and was perpetuated by the housing market collapse, phase two began in the third quarter of 2007 with the credit squeeze & credit market disruption which was triggered by uncertainty in the financial markets. The third phase began the first quarter of 2008 & has been characterized by market failures in the financial sector which were brought about by high exposure to toxic mortgage instruments by banks, particularly Investment banks on Wall Street. As the recession matures, GDP will invariably trickle to a halt with the worst case scenario being a spillover into a depression. It indeed would be unwise for anyone not exercise foresight, caution and seek mitigation remedies.

1.0 BACKGROUND

The U.S. economy is commonly referred to as the world's driving engine, we all have heard of the saying, when the U.S. economy sneezes, the whole global economy catches a cold. While this may have held true for many years, this notion more and more seems suspect at the very least. The current U.S. economic slowdown has been stunning, the 2007 overall growth rate was a dismal 2.2%, the weakest rate since 2002 when the U.S. economy was just emerging from an earlier recession. The U.S. Department of Commerce figures state between July and September, the economy was growing at an annual rate of 4.9%, however the rate of growth between October to December was a meager 0.6%. Experts are pessimistic for the future outlook and project the growth rate in 2008 to hover around 0.8%-1%. A former Federal Reserve chairman in an interview characterized the current U.S. woes as the worst credit crisis in the last 50 years. The United States has had ten recessions since World War II with the typical recession (if there is such a thing) lasting between 8-16 months. On average, recessions account for a 2% decline in gross domestic product within the economy. By and large the most brutal of these recessions (aside the great depression) would have to be the 1973-1975 slow-downs due to the Arab oil crisis. The following chart illustrates the economic growth trends in the U.S. from 2004-2008

FIGURE 1: QUARTER TO QUARTER GROWTH IN REAL GDP

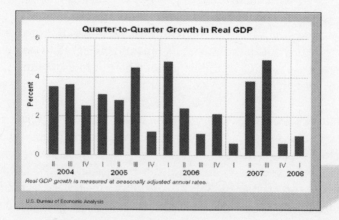

Source: U.S. Bureau of Economic Analysis [1]

1.1 CONSUMER SPENDING

The U.S. economy to a large extent is driven by consumer spending often referred to as the engine of the economy & accounting for two thirds of GDP. This trend of relying on discretionary consumer spending to sustain the economy has become more prominent in the last 10-15 years which by its own merits is an unsettling trend. As consumers have continued to pull back on their spending, the results have been rather troublesome to retailers. Housing prices have also been experiencing a free fall with an average nationwide decline of 8 percent and as much as 40 percent in some markets. Unemployment rates have also been climbing, in December 2007, the unemployment rate rose to a two year high of 5% and is now creeping within a few points of the 7 percent mark which would mean the highest rate in over 16 years and more significantly translates into 3 million Americans without a job. Amid all these gloomy conditions, (job worries, high gas prices, high energy prices, foreclosures, increased credit card delinquencies, etc), consumer confidence has suffered and taken a beating, according to the RBC index [2] consumer confidence is at its lowest level in six years. As the U.S. economy has suffered losses in manufacturing to overseas competitors in South America, Asia, etc and migrated service employment such as call centers to India, the economy has increasingly come to rely on consumer spending.

Another consequence of the economic slowdown is that, as more people are starting to feel the pinch, it is becoming harder for consumers to keep up with the bills. In fact, AT & T a large U.S. telecommunications company reported that it was disconnecting more customer telephone accounts recently due to delinquencies. American Express Company a highly renowned blue chip financial services company which generally has a customer base of affluent customers stated that it was projecting reduced spending and more delinquencies for 2008, delinquency rates rose 29 basis points to 3.71% in August, while the default rate rose 51 basis points to 6.14% according to an American Banker report. In October 2008, the company had its highest monthly increase in credit card delinquencies on record as jobless claims rose according to FBIR Capital Markets. A basis point is 0.01 percentage point. American Express is not alone, throughout the industry, credit card issuing companies are being battered by rising delinquencies as unemployment claims rise. Bank of America Corp Chief Executive Kenneth Lewis forecast record losses for the credit card industry. U.S. card losses are expected to increase to 7.95 percent in 2009 from 6.35 percent in 2008 according to Goldman Sachs Group. The overall credit card losses will rise by 25 percent in 2009 as unemployment climbs and customers are unable to pay their credit card bills. Some have already raised the alarm bells suggesting the credit card industry is the next domino to tumble. The arguments are compelling, the credit card industry has traditionally been able to weather the storm by compensating the short-comings via late fee or over limit fee adjustment and so forth. However, now they are confronted with rising unemployment where consumers simply stop paying due to inability, this translates to record losses for the credit card industry. The parallels are eerily similar to the subprime mortgage meltdown which represented about $900 billion in questionable securitized debt. The credit card industry has about $915 billion in outstanding debt. This slow down has hit all ranks, the affluent as well as the working class, everyone is tightening the belt as food costs rise, gas prices skyrocket, energy prices are also rising and the list goes on. Amidst all these rising consumer prices, income levels on the other hand have remained flat, thus the dollar is being stretched to its limits until a snapping point is reached. When consumers reach what I phrase the "snapping point" they start seriously prioritizing their bills, paying necessities first and whatever they cannot payoff they dump on their credit cards, eventually their credit cards become exhausted, at this juncture consumers start juggling bills until the juggling act is unmanageable and catches up with them and thus the onset of delinquencies.

1.2 SUBPRIME CRISIS

The elephant in the room here is clearly the subprime mortgage industry collapse, this $1.3 trillion market sector saw a monumental debacle beyond conception. In brief, the subprime market is the segment of the mortgage industry that dedicated itself on extending home mortgage loans to borrowers with poor credit histories who otherwise would not meet the minimum requirements to qualify for a conventional mortgage instrument. According to the Mortgage Bankers Association [3], subprime borrowers are likely to default on their loans at a rate of five times more than borrowers with good credit histories. Naturally, because of the clientele at play, the risk exposure was magnified. In the short-term, the subprime market sustained under the radar and the industry flourished realizing a huge boom we all came to know as the "housing market boom". Inevitably, the boom was destined to collapse, economist's in fact point to what is known as a "stopgap measure" as to what sustains questionable booms in the short run. Similar to holding a leak with a bandage, it works in the short run but inevitably the floodgates burst wide open. In essence, the housing boom sustained and maintained the subprime market, however as interests rates continued to increase over a two year period, it became difficult and in many cases downright impossible for borrowers to keep up or let alone afford their monthly mortgage payments which in turn led to mortgage defaults and the onset of the "subprime" collapse and the resulting credit woes. Home owners found themselves with negative home equity where they owed more than what their house was worth, faced with this scenario, homeowners make the difficult decision to wash their hands and walk away from their homes. Foreclosure rates as a result go up and banks find themselves with excess homes on the market and subsequently begin losing money as home prices continue to decline and thus the synopsis of the mortgage squeeze.

States such as Florida, California, Nevada and Texas were especially hard hit with high foreclosure rates. South Florida in particular was at the epicenter of upside-down mortgages or what has come to be termed as underwater borrowers. An analysis conducted by First American Core Logic had the combined South Florida (Broward, Miami-Dade & Palm Beach counties) homeowners owing $62.7 billion more than what their homes were worth as of September 2009. Homeowners who bought homes in 2006 were registering a median negative equity of $75,000 while the figure in Miami-Dade county was pegged at $63,000 according to web based real-estate outfit Zillow. com. These are frighteningly high numbers and have greatly manifested into increased foreclosures or strategic defaults, a phenomenon where homeowners simply stop making their mortgage payment obligations and ride it out as long as they can until they are thrown out of their homes. In the fourth quarter of 2008, strategic defaults represented about 28% of defaults in South Florida according to an Experian-Oliver Wyman consumer report.

During the inflated home boom, many homeowners practically used their homes as cash machines when faced with any financial constraint. Between 2001 and 2006, homeowners cashed over $1.2 trillion against their home equity. According to Business Week [4] the average debt to income ratio for middle class Americans is now 141%, which is double since 1983. Consumer Credit Counseling Service of San Francisco [5] states that the average balances for people seeking credit help jumped from $14,000 to $27,000 in 2007.

To put it context, it is worthwhile to have a brief comprehension of how the subprime market works in the underbelly. The subprime market is composed of three main players; investors who put up or front the cash to set the ball rolling, mortgage servicing outfits who are the middlemen or bridge between the investors and the borrowers make up the third party of the component. Moody's [6] Investors Services estimates around sixteen major mortgage servicing companies' account for 80% of all sub-prime loans. In most cases, mortgages are originated by a single financial institution. The mortgages are then bundled into packages then pooled and sold to investors in the form of securities. The subprime equation begins with a group of investors who provide the financial resources to buy these mortgage portfolios, the investor's contract with a mortgage service provider who assumes the responsibility of managing these portfolios, collecting monthly payments, effectively satisfying and protecting the interests of investors. If the homeowner does not make their home payment, the servicing company absorbs that loss and still has to pay the investors on the backend. To make up and compensate for gaps like this, servicing companies will charge delinquency fees on the front end and may refinance loans, re-write or restructure loan terms and as a last resort may move to foreclosure, sell the property, recoup its share and pay the investor. Mortgage servicing companies make their money by charging investors monthly service fees on monthly payment collected, generally about 0.5%.

One of the biggest casualties of the subprime collapse undoubtedly is Citigroup, the largest financial institution in the U.S. with a global presence in over 100 countries. Traditionally, Citigroup was a deposit lending institution with a lesser role in the business of originating and servicing mortgages via its consumer banking division. Things were business as usual at Citigroup, however things would take a dramatic and drastic turn when the investment banking division of Citigroup bought a company called ACC Capital which was deep to its head in the subprime mortgage business. Citigroup investment bankers were convinced this was a prudent strategy and based their rationale on the premise that by getting full-scale in this arena, it would compliment its existing mortgage securitization wing. This strategy by the investment bankers would have catastrophic consequences and implications. The decision to diversify into these complicated security housing bonds was ill advised in retrospect. To be fair to Citigroup, many of these mortgage bonds were rated triple (AAA) by rating agencies, so from the outset, such bonds could be perceived as good investments. However, when the housing market imploded and home prices collapsed, it effectively made such bonds junk & worthless. So for companies like Citigroup that were heavily leveraged in such instruments, the consequences were punishing. Citigroup in part places blame on the rating agencies for over inflating the value of the bonds but ultimately the finger comes back to Citigroup risk managers for not conducting sufficient risk analysis and stress tests on these bond instruments. To put it in context of what Citigroup was dealing with, consider these numbers from the Mortgage Bankers Association [7], at the end of December, Citibank had a loan portfolio of about 280,000 and of these, about 16.4% or about 46,000 where in default (two or more months past due). Not a very good outlook from a business standpoint.

1.3 CREDIT SQUEEZE

The mortgage crisis has manifested many unintended consequences, one such result being a tightening of credit availability by lenders. This began in the third quarter of 2007 as the effects of the crisis dug-in, underwriters in lending institutions begun closely scrutinizing who they were giving access to funds by combing through financial documents, credit scores and so forth. Credit card issuing companies also got proactive and started weeding out risky borrowers with poor credit scores, bad payment histories, negative derogative records, high debt to credit ratios etc. Borrowers who fell into this category had their credit lines reduced or in adverse circumstances had their accounts cancelled. The credit squeeze will undoubtedly have a direct impact on economic growth levels, however a bigger implication or fear of the credit squeeze is a phenomenon called the "Negative Feedback Loop". This circumstance refers to the inverse relationship between financial markets and the real economy. In this relationship, tighter liquidity measures imposed by lenders result in lower asset values, distorted capital markets, reduced credit supply and ultimately fosters mistrust between the borrowers and lenders. To circumvent the punishing hardships, lenders in turn pass along the cost to borrowers through higher interest rates which subsequently result in increased delinquencies which invariably come back to roost and burden the lenders. This in a nutshell is the "negative feedback loop", a vicious cycle.

The second outcome of the credit squeeze is a situation called the "Debt-Deflation Spiral". Many will indeed remember this nasty circumstance from the Japanese economic crisis in the 1980's. This essentially is a scenario where there is an increased level of savings in times of distress by consumers as they are surrounded by paranoia, uncertainty, job fears, difficult access to credit and so forth. Subjected to all these constraints, consumer's naturally horde nickels and dimes which results in lower prices and an increased burden on debt.

1.4 WALL STREET & THE SPECULATIVE HOUSING BUBBLE

Wall Street never blinks or misses an opportunity to make a buck and the subprime market provided a perfect goldmine. Traditionally, mortgages were overwhelmingly underwritten through in-house settings by banks and lending institutions, this arrangement meant the loans were kept internally on the institutions books. Due to this accountability on the balance sheet, most granting lenders were very prudent and stringent as to who loans were issued. After the 2000 deregulation and liberalization of the mortgage industry, the parameters and the playing field changed, opportunists with dollar signs in their mind smelled and sensed a perfect opening. Many Investment Banks & Securities firms inserted themselves into the sub-prime mortgage business and it's no surprise that as of 2008, only two out of the five major investments banks are still in existence. (Goldman Sachs Group Inc. & Morgan Stanley). Unlike traditional commercial banks which are subject to heavy government regulation, investments banks have less stringent regulation since they do not hold consumer bank deposits. One can argue that the lax regulation in many respects played a major role with the sub-prime debacle. Many observers also point to the elimination of the Glass-Steagall Act as a major contributing factor to the sub-prime meltdown. The Glass-Steagall Act was a Depression era law that prevented commercial banks from doing investment banking business, the law was repealed in 1999 and opened the floodgates. The "house" in American society as in many societies is much endeared and in many cases owning a home for many represents the quintessential "American dream". Recognizing the fact that the "house" in many respects represents the biggest financial investment to many, Wall Street financial gurus concocted a convoluted way to cash-in. The premise was seemingly simple on the outer edges, basically pool loans and sell them on the open market.

Wall Street created a market of over $2 trillion in securities backed by mortgages according to the Wall Street Journal [8]. Wall Street essentially convinced lending underwriters that they could repackage mortgages into securities that could be traded in the same fashion as bonds. The large traditional underwriting lenders were convinced this deal was to sweet to pass up on, the financial lenders were able to sell-off mortgages and dispose them from their books, for many originating loan lenders, it was a good way to wash their hands off the responsibility of these loans. All was dandy as home prices kept skyrocketing and credit accessibility was made seamless. Wall Street firms were making their cut by earning a percentage of about 1% on securities they underwrote. The reasoning and selling point from the Wall Street gurus was that since the home constituted a major investment of value in one's life, people will always do whatever it takes to pay-off their mortgage, always paid first before all other debts, the other premise and contention was the assumption that home prices would always continue to rise therefore making for a win-win scenario, this assumption as we now know in hindsight would have catastrophic consequences, in contrast the opposite outcome would manifest as home prices plummeted.

FIGURE 1.1 U.S. HOME PRICES

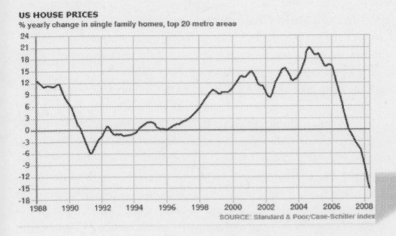

Source: Standard & Poor/Case-Schiller index

The traditional mortgage loan arrangement from in-house lending originators was now shifted to this new ingenious securitization scheme. Under this arrangement, loans were packaged into over 10,000 loan pools and sold to thousands of investors on the global market. The investors that purchased these loans would further slice and dice the loan portfolios and resale them to other investors., these repackaged loan instruments were referred to as Structural Investment Vehicles (SIV's) and Collateralized Debt Obligations (CDO's). This strategy saw the subprime industry explode from $160 billion in 2001 (7.2% of new mortgages) to $600 billion in 2006 (20.6% of new mortgages) according to Inside Mortgage Finance [10], clearly a phenomenal leap by any measure, this in essence was the forbearer to the home market boom. Amongst the largest underwriters of CDO's were Merrill Lynch and Citigroup. SIV's and CDOs in effect were used by banks and other lending institutions as hedge funds, the banks were betting or speculating on bad mortgage instruments and to further compound to the dilemma, the institutions added speculative value as assets to their books.

Wall Street financers and bankers alike in principle gave mortgage brokers the assurance that their assets would not fail through what came to be known as "credit default swaps", which essentially implied the loans were insured, the masterminds were careful not to implicitly use the word "insurance backed loans" since such loans are government regulated and backed. They could by-pass this sticking point by utilizing instruments such as credit default swaps which are unregulated and offer great leverage. The credit default swap in effect was the collateral backing these loans, one can relate this to junk bonds. A slight variation called "credit derivatives" was also used by investors to hedge credit risk. In principal, the mortgage originators passed the bulk of the repayment risk to investors through the use of these mortgaged backed securities.

Many attribute the problems with Wall Street & Sub-Prime mortgages largely due to relaxation of U.S. regulation when the mortgage industry was deregulated which saw many brokerage and investment banks thrust themselves in the business. Traditional banks that typically underwrote mortgages were heavily regulated and that created a lot of oversight fiscal responsibility, Investment banks on the other hand did not fall under the same regulations by Federal authorities, so when they entered the mortgage market, they were able to cut a lot of corners and devise all sorts gimmicks under the radar. Many fault the elimination of the "Uptick Rule" by the Securities and Exchange Commission (SEC) which was a rule that regulated short selling as a major contributor to the financial meltdown. In the absence of the Uptick rule, a loophole in the practice of short-selling of financial shares was exposed. Short selling is a practice where investors bet or hedge that prices will decline. Many hedge funds were very active in the trading of derivatives such as Credit Default Swaps which ignited the sub-prime debacle. Such derivatives are not traded on the open market, therefore unlike regular stocks on the open market, they lack transparency, are very complex & unregulated. The Securities and Exchange Commission (SEC) faced by pressure under the recent financial market turmoil has stepped up scrutiny of such instruments. The distinction between commercial banks and investment banks stems from the depression era, during the depression the U.S. congress separated commercial banks which take deposits & offer loans from investment banks which handle the underwriting and trading of securities. However, this distinct separation of turf changed after the U.S. Congress in 1999 repealed the depression era laws which opened the flood gates for investment banks to enter the mortgage arena, at the crest of the home market boom, investment banks were borrowing $32 to $1 of their assets.

TABLE 1.2
MAIN SUBPRIME MORTGAGE COLLAPSE CASAULTIES

COMPANY NAME	LOSSES (billions usd)
Citigroup	$18 billion
USB	$13.5 billion

Morgan Stanley	$9.4 billion
Merrill Lynch	$8 billion
HSBC	$3.4 billion
Bear Stearns	$3.2 billion
Deutsche Bank	$3.2 billion
Bank of America	$ 3 billion
Barclays	$ 2.6 billion
Royal Bank of Scotland	$2.6 billion
Freddie Mac	$2 billion
Credit Suisse	$1 billion
Wachovia	$1.1 billion
IKB	$2.6 billion

Source: Company Reports [11]

WALL STREET & THE FINANCIAL MARKETS MELTDOWN

March 16: BEAR STERNS

A once mighty titan on Wall Street finally circumb to the plague of what has come to be known as "toxic subprime loans. Faced with high exposure of bad risky mortgage backed loans on its books, the weight was too much to contend with and the company was under collapse until the Federal Reserve on March, 16 2008 stepped in with a rescue plan. The Federal Reserve facilitated an extension guarantee of $29 billion in order to persuade J.P. Morgan Chase to buy Bear Sterns, the acquisition did eventually go forward.

July 11: INDY MAC

The large mortgage company under the strain of the housing crisis failed to meet its minimum required holding reserves. Federal regulators took control of the bank on July 11, 2008, the company subsequently filed for bankruptcy. At the time of Federal seizure, the bank had $32 billion in assets.

September 6: FANNIE MAE & FREDDIE MAC

The nation's two largest mortgage finance companies like many others in the industry were not spared the fallout precipitated by the sub-prime meltdown, in September 2008, the two entities were the latest to be bailed out by the Federal Government. On September 6, 2008, Federal Reserve effectively seized the companies under a government conservatorship Rather than allow the companies to fail under bankruptcy. The government in justifying it's action felt allowing the companies to collapse would have more devastating effects to consumers as they would not be able to get residential, auto & a host of other loans. It's yet another unusual and troubling approach of government interfering with the free-market system as opposed to letting the markets self correct. The rational from government authorities is the same as in the Bear Sterns, Citigroup and AIG bailouts, i.e. allowing a failure of these titanic entities would have catastrophic consequences for the economy, a question of opportunity cost at the highest unprecedented scope. These market interventions and bailouts are historic by any measure. The bailout plan is complicated as such arrangements always are, essentially, the government will replace the top management brass, handover control of the company to Federal regulators. The Treasury Department will inject approximately $100 billion to each company by acquiring preferred stock allowing the companies to have operating capital to meet short term obligations. The government will also assume responsibility of the trillion dollars of debt. A host of other stipulations are contained in the plan including the freezing of dividend payments to stockholders. The short-term implications of this move are unclear, investors who are shareholders may see a bump in the stock price following the news. Taxpayers will unlikely know how much this will ultimately cost them as future housing prices & mortgage default rates will bear the true cost. Consumers might be the biggest beneficiaries in the immediate future as such a move spurs low interest rates since the markets are reassured.

September 14: LEHMAN BROTHERS HOLDINGS INC

The 158 year old blue chip premier investment bank finally gave in to the web of the sub-prime crisis as it entered bankruptcy reorganization proceedings on September 14, 2008. A segment of its business unit was purchased by Barclays bank for $1.75 billion. Barclays was careful in securing only the large fixed income segment and staying away from the real estate assets which drove

Lehman into bankruptcy. The acquisition by Barclays may salvage some 8000 jobs. Lehman filed for Chapter 11 protection in the U.S. Bankruptcy Court for the Southern District of New York in September 2008. With over $630 billion in assets, this bankruptcy filing represented the largest in U.S. history far surpassing the Enron debacle. Lehman is as Wall Street as they come. The company was founded in 1850 and went public on the New York Stock Exchange in 1994

September 15: MERRILL LYNCH

Faced with plummeting stock values, Merrill Lynch a prominent Wall Street brokerage house was yet another victim done in by the housing market collapse. The sub-prime market failure cost the company over $45 billion in 2007 according to a New York Times report. The writing was clear on the wall, rather than wait for the inevitable, the company offered itself for sale on September 15, 2008 and was quickly scooped up by Bank of America at a bargain price of $29 a share considering a year earlier the share price was $78 according to Dow Jones reports.

September 16: AMERICAN INTERNATIONAL GROUP (AIG)

AIG is one of the world's largest insurance related companies and this segment represents the core of the company's activity. The company is however very heavily diversified with it's tentacles in all directions and in fact the nature of it's demise had nothing to do with it's mainstay insurance business but rather stemmed from it's financial products unit which was heavily involved in the trading of credit default swap contracts which took a beating with the housing mortgage debacle and eventually took down anyone within reach. Credit Default Swaps (CDS) are primarily insurance contracts against default on mortgage loans; AIG had vested and written CDS on huge volumes of mortgage securities. So when the home market was distressed, AIG was obligated to pay for investor losses on these instruments. As the housing market collapsed, the value of the of the credit default contracts it had on it's books dropped drastically becoming almost worthless, the company was then forced to borrow against it's assets in order to raise cash to cover the losses. The losses from these contracts resulted in $18 billion in losses over three quarters, which eventually overwhelmed the company and took it under like the fate of many involved in credit default swap contracts.

WASHINGTON MUTUAL

The Seattle, Washington based financial institution was not spared the brutal knockout punch of the sub-prime crisis. WAMU was the largest Savings and Loan bank in the U.S. and sixth largest bank in the U.S. The company was founded in 1889 and as of September 2008 had over 43,000 employees & $309.7 billion in assets. The bank has 700 branches in California and 2,300 nationwide. The bank in September 2008, (a month many on Wall Street pray for temporary amnesia) like so many other victims solicited itself up for purchase. WAMU like many afflicted with the mortgage crisis saw its stock price decline 13%, it lost $3.3 billion in the second quarter of 2008 due to bad sub-prime mortgages. WAMU's problems were exacerbated by its high exposure to "pay-option adjustable rate mortgages, these are loans that initially allow borrowers to make very small minimal monthly payments, then reset at higher rate a few years later, often referred to as balloon loans. These loans are typically packaged and targeted toward the riskiest borrowers by coaxing & reeling them in with the low introductory rates. According to a LA Times report. $52.9 billion of WAMU's $181.5 billion single family mortgage were pay option adjustable rate mortgages. So naturally, when the sub-prime meltdown manifested, the gamble WAMU took exploded in their face. As of September 15, 2008, WAMU's stock closed at $2 per share, 95% off its 52 week high according to a Washington Post report. WAMU with recorded assets of $310 billion was eventually seized by the Federal Deposit Insurance Corporation (FDIC), the biggest bank failure in U.S. history. The FDIC is a federal agency that insures bank deposits against bank failures. WAMU was heavily invested in bad mortgage loans, so when the home market collapsed and borrowers went into default and stopped paying, the strain was too much for WAMU to withstand. Faced by heavy pressure from FDIC to liquidate, WAMU was purchased by J.P. Morgan Chase bank for $1.9 billion at the tail end of September, 2008. The buyout included a plan for J.P. Morgan Chase to write-down approximately $31 billion and make available $8 billion in common stock sale offering as a way of raising capital. This is the second major acquisition by J.P. Morgan Chase in six months since it bought Bear Sterns in March.

MORGAN STANLEY

The Investment bank founded in 1935 and headquartered in New York with over 46,000 employees and over $1 trillion in assets saw its share value drop 46% through the course of 2008, the bank is reportedly exploring possible merger alternatives according to media accounts. The bank also changed its status from strictly being an Investment bank to becoming a bank holding company which allows it to accept deposits from investors, a measure taken to facilitate more ways of raising capital. The change in status also means the bank will be subject to more intense scrutiny by regulators and the Federal Reserve, the heavy regulation is in place to protect consumer deposits, a luxury Investment banks have.

1.5 EMPLOYMENT SECTOR EFFECT

Depending on the nature and extent of the economic downturn, the employment sector usually is not spared from the forces at play. In January 2008, the U.S. Labor Department [12] reported the U.S. economy experienced 17,000 non-farm job losses, this was the first monthly loss recorded since August 2003. The biggest losses were recorded in the manufacturing and residential-construction industry. In contrast, wall-street economists were forecasting and projecting the economy would add over 75,000 during the same period. The national unemployment rate was down to 4.9% and amid all this uncomfortable & unsettling news, the U.S. national economic growth rate shrunk to an abysmal 0.6% annual fourth quarter rate compared to a rate of 4.9% in the previous quarter. The numbers for march 2008 were not any better, non-farm payrolls fell by 80,000 jobs The manufacturing sector has had its share of problems, it's been especially hit hard as a direct "cause & effect" correlation to the housing slump, as home prices and subsequent sales have continued to fall, construction of new homes has drastically diminished. The U.S. Labor Department reported that the construction industry had lost 284,000 jobs since a high mark reached in September 2007. In January 2008, the construction industry lost 27,000 jobs. Conversely, spending in the construction sector fell by a record of 2.6% in 2007, a far cry from the 5.3% increase in 2006. Consequently, the unemployment rate rose to 5.3%, the highest rate increase in 3 years. In November 2008, the Labor Department reported claims for unemployment benefits jumped to a 16-year high. Employees who are laid off are eligible for employment benefits but those who are fired or quit are exempt from receiving benefits. The unemployment rate for 2008 is anticipated to reach 7 % and top 8% in 2009.

FIGURE 1.3 U.S. UNEMPLOYMENT RATE

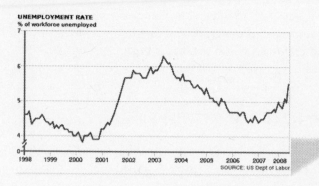

Source: U.S. Department of Labor [13]

1.6 INFLATIONARY FORCES

The economy is feeling the strain of the high oil and energy prices, while incomes for the most part have remained constant and flat the last few years, the opposite can be said for the other intangibles. Oil prices have surpassed $119 per barrel, home heating energy costs are off the roof, home rental prices are up and clearly the picture is skewed with little optimism. The Federal authorities have somewhat underplayed this variable, but this to me seems to be a gross miscalculation, the sound alarm inflation mark is crossing the 2% mark and over the last five years this mark has been routinely passed.

FIGURE 1.4 U.S. INFLATION RATE

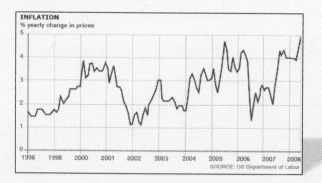

Data source: U.S. Department of Labor [14]

1.7 CRUDE OIL PRICE RECORD HIGHS AND BROADER IMPLICATIONS

The price of crude oil on April 22, 2008 was trading at $119.39 per barrel on the New York Mercantile Exchange, unbelievable by any measure but such is what we are confronted with in this age. This development has had punishing effects on the U.S. economy, possibly the most devastating effect behind the mortgage crisis. The effects of the high crude oil prices is essentially two-tier, one can recognize the effects on the consumer level and the effects on the business sector. The three main factors driving oil prices in the U.S. are: Demand & Supply (upward pressure), declining dollar value and the role of speculators. These by far are not the only factors driving oil prices, other external & global forces play a crucial role as well, below is a brief summation of the main drivers to the global oil price spike.

FIGURE 1.5 CRUDE OIL FUTURES

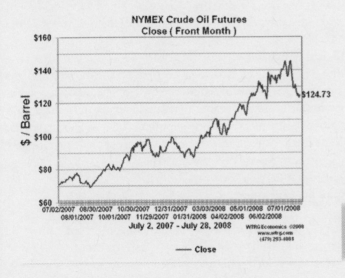

Global oil demand & supply market disparities

The overall global demand for oil has grown by leaps and bounds as economies across the globe continue to expand. Global consumption across the globe has increased by over 3 million barrels a day since 2005. While the U.S. continues to be the world's largest consumer of oil, other major players are rapidly emerging and rapidly fueling an upward pressure on demand. The two principle culprits fueling this upsurge as one would expect are China and India which are experiencing rapid economic expansion.

U.S. Dollar decline

- The sustained decline of the value of the dollar also plays a role particularly since oil is traded in dollars.

Role of oil commodity speculators

- The explosion of market speculators in the oil trading market is a factor in the sky high commodity prices. By virtue of their business, speculators are betting on futures market that prices will increase which observers contend artificially balloons the true value of oil and forces prices in a sustained increase. The role of U.S. trading speculators has received wide scrutiny in the U.S. as many consumers blame these traders for price manipulation by over inflating market prices, the concern is so grave it's a recurring debate in the U.S. presidential campaign and legislators threatening to hold hearings.

Oil supply and political concerns

- The irony of the oil crisis lies in where the bulk of the oil comes from, most of the suppliers are in volatile places where political shake up's affects the global price of oil. Major suppliers such as Saudi Arabia, Iran, Iraq, Venezuela, Nigeria and Angola share tense political climates which only plays into the market insecurities.

Effect of the oil spike on consumers

As oil prices surpass the $140 mark per barrel, consumers are being hit where it hurts the most, their wallets. In a society where commuting is a way of life, this development for many has naturally been devastating, the paycheck is not covering as much terrain as what most consumers are accustomed to, the paycheck has been stretched to breaking points. Unfortunately, it is hard if not impossible to escape the grips of the gas price strangle hold; people need to drive to work, drive to the grocery store, shuttle the kids around, and so forth. For many, it is merely impractical to park the car and walk or cycle 30 miles to work, while measures are out there such as hybrid fuel efficient vehicles, such options still are beyond the reach of many and simply out of consideration.

Business sector effect of oil price spike

On the business end, airlines by far have bared the brunt of the high fuel prices. Jet fuel prices have more than doubled since 2007, faced with such sky rocketing prices, U.S. airline carriers have posted over $1 billion losses for the first quarter of 2008. All the top 5 U.S. carriers posted losses in the first quarter of 2008. The losses across the industry have been astounding, according to a news report by the Washington Post:

UAL, the parent company of United Airlines reported a loss of $537 million in the first quarter of 2008. AMR, the parent of American Airlines reported a $328 million loss in the first quarter as well during 2008. United has also announced job cuts of 500 workers across the board, it also reported its shares dropped a third of it's value with share prices dropping $7.88 to $13.55 due to lack of investor confidence, this according to a Chicago Sun Times report. [16] Continental Airlines posted an $80 million first quarter loss, Air Tran registered $34.8 million or 38 cents per share in losses, while Jet Blue posted a loss of $8 million in the first quarter as well.

The woes continue, Northwest airways reported a $191 million or 73 cents per share loss and blamed high jet fuel as playing a major contributing factor, similarly, Delta airways, the U.S. third largest carrier also attributed high fuel costs to it's $274 million or 69 cents a share first quarter loss. Within all this turmoil, Delta which just emerged from bankruptcy a year ago announced a buyout of Northwest to form what will be the world's largest airline. My opinion on this move is skeptical at best, a little too ambitious, Delta has too much baggage and issues to take up a venture of this magnitude.

The high fuel costs will trickle down to the consumers as airlines will have to raise fares in order to offset these costs. Since airlines by law are prohibited to signal fare changes in advance, airlines will circumvent this obstacle by reducing the availability of seats, airlines do this by parking older planes with higher operational costs and decrease less profitable regional routes. The higher air fares are already apparent, in the 4th quarter, U.S. airfares rose 4% which according to the U.S. Department of Transportation Bureau of Transportation statistics [17] was the highest quarterly increase in six years. Airlines are also resorting to charging extra for itinerary changes, baggage fees and so forth. Another inevitable consequence will be resulting job cuts to curb costs. Sadly, some airlines will not be able to survive this setback particularly the small regional discount carriers, such outfits will very likely be forced to close their operations. So the effects will be felt from top to bottom. The airline CEO's to their defense in congressional hearings contend that they do not control market conditions, they point out that price is determined by consumer search engines and also raise the point that in addition to high fuel costs, what is being overlooked are the currency attributes. U.S. carriers insist that due the decline of the dollar, jet refinery costs are not being accounted for. U.S. refining costs are at $30 which when compared to European carriers set's them at a disadvantage, $80 aggregate for European carriers vs., $150 for U.S. carriers.

1.8 THE CHINA IMPACT

The dawn of the new global superpower vis-à-vis "China" has been a double edged sword for the United States, on one hand China as today's world factory is good to the U.S. economy because it provides cheap goods to the U.S. consumer which in turn boosts the U.S. consumer confidence & spending. The drawback to this situation is the loss of the manufacturing sector. Another underlying and unintended consequence of this dynamic lies in the fact that China has become increasingly wealthy due to this arrangement, increased wealth has meant that there is a larger supply of U.S. dollars in circulation across the global market, which in turn has manifested the collapse of the dollar exchange rate further exacerbating the strain on the U.S. economy.

A new development of China's growth is that China is becoming less and less dependent on exports to the U.S. for it's survival, instead as China becomes more and more wealthy, a new middle-class consumer demand segment has emerged. China is now focusing on this rapidly growing market to the effect that they can withstand the U.S. recession, its all in the numbers and inevitable 250 million U.S. consumers vs. 1.3 billion Chinese consumers.

1.9 DOTCOM AFTERMATH

In the last few years, the economy has struggled to maintain and sustain consistent positive economic performance since the heydays of the 1990's high-tech boom, it's been a bumpy road since that period. This boom period was followed by the "bubble bust" or dot-com bust. The markets suffered a great deal, however they were able to recover as a result of monetary fiscal policy intervention which adjusted and reduced interest rates. Indeed we saw that the dot.com bubble bust was accompanied by an economic down-turn that was followed by a brief reprise of stability.

1.10 CURRENCY FLACUTATIONS

The U.S. Dollar (USD) has continued to struggle with major currencies and has been in a downward spiral against the major currencies as confidence in the U.S. market globally is skeptical.

FIGURE 1.6 EURO V. DOLLAR

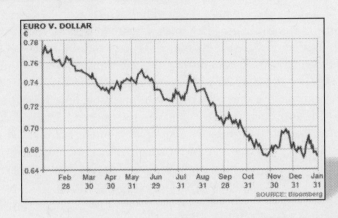

[18] Bloomberg

1.11 POST 911 CONSEQUENSES

The 911 economic scares were mitigated with fiscal policy short-term measures which utilized Federal Reserve interest cuts and government mandated tax rebates intended to stimulate consumer spending. Now in 2008 we find ourselves in the mist of the mortgage lending collapse, Wall Street wild gyrations and a weak dollar on the global market amongst other factors.

1.12 BROADER SLOWDOWN CATALYSTS

Without question or dispute, the subprime mortgage collapse was the spark that lighted the fire, from an economist viewpoint, risk was being inappropriately priced, lending structures were too liberal and Asset managers took on too much risk than they could handle (got too greedy) However, economic downturns always have underlying factors that operate in the sidelines but non-the less have significant indirect consequences. In the following section we look at a few such factors at play.

Business Cycle Fluctuations

Critics who loath the notion of a recession and are often cynical of slowdowns take the view of cyclical trends. They down-play economic slowdowns and view them as mere mild speed bumps which are inherent to an economy as normal business cycles. They further contend that business cycle fluctuations are in fact healthy for the economy as every recession spawns new business opportunities. For instance, during this current economic crunch, the value of the U.S. dollar has declined drastically against the British Pound, they would argue that this trend would spawn a mini-export boom as exports of U.S. manufactured products become cheaper to export to Europe thus creating an opening for a cottage industry. Another argument follows that it's been over 8 years since the U.S. experienced a capital turmoil and therefore only natural that the economy is going through a slowdown as part of inherent business cycles.

Global Imbalances & Strong global performance

Imbalances across the globe lend a hand to the economic outlook, the main imbalance as expected lies with China. The Chinese economy has been expanding at a staggering rate for the last 10 years with double digit annual growth rates, this unprecedented expansion has injected billions upon billions of foreign reserves in the Chinese economy. These reserves invariably trickle down to the people and therein lies the contradiction. China as a nation is saving at 50%, a truly astonishing amount by any measure, thus said, the U.S. feels that China is playing unfair because it's dumping Chinese made goods in the U.S. and becoming very, very wealthy but as a society China is not spending back the newly found wealth buying U.S. products but rather hoarding their cash in savings which further widens the imbalance of trade. The argument for the high level of Chinese savings follows the premise that China unlike the United States does not have an established social structure, such as social security benefits, therefore the Chinese family has to create their own social safety net and the way to do that is by saving every single penny available and just spend for the bare essential necessities. The strong global performance is more pronounced in China, but globally, the trend is similar, in Latin America economies are rapidly expanding, in Africa, most economies are growing over 7% per year, all this has meant there is greater liquidity of foreign currency globally. The high oil prices which we have seen reach $140 per barrel have also added to the large influx of the dollar supply on the world markets. While this is good for the countries at the receiving end of these cash-flows, it has had a negative impact on the U.S. economy. An unintended consequence of the vast dollar liquidity globally has been it's impact on the value of the U.S. dollar, the value of the U.S. dollar has been drastically reduced due to saturated dollars globally.

Economic misdiagnosis

Many leading economists and economic planners made a miscall by predicting the mortgage crunch would be short lived and bottom up sooner, we all know what transpired was anything but short-lived. Economist's also miscalculated global economic growth, they projected a much subdued global expansion but it turned out global economic growth was red-hot and sizzling. Global economies were much better run and more efficient therefore maximizing returns.

1.13 OPTIMISTIC VIEW POINT

- US economy will always have it's ups and downs, no need for panic, all will be fine through forces of the invisible hand in the economy.
- Rapid accumulation of foreign reserves globally is good for the U.S. economy since most foreigners will invest their capital in the U.S. (foreign capital infusion) or what is commonly referred to as foreign sovereign funds.
- Jobs lost in the U.S. are not due to trade inequities but rather a result of technology enhancements in global markets, they site an example that in 1950, there were 50 million manufacturing jobs and today we still have roughly the same number but the inequity is in productivity, visa vie technology.
- The rapid global expansion can only sustain for so long, sooner or later the global economy is going to overheat particularly since the focus of these economies has centered on growth alone and ignoring monetary policy.
- Overall trade imbalances declining
- Exports driving growth to U.S. economy
- US economy benefiting from global economic growth
- People need to shy away from pessimistic views of global trade and instead enhance their skills in order to compete in a vibrant global economy.

1.14 GOVERNMENT & MONETARY INTERVENTION EFFORTS

GOVERNMENT STIMULUS PACKAGE

The U.S. House of Representatives just approved an emergency economic stimulus package proposed by president Bush that includes more than $146 billion in tax relief designed to encourage spending and investment. The Senate is considering a different measure, the stimulus is intended to boost consumer spending and jumpstart the sagging economy, unfortunately with the extent of this slowdown, my view is this initiative will have minimal to inconsequential effects. The wound is too big to patch up with a bandage.

INTEREST RATE CUTS

The U.S. Central Bank has continued cutting short-term interest rates to help mitigate the effects of the declining home prices. The Federal Reserve Board cut interest rates by a 0.5 percentage point bringing the rate to 3%. These are the most aggressive and deepest cut undertaken by The Feds since the 1980s. The Fed hopes that interest-rate cuts will help stimulate consumer and business spending, since lower rates make borrowing more attractive and saving less attractive The Fed also anticipates these rate cuts will reduce payment amounts on things such as home equity loans, credit cards and car loans. To justify the rationale behind these cuts, the feds pointed to the stress in the financial markets, falling real-estates values and rising unemployment.

MARKET INTERVENTION BAILOUTS

The Central Bank has also been embroiled in a highly publicized controversial move to bail out the troubled financial company Bear Sterns, In brief, Bear Sterns like many companies suffered a fatal blow from involvement with the sub-prime mortgages and was essentially doomed, the government in its assessment felt the collapse of a powerful entity such as Bear Sterns would be too detrimental for the markets and have larger trickle effects. Through their cost benefit analysis, the government released an emergency loan of $30 billion to facilitate the company's take over by JP Morgan Chase bank. This move prompted an outcry from all ranks as many viewed this as preferential treatment for a Wall Street blue chip company while common folks were being thrown out of their homes through foreclosures with just the clothes on their backs. The sounding bells were so loud to the effect the Federal Reserve chairman and top brass were summoned to congress to explain the justification of this action. Paul Volcker, former Federal Reserve chairman from 1979-1987 in a statement to the economic club of New York characterized this move as transcending the long-embedded central banking principles. In September 2008.The U.S. government also stepped in to rescue failing global insurance giant American International Group Inc. by seizing control and granting the company a two year emergency loan of $85 billion. The Federal government argued that the risk of letting AIG collapse would have far reaching catastrophic effects to the financial system. While such measures are very unusual, they ate in fact authorized under the Federal Reserve Act which essentially allows the government to lend money to non banks provided "unusual and exigent" circumstances exist.

Following the financial market collapse in 2008 which saw powerhouses such as Bear Sterns, Lehman Brothers, Washington Mutual, Merrill Lynch, Fannie Mae & Freddie Mac, etc, the Bush Administration literally saw the writing on the wall, a sinking ship. In the land of the free market system, no one could have seen this boomerang coming, any student of economics and business knows that the cardinal rule of the free market system is a "laissez-fait" approach. In other words, a capitalistic free market system at its very core is supposed to be self correcting where demand and supply on the open market are king. The year 2008 brought new connotations to the free market principal, if there is one lesson from this crisis, it can be summarized as follows: no one economic paradigm is perfect and indeed the imperfections were really brought to the forefront, the irony always lies in the details. The free market ideal that for long despised government regulation & oversight went running back to government to be bailed-out.

In October 2008, the U.S. congress enacted the Emergency Economic Stabilization Act of 2008. The legislation created a relief fund and gave authority to the United States Department of Treasury to manage what was called The Troubled Assets Relief Fund (TARP). This is the commonly referred to $700 billion government bailout proposal by the Bush Administration. It is of historic proportions and very controversial. It is intended to absorb the toxic mortgage loan exposure hampering banks. On paper it's a very simplistic proposal one could spell out on one page, but as always, the devil lies in the details. The proposal essentially calls for the U.S. Treasury Department initially buying $450 billion of the so called "toxic mortgage assets" from the books of failing financial banks. The money from this plan is to be sourced via the U.S. Treasury Department, which in turn will have to borrow this money from Treasury Bills. The other segment of the $700 billion proposal calls for the supplemental funding of the Federal Deposit Insurance Corporation (FDIC). The FDIC is federal regulatory agency which guarantees consumer bank deposits up to $100,000 from bank default or failure. The FDIC has

$45 billion on hand to cover bank failures. With so many banks failing, $45 billion would fall far short and effectively put the FDIC in the red resulting in consumers loosing their money. Given this grim outlook, the proposal would cover this shortfall to avoid turmoil and collapse of the FDIC. Naturally, they are a wide array of provisions and stipulations in the entire context of the proposal such as more government oversight, regulation overhaul, capping of CEO compensation, and so forth. Public outrage against this proposal has been rife and heated, many taxpayers on mainstream feel they have maintained their end of the bargain and should be forced to bail out the wealthy Wall Street elite bankers who through their greed did not play by the rules.

Initial results of the TARP bailout have been lackluster and disappointing. The brunt of the plan was to inject capital in stressed out financial companies so in turn they could free up frozen capital in the market thus averting a complete collapse. However, a couple of months since its inception, the credit market is still as frozen and loans are even harder to get, which in part means consumers & small businesses cannot borrow short-term loans, thus stimulating the economy. Some rates such as Commercial paper rates have subsided and so has the London Inter-bank Offered Rate (LIBOR). The three month LIBOR rate dropped to 2.15% from 4.82% in October. Home mortgage rates which were anticipated to come down due to the capital infusion have remained the same. Libor is similar to the Federal Funds rate in that it's a benchmark rate that banks lend each other money. It's too early to make any meaningful conclusions, in the grand scheme of things, only time and history will render a verdict on this government rescue plan. While government bailouts are very rare, they are certainly not unheard off.

LESSONS FROM THE JAPANESE BAILOUT

Government economic bailouts are not only confined to the U.S. In fact, the $700 billion bailout package has many eerily similar characteristics as the Japanese government rescue package in the 1990s. During the 1990s, the Japanese economy was confronted with banking & real estate collapse which brought the economy to a halt and forced government authorities to inject billions to jumpstart the economy. The nature and extent of the Japanese collapse differed from the U.S. collapse in that unlike the U.S. bubble which was sustained by borrowed money primarily from China, the Japanese debacle was internally sourced with low interest rates acting as a catalyst for the meltdown. Determining an assessment of whether bailouts work or not are always a mixed bag and are often ambiguous. Bailouts offer a classic cliché, "the glass is half-full or half-empty" depending on ones perspective and vantage point. What is evident from the Japanese situation is how long it took for Japan after the bailout to get back on track. The economy suffered a prolonged recession for years with no growth and during a ten year span had four recessions. Unemployment was rampant, the Yen value was at an all time low, investment capital and lending came to a standstill as well. So whatever side of the fence one sits, there are lessons to be learned from the Japanese circumstance to ensure the pitfalls are not revisited. Economists in many circles have rendered verdict on the Japanese bailout as a failure with gross mismanagement. My own analysis and assessment seems to concur with that conclusion, I am a fiscal conservative and subscribe to laissez-faire aspect of the free-market system. The private sector should be allowed to bear consequences of their actions and not be offered a golden parachute for the bad decisions. As I stated earlier, there are compelling arguments for bailouts which warrant merit, but ultimately, the cost of massive bailouts seems to exceed the intended benefits.

NOTABLE U.S. GOVERNMENT BAILOUTS (SOURCE: PROPUBLICA.)

- PENN CENTRAL RAILROAD (1970)—The Nixon Administration facilitated $676.3 million loan guarantees The Company was consolidated in 1976 with five other railroad outfits forming Consolidated Rail (Conrail). The company became profitable by 1981 and the government subsequently sold the outfit in 1987.
- LOCKHEED (1971)—Recipient of relief under the Emergency Loan Guarantee Act. Lockheed paid off its loan obligations by 1977 and government realized about $112 million in loan fees.
- FRANKLIN NATIONAL BANK (1974)—Rescued by a loan package of $1.75 billion from the Federal Reserve. The bank was subsequently plagued with corruption allegations which resulted in convictions of bank executives. FDIC sold the bank in 1981 for about $5.1 billion with a deficit of $185.3 million in owed interest.
- NEW YORK CITY (1975)—Under the Ford Administration, the City received $2.3 billion in loans via the New York City Seasonal Financing Act. The city utilized this aid until 1986 and has since settled all obligations.
- CHRYSLER (1980)—Recipient of $1.5 billion in loans from the Chrysler Loan Guarantee Act. Chrysler paid back its loan by 1983, seven years earlier. The government reportedly made $660 million profit from the bailout.
- CONTINENTAL ILLINOIS NATIONAL BANK & TRUST CO (1984)—Received relief from FDIC and the Federal Reserve after suffering significant losses from investments in energy loans. Government had 80 percent ownership under the bailout arrangement.

Company was privatized in 1991 with the government a $1.8 billion loss.

- SAVINGS & LOAN (1989)—In response to the collapsed S&L banks, Congress under the George H. W. Bush administration enacted the Financial Institutions reform recovery and Enforcement Act in 1989 to rescue the failing S&L banks. Failed S&L banks received about $220 billion. Tax payers were responsible for about $178.56 billion.
- AIRLINE INDUSTRY (2001)—After the 2001 terrorist attacks, President George W. Bush signed the Air Transportation Safety and Stabilization Act, a law which offered compensation for the mandatory grounding of planes during the ordeal. The government released $5 billion in compensation and an additional $10 billion in other guarantees. Reportedly, the government realized a profit even though the figures are murky (between $141 to over $300 million)

FEDERAL RESERVE AND LEGISLATIVE MITIGATION PROPOSALS

The Federal Reserve working with other banking regulators have unleashed a host of proposals and regulations intended to address deceptive credit practices which many blame as a major catalyst in the mortgage crisis. Washington policy makers in response to consumer outcries over fees and interest rate hikes are moving to put restrictions on credit card lenders. The senate banking committee is also pushing legislation aimed at making credit card billing, marketing and disclosure practices more transparent. The proposed senate bill calls for lenders to apply payments to card balances with the highest interest rate first. The proposal also bans interest charges on debt paid on time and also addresses fee penalties. Legislators are also proposing restrictions on lenders from raising interest based on delinquencies with other creditors. The proposed senate bills include, The Credit Cardholder's Bill of Rights, The Credit Card Accountability Act and The Responsibility and Disclosure Act. In similar fashion, the Securities and Exchange Commission (SEC) has made recommendations for broad changes on how bonds are rated. The proposals call for more transparency and thorough disclosures to the public. Other regulatory bodies such as The Office of Thrift Supervision have also put forward proposals as well.

1.15 DESCRIPTIVE COMPONENTS OF THE ECONOMY

The U.S. economic activity can be summarized by collectively gathering information from various indexes at play in the market place, economists and various agencies compile quantitative data on a monthly or quarterly basis. This data once studied can offer an insight into how the economy is performing, where the economy is trending and so forth, the data is especially useful because past trends offer an abundant resource. They are three main index categories, Leading indicators historically have cyclical turning points that manifest before the overall economy, thus are a good forbearer of things to follow, much like a crystal ball. Coincident indexes have turning points that occur at about the same time as the overall economy and the third index is the Lagging index which as the name suggests has turning points after those of the overall economy. The Conference Board [19] a renowned global non-partisan organization compiles and produces this data from various outlets.

LEADING INDEX COMPONENTS

Average weekly manufacturing hours

The average hours worked per week by production and factory workers in manufacturing industries tend to lead the business cycle because employers usually adjust work hours before increasing or decreasing their workforce.

Average weekly initial claims for unemployment insurance

This component addresses the number of new claims filed for unemployment insurance. It has a direct relationship with employment levels in that when the unemployment rate is low, claims filed are low and during depressed times of layoffs and high unemployment rates, claims will skyrocket.

Manufacturers' new orders, consumer goods and materials

This is a composite tally of new orders of consumer goods. The inflation-adjusted value of new orders leads actual production because new orders directly affect the level of both unfilled orders and inventories that firms monitor when making production decisions.

Vendor performance, slower deliveries diffusion index

This index calculates or measures the speed at which vendors or manufactures are receiving their orders. The logic is as follows, if the deliveries timeframe shows a marked decrease or slowdown, such an occurrence is associated with increases in demand for manufacturing supplies This measure is based on a monthly survey conducted by the National Association of Purchasing Management (NAPM) that asks purchasing managers whether their suppliers deliveries have been faster, slower, or the same as the previous month.

Manufacturer's new orders, non-defense capital goods

Measures number of new orders received by manufacturers in non-defense capital goods industries (in inflation-adjusted dollars)

Building permits, new private housing units

This measures the number of new residential or home construction permits issued. This offers an insight into the construction industry, more permits issued would imply a good sign for the construction sector and vice versa.

Stock prices, 500 common stocks

The stock index looks at trading activity of common stock on the New York Stock Exchange, this gives a good indication on the outlook investors have in the present and future market.

Money supply (M2)

Under this category, inflation adjusted dollars are considered or what is commonly called the M2 segment of money supply. M2 inherently looks at the liquid part money, this includes currency as in cash, deposits such as paper checks, money market funds, savings deposits, mutual funds, travelers checks and the like. This is an important category because it keeps a gauge on the balance of money supply and inflation levels or tendencies.

Interest rate spread, 10-year Treasury bonds less federal funds

This segment basically measures the difference or what's called the spread between long and short term rates, the resulting difference is thus called the yield curve. To derive this spread, the 10 year Treasury bond and the federal funds rate (overnight inter-bank borrowing rate used by banks) are used as a benchmark When this index becomes negative (i.e., short rates are higher than long rates and the yield curve inverts) it implies a good propensity or likelihood of an recessions.

Index of consumer expectations

The University of Michigan Survey research Center collects data monthly based on consumer expectations. This index shows changes in consumer attitudes concerning future economic conditions. It is the only indicator in the leading index that completely relies on consumer expectations. Responses to the questions concerning various economic conditions are classified as positive, negative, or unchanged. Three primary questions yield the responses. (1) economic prospects for the respondent's family over the next 12 months; (2) the economic prospects for the country over the next 12 months; and (3) the economic prospects over the next five years.

COINCIDENT INDEX COMPONENTS

Employees on nonagricultural payrolls

This component refers to data compiled by the Bureau of Labor Statistics, it is often referred to as payroll employment. The data details full-time and part-time workers and does not distinguish between permanent and temporary employees. This is a very critical measure on the status of the economy because it is very specific in that it implicitly looks actual hiring and firing statistics.

Personal income less transfer payments

This inherently looks at what is called real income or salaries. It includes real dollar earnings & wages in inflation adjusted dollars. The wages measured are from both traditional earnings and non-traditional earnings, essentially looks at the value of all incomes by the society. It is important to note that this series does not include income from government transfers such as social security. It's an important indicator because it offers an insight into the income levels and gives an indication of what consumer spending may be, it also offers an idea of consumer saving levels when income levels are pegged against spending levels.

Index of industrial production

This category looks at the overall physical output of all factories and manufacturing. It is compiled from a variety of sources that measure physical production numbers, shipment values and employment levels.

Manufacturing and trade sales

This is a collection of sales numbers from sales, manufacturing, wholesale, and retail sectors. The numbers are inflation-adjusted to represent real total spending. The information from this compilation is part of the National Income and Product Account.

LAGGING INDEX COMPONENTS

Average duration of unemployment

This segment measures the average length of time employees have been unemployed in weekly intervals. This segment has an inverted relationship, meaning this measure tends to be higher during recessions and lower during expansions or boom times.

Ratio, manufacturing and trade inventories to sales

The Bureau of Economic Analysis compiles this data, it essentially is a ratio of inventories to sales of businesses, it is a popular tool of measuring the outlook of overall business conditions for individual firms, entire industries, and the whole economy. When the economy is struggling or in a downturn, inventories typically tend to increase, this is because sales numbers fail to meet projected numbers. The ratio usually reaches its cyclical climax in the middle of a recession and conversely will decline at the beginning of an expansion as firms meet their sales due to increased demand.

Change in labor cost per unit of output, manufacturing

This segment measures the rate of change when labor costs for manufacturing firms rise faster than their production, it also looks at the reverse effect. The survey & index determination is compiled by the Conference Board.

Average prime rate charged by banks

This looks at the average monthly prime rate which is the benchmark that banks use to establish their interest rates for different types of loans. It is compiled by the Board of Governors of the Federal Reserve System.

Commercial and industrial loans outstanding

Measures the volume of business loans held by banks and commercial paper issued by non financial companies. The bulk of the data is compiled by the Board of Governors of the Federal Reserve System.

Ratio, consumer installment credit outstanding to personal income

Measures the relationship between consumer debt and income. Consumer installment credit outstanding is compiled by the Board of Governors of the Federal Reserve System and personal income data is from the Bureau of Economic Analysis. it's a lagging indicator because its effects are after the fact, in practice, borrowers or consumers will traditionally withhold borrowing in adverse economic times and only resume borrowing after the downturn ends.

Change in Consumer Price Index for services.

The Bureau of Labor Statistics compiles this data which measures the rates of change in the services component of the Consumer Price Index.

1.16 FUTURE OUTLOOK & OBSERVATIONS

- The sub-prime effects will persist all through 2008 and possibly spillover into the onset of 2009 particularly as option ARM (Adjustable Rate Mortgages) are due to reset at higher rates. The numbers are staggering, industry experts estimate in January, $80 billion worth of loans reset, $90 billion in February and $110 billion in March. The cumulative effect of all these resets will be increased default levels and consequently foreclosures as homeowners struggle to meet higher mortgage payments.
- The economy particularly banks and financial institutions will see more foreign investment through "sovereign wealth funds". Foreign governments through these funds are already bailing out several companies similar to what the Japanese companies were doing in the 1980 U.S. financial troubles, the main distinction though being that the Japanese companies were private and not government entities. This trend has already started. Citigroup in November 2007 was bailed out by the Arab nation of Abu Dhabi with a cash capital infusion of

$7.5 billion. Merrill Lynch also received a capital bailout of over $7 billion from Singapore. UBS has also sought the help of Singapore for a life-line. Morgan Stanley was reeled in by China. The Chinese have deep pockets and are keen on heavy foreign investments. China has a sovereign wealth fund of $200 billion which is managed by China Investment Corporation. The Gulf nations with billions of dollars dripping from their coffers are also jumping into the game and the main players in this region are Qatar, Kuwait and UAE.

- The Chinese will inevitably spend more in the long-run as their capital markets become more developed and a social safety net is in place. By the same token, the U.S. as a people need to save more and not just live to spend.

- The U.S. needs to have more strategic dialogue with Asia (China in particular).especially as relates to currency policy and balance of trade.

- There needs to be more transparency between the Federal reserve, Banks, Hedge Funds, private equity firms and similar entities in order to develop clear and concise regulation. There is a need for comprehensive regulatory blue prints, Rating agency reform and a closer scrutiny of mortgage originating policies to close the loopholes that resulted the mortgage collapse.

- The U.S. also needs to continue being vocal on the subject of import safety, product safety and environment agreements. They also need to push hard on caps on emissions, illegal trading tariffs, child labor laws and so forth.

- The Federal Reserve will continue with aggressive rate cuts in trying to mitigate the economic forces, however the Fed should be cautious and very judicious in its exercise of continuous interest cuts as this can trigger inflation rates.

- I expect the economy to be in mild recession mid 2008, full blown recession at the tail end of 2008 and start to decent at the onset of 2009 and finally bottom up summer of 2010 with a soft landing. The U.S. dollar will continue it's downward spiral throughout 2008 and reach it's true value based on the global market supply & demand of dollars on the world market. At this point the U.S. economy will start appreciating due to large infusions of Sovereign Wealth Funds by passive investors from booming sources such as Singapore, Middle East and China. Foreign investors with dormant liquidity assets will naturally take advantage of the reeling U.S. economy by acquiring U.S. companies or making substantial investments particularly with low dollar rate. The U.S. economy is projected to be in a recession until the end of 2009.

- Foreign governments from a fiscal policy standpoint will continue to artificially keep their currencies low and keep on buying dollars in bulk as the case with China. They will do this to stimulate their export positioning by making their exports cheap
- Trading instruments such as collateralized debt obligations (CDOs) structural investment vehicles (SIVs), hedge funds, etc will all exhibit a diminished leverage capacity as huge write down losses by lenders continue. Similarly, the credit derivatives market will have a tough road ahead since the underlying credit default swaps (CDS) are tanking and in freefall. This presents a sounding bell for JP Morgan Chase, a principal leader in this derivative trading arena. CDS are contracts effectively that allow investors to take a credit risk without buying the specific bond.
- The struggling economy will force growth to hover between 2.5-3% annually as the markets remain volatile and unstable.
- As the markets continue to deteriorate, new opportunities to buy will arise as we approach the Bear Market, which is traditionally categorized by the Dow Jones Industrial Average dipping to 20% below its peak rate. Based on data from the last 19 bear markets, each bear market lasts for about a year and a half [20]. A bear market can represent a buying bonanza for investors with disposable capital, following the golden rule of investment: always buy when rates bottom out. Cautionary tales to the wise, even though economic downturns can be a bonanza to investors, don't be quick to jump the gun, carefully weigh all options before pulling the trigger.
- Rising oil prices will continue to be a noose around the neck for the entire global economy throughout 2008 and 2009 as emerging markets continue to expand especially China and India with their blood thirst appetite for oil.
- I anticipate home equity and credit card loan delinquencies to mount in 2008 and 2009 as consumers are faced with rising prices and stagnant incomes. The American Bankers Association is already noticing an upward shift in delinquencies.
- Expect banks and other lenders to cut dividend payouts as they feel the pinch of the economy slowdown, particularly those that were heavily untangled and hedged in the subprime market. Many large U.S. banks had to write down millions of dollars from the subprime debacle so most of such bank's need all the cash on hand and thus paying dividends can wait for now until they sort out their affairs. Wachovia Corp and 13 other U.S. lenders have already cut dividends this year, Bank of America, Deutsche Bank and Goldman Sachs are reportedly following suit. [21]

KEY TERMS AND DEFINATIONS

Economic Growth Rate:

Measures economic growth from one period to another in percentage terms. This measure does not adjust for inflation and it is expressed in nominal terms.

$$\text{Economic Growth} = \frac{GDP_2 - GDP_1}{GDP_1}$$

In practice, it is a measure of the rate of change that a nation's gross domestic product goes through from one year to another. Gross national product can also be used if a nation's economy is heavily dependent on foreign earnings.

Gross Domestic Product (GDP):

The monetary value of all the finished goods and services produced within a country's borders in a specific time period, though GDP is usually calculated on an annual basis. It includes all of private and public consumption, government outlays, investments and exports less imports that occur within a defined territory.

$GDP = C + G + I + NX$
where:
"C" is equal to all private consumption, or consumer spending, in a nation's economy
"G" is the sum of government spending
"I" is the sum of all the country's business spending on capital
"NX" is the nation's total net exports, calculated as total exports minus total imports. (NX = Exports - Imports)

Gross National Product (GNP):

An economic statistic that includes GDP, plus any income earned by residents from oversea investments minus income earned within the domestic economy by overseas residents.

Real Gross Domestic Product:

This inflation-adjusted measure that reflects the value of all goods and services produced in a given year, expressed in base-year prices. Often referred to as "constant-price", "inflation-corrected" GDP or "constant dollar GDP".

Nominal GDP:

A gross domestic product (GDP) figure that has not been adjusted for inflation
Also known as "current dollar GDP" or "chained dollar GDP".

Recession:

A significant decline in activity spread across the economy, lasting longer than a few months. It is visible in industrial production, employment, real income and wholesale-retail trade. The technical indicator of a recession is two consecutive quarters of negative economic growth as measured by a country's gross domestic product (GDP).

Boom:

A period of time during which sales or business activity increases rapidly

Inflation:

The rate at which the general level of prices for goods and services is rising, and, subsequently, purchasing power is falling.

Interest Rate:

The monthly effective rate paid (or received, if you are a creditor) on borrowed money. Expressed as a percentage of the sum borrowed.

Nominal Interest Rate:

The interest rate unadjusted for inflation.

CONCLUDING REMARKS

The Subprime mortgage collapse stems from irresponsible lenders who put greed motives ahead of moral, ethical and commonsense business practices. Essentially, lenders extended credit, in this case mortgage loans to applicants who ordinarily would not be able to meet the repayment obligations, lenders used a lot of tactics in many cases targeting low-wage earners, setting them up with unrealistic, unconventional loans laced with low teaser introductory rates which ballooned to very high unrealistic rates. For a while what was phrased as the "home-market/real-estate boom" was unstoppable, every Jim and Jack was getting a mortgage and becoming a homeowner, the uncontrolled expansion was further compounded by the ease at which homeowners could refinance their existing loans. This meant when homeowners were faced with any financial constraint, they used their home equity (in this case, negative equity) as a personal cash dispensing asset, mortgage lenders were eager to refinance loans and make their commissions while the borrowers (homeowners) sunk further and further into debt. It was just a matter of time before this fantasy would self-implode. Home owners inevitably fell further and further back on the mortgage payment obligations, ultimately ending up in default and foreclosure. The culminating effect of these defaults resulted in many sub-prime lenders going out of business which meant laying-off thousands of employees, all these manifestations had what we economists call the trickle-down effect ultimately, the financial markets crushed, unemployment figures were up, foreclosure rates were up, crime rates rose, all these indiscretions were a result of the "Sub-prime market collapse".

Unlike other economic slumps we have seen in the past, this down-turn is very concerning because not only has it hit consumers hard, but more significantly has been the hit "investors" have taken, we have seen the big guns such as Merrill Lynch (U.S. largest brokerage firm) and Citigroup experience monumental losses and announce large job cuts. Lessons should have been learnt from the monumental collapse of Long Term Capital Management (LTCM) in 1998. LTCM was hedge fund which was heavily invested in the derivative bond market. The company was the forbearer of the now infamous derivative market with complex mathematical models. Recovering from this down-town may not just be as easy as business as usual, the proposed $150 billion tax relief in the form of rebates may not cut it this time, giving $800 per person is just a bandage solution, all this relief is borrowed money growing deficits which someone else down the line has to deal with. Giving $800 back to consumers hoping that this will stimulate consumer spending is self-defeating if at the very core of the problem the U.S. is concerned about the imbalance of trade with China as inevitably, a good portion of these rebates will be used to purchase "made in China" commodities. The solution to managing this recession (which is what it truly is in the classic economist sense, terms such as slow-downs, down-turns etc are merely a mask of what is really happening) calls for long-term well thought out fiscal and monetary policy. U.S. spending with all these global wars has been irresponsible, heavy reliance on foreign capital is another burden, bad fiscal policy is another contributor, unless a realistic approach is followed, the solution will just be a temporary patch-up job before the flood gates open again.

APPENDIX 1

Business Cycle Expansions and Contractions

US Business Cycle Expansions and Contractions[1]

Contractions (recessions) start at the peak of a business cycle and end at the trough.

BUSINESS CYCLE REFERENCE DATES		DURATION IN MONTHS		Cycle	
Peak	Trough	Contraction	Expansion	Cycle	
Quarterly dates are in parentheses		*Peak to Trough*	*Previous trough to this peak*	*Trough from Previous Trough*	*Peak from Previous Peak*
	December 1854 (IV)	—	—	—	—
June 1857(II)	December 1858 (IV)	18	30	48	—
October 1860(III)	June 1861 (III)	8	22	30	40
April 1865(I)	December 1867 (I)	32	46	78	54
June 1869(II)	December 1870 (IV)	18	18	36	50
October 1873(III)	March 1879 (I)	65	34	99	52
August 1918(III)	May 1885 (II)	38	36	74	101
January 1920(I)	April 1888 (I)	13	22	35	60
May 1923(II)	May 1891 (II)	10	27	37	40
October 1926(III)	June 1894 (II)	17	20	37	30
August 1929(III)	June 1897 (II)	18	18	36	35
May 1937(II)	December 1900 (IV)	18	24	42	42
February 1945(I)	August 1904 (III)	23	21	44	39
November 1948(IV)	June 1908 (II)	13	33	46	56
July 1953(II)	January 1912 (IV)	24	19	43	32
August 1957(III)	December 1914 (IV)	23	12	35	36

April 1960(II)	March 1919 (I)	7	44	51	67
December 1969(IV)	July 1921 (III)	18	10	28	17
November 1973(IV)	July 1924 (III)	14	22	36	40
January 1980(I)	November 1927 (IV)	13	27	40	41
July 1981(III)	March 1933 (I)	43	21	64	34
July 1990(III)	June 1938 (II)	13	50	63	93
March 2001(I)	October 1945 (IV)	8	80	88	93
	October 1949 (IV)	11	37	48	45
	May 1954 (II)	10	45	55	56
	April 1958 (II)	8	39	47	49
	February 1961 (I)	10	24	34	32
	November 1970 (IV)	11	106	117	116
	March 1975 (I)	16	36	52	47
	July 1980 (III)	6	58	64	74
	November 1982 (IV)	16	12	28	18
	March 1991(I)	8	92	100	108
	November 2001 (IV)	8	120	128	128

Average, all cycles:				
1854-2001 (32 cycles)	17	38	55	56*
1854-1919 (16 cycles)	22	27	48	49**
1919-1945 (6 cycles)	18	35	53	53
1945-2001 (10 cycles)	10	57	67	67

* 31 cycles
** 15 cycles

Source: NBER

The determination that the last contraction ended in November 2001 is the most recent decision of the Business Cycle Dating Committee of the National Bureau of Economic Research.

The NBER does not define a recession in terms of two consecutive quarters of decline in real GDP. Rather, a recession is a significant decline in economic activity spread across the economy, lasting more than a few months, normally visible in real GDP, real income, employment, industrial production, and wholesale-retail sales. For more information, see the latest announcement on how the NBER's Business Cycle Dating Committee chooses turning points in the Economy and its latest memo, dated 07/17/03.

REFERENCE NOTES

1. US Bureau of Economic Analysis
2. RBC index
3. Mortgage Bankers Association
4. business week
5. Consumer Credit Counseling Service of San Francisco
6. Moody's
7. Mortgage Bankers Association
8. Wall Street Journal
9. Standard & Poor's
10. Inside Mortgage Finance
11. Company Reports
12. US Labor Department
13. US Department of Labor
14. US Department of Labor
15. NYMEX
16. Chicago Sun Times
17. U.S. Department of Transportation Bureau of Transportation statistics
18. Bloomberg
19. Conference Board
20. Wall Street Journal
21. Bloomberg

CHAPTER II

U.S. MORTGAGE OVERVIEW & INSTRUMENTS

Before we look at the various types of mortgage instruments, it is essential to get an understanding of what a mortgage instrument entails. A mortgage is essentially a loan to repay a debt obligation secured against real-estate or personal property. In practical terms, a mortgage is described as a pledge of property as security for a debt. The drawn out document entailing this agreement is widely kwon as a "Deed of Trust". The term "mortgage" is of French law origins loosely translating as a form of a pledge. The term is now widely accepted as relating to a loan secured or guaranteed against a physical building structure (residential or commercial), where the building is a means of collateral and buffer against default. Conversely, the word "mortgage" is synonymously associated with either a home purchase or refinance.

The two main principles involved when drawing up a mortgage note or arrangement are the borrower or commonly referred to as the debtor, whilst the second principle being the lender also known as the creditor. The creditor maintains full legal rights to the property used as security until all mortgage terms are satisfied, failure to uphold the terms of the agreement, the creditor may penalize the debtor through fines and ultimately as a last resort may retake the property and initiate foreclosure procedures to recoup the investment. Common creditors are normally banks and financial companies. Other auxiliary parties in the mortgage transaction may include but are not limited to, mortgage brokers, property or structural inspectors, attorneys, etc.

Mortgage rates like any loan instrument are driven by many factors on a macro and micro level which include Federal interest rates, employment levels, economic growth levels and other activity. Mortgage rates are typically cyclical similar to economic trends and usually mirror economic boom or decline trends. In the current economy, the U.S. mortgage industry is in dire straits going through a mortgage downturn after a remarkable sizzling growth period that lasted 10 years or so, what was referred to as the "mortgage boom". The days of the boom are long gone and now the industry is undergoing what has been phrased as the "mortgage bubble bust". The "mortgage bubble bust" is mainly a victim of its own success as extensively detailed in the previous section.

2.0 MORTGAGE FIT

Understanding the different types of mortgages circulating in the market place is very critical, whether a first-time buyer treading the waters or a seasoned pro, choosing the wrong loan type can have punishing consequences. People take out mortgage loans for different reasons, but the most common reason of securing a mortgage is for the sole purpose of buying property such as a residential house, business building, land and so forth. Other reasons such as refinancing, equity withdrawal or pull-out, move-up buyers, retirement, etc explain the need for mortgage loans as well. Therefore the process and ultimate decision of selecting a mortgage should be a very thoughtful meticulous decision and not merely based on the best interest rate, the need of the loan should preclude all factors and be the overriding variable. Smart informed consumers should therefore do their due diligence and research the market to find the best product based upon their needs. For instance, it may make perfect sense for a retired elderly couple in their seventies to seek a reverse mortgage as a retirement option where as this option is definitely not practical for young couple in their prime professional careers, a fixed-rate long term loan may be more practical.

2.1 CONVENTIONAL MORTGAGE

A conventional mortgage is a fixed or adjustable rate residential mortgage that is directly insured by the lender and not backed by the government through the Federal Housing Administration (FHA) [1], the Department of Veterans Affairs (VA) or the Rural Housing Services (RHS). They make up 35-50 % of the market share of mortgages contingent on the economic climate. Conventional loans are commonly referred to as Fixed Rate Mortgages (FRM). Fixed-rate mortgages are available for 40, 30, 25, 20, 15 years and 10 years. Generally, the shorter the term of a loan, the lower the interest rate you could get. To qualify for this type of loan, borrowers need an excellent credit history which typically calls for 20% down and does not require government insurance as the insurance is provided directly from the lending bank institution.

Conforming loans are effectively loans eligible for sale to Fannie Mae & Freddie Mac, i.e. "*conform*" to the set guidelines, the original mortgage amounts cannot exceed the stipulated thresholds (see table below). Fannie Mae was founded in 1938 by the government to boost home ownership, it functions in the secondary market buying loans from lenders, in 1968, it was restructured by congress to operate as privately held stockholder company responsible for its own funding.[2] Freddie Mac was created in 1970, it is a privately owned corporation chartered by Congress to increase the supply of funds to mortgage lenders, such as commercial banks, mortgage bankers, savings institutions and credit unions, these institutions consequently are able to make funds available to homebuyers and multifamily investors.[3] These are the two lending corporations who buy loans that meet their set criteria from various lenders and then repackages them into securities which are sold to investors. Together, these two entities own more than 50% of residential mortgages representing more than $5 trillion in mortgages underwritten.

TABLE 2
HISTORICAL LOAN LIMITS FOR CONFORMING LOANS

Loan Limits for:	2006	2005	2004
One-family	$417,000	$359,650	$333,700
Two-family	$533,850	$460,400	$427,150
Three-family	$645,300	$556,500	$516,300
Four-family	$801,950	$691,600	$641,650

Loan Limits for:	2003	2002	2001
One-family	$322,700	$300,700	$275,000
Two-family	$413,100	$384,900	$351,950
Three-family	$499,300	$465,200	$425,400
Four-family	$620,500	$578,150	$528,700

Loan Limits for:	2000	1999	1998

One-family	$252,700	$240,000	$227,150
Two-family	$323,400	$307,100	$290,650
Three-family	$390,900	$371,200	$351,300
Four-family	$485,800	$461,350	$436,600

Source: *http://mortgage-x.com/library/loans.htm*

2.2 NON-CONFORMING MORTGAGE

Non-conforming loans encompass the rest of all the other mortgages that do not meet the requirements set forth by Freddie Mac & Fannie Mae. Effectively, a non-conforming loan is a product where the amount of the loan exceeds the minimum amounts stipulated. Lenders thus are left with these loans or have to dispose of them in the secondary market to investors willing to buy them. Consequently, these loans have a premium associated with them which in-turn is passed along to the borrower, the mark-up on the loan price represents about 25%. Non-conforming loans are referred to by many names such as "subprime" (less than normal), BCD loans (not "A" paper loan), Equity Lending loans (since loan is based on the equity of the collateral rather than the credit of the borrower). The main reasons people do not qualify for conforming loans are typically associated with a poor credit history or standing, high levels of DTI (Debt to Income ratio), public records etc. Because lenders view such borrowers as high risk with a higher incidence of default, they cover this risk threshold by passing the exposure to borrowers. Below I outline some of the more common precluding factors that throw borrowers into this category:

- Score of less than 620 from the 3 main reporting credit bureaus (Equifax, Transition & Experian)
- No credit history at all
- Balances too high
- Recent BK (bankruptcy)
- Foreclosure past
- Too much credit (overextended)
- Repossessions
- Federal or State Tax Liens
- Unpaid Student Loans
- Unverifiable stated income
- Excessive credit inquiries
- Inconsistent documents

- High DTI (debt to income)
- Derogative public records/character issues
- Too many job changes

The following graph points out the level of mortgage activity as a percentage industry wide based on credit scores. The three major credit bureaus (Equifax, Transunion and Experian) rate consumers based on various factors such as open credit balances, loan to value rates, payment history, delinquencies, etc and calculate a numerical credit score which implies how credit worthy a borrower is. The higher the score, the less the risk posed by this borrower, consumers with a lower credit score on the other hand present a greater risk of default. and so to compensate for the risk threshold, such borrowers are charged higher interest rates.

FIGURE 2.1 MORTGAGE ACTIVITY BY CREDIT SCORE

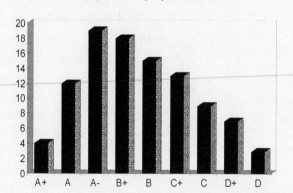

Mortgage Activity by Credit Grade

Conforming: A+ = 700-899, A = 675-699, A-=650-674, B+=625-649
Nonconforming: B=600-624, C+=575-599, C=550-574, D+=525-549, D=500-524

2.3 FHA MORTGAGE

FHA mortgages are loan products administered by the Federal Housing Administration which was created in 1934 and now falls under the jurisdiction of the U.S. Department of Housing and Urban Development. FHA is a federal agency that insures residential mortgages from its various approved lenders, this arrangement means lenders are protected from bearing the brunt in the event of loan default, if a borrower defaults on the loan, the FHA will pay the lender for the loss, the insurance cost is passed along to borrowers by incorporating it within the mortgage monthly payments. It is worth noting that this passed along insurance cost will typically drop of after five years or if the LTV is at 78% (balance of the loan is 78% of the value of the property). [5] This allows these loan products to have a lot of flexibility in terms of down-payments, typically the down payments can be adjusted and lowered to allow for people who would not be able to come up with conventional down payment amounts. Essentially this agency was put in place to assist home buyers who are not able to obtain financing through conventional mortgage lenders such as banks, savings & loans, finance companies, etc. The agency through its approved lenders offers a variety of flexible loan options. FHA loans have maximum limits for the loan amount. These limits are constantly updated and vary from state to state, by county or municipality

2.4 VA MORTGAGES

VA loans are mortgage loans partially guaranteed as relates to default on the principal by the Department of Veterans Affairs. The United States government offers a variety of benefits to its service personnel in appreciation for their service to the country whether active or inactive. None is more prominent than the VA Home Loan Guarantee Program. The main incentive for lenders lies in the notion that the Veterans Administration guarantees 80% of a 30 year residential mortgage against default. The VA loan was primarily designed to offer active, retired or discharged U.S. military personnel an affordable way of realizing the goal of home ownership by making available to them no down-payment loans, as of 2006, the loan amount qualifying for no-down payment was $417,000. These loans are sometimes called GI loans, in addition to 0 down-payments, these loans typically carry lower interest rates than conventional loans.

2.5 ADJUSTABLE RATE MORTGAGE

An Adjustable Rate Mortgage is a mortgage where the interest rate can change and is not fixed as opposed to a Fixed Rate Mortgage. The interest rate is calculated and adjusted against an index and may fluctuate upwards or downward depending on the behavior of the index. The index may for instance be pegged against the six-month Treasury bill. Adjustable rates are calculated by factoring in the Index + Margin x Rounding Factor. The Index represents a statistical coefficient derived from the general economic conditions, the margin is a fixed set amount compounded to the index and the rounding factor is a cumbersome percentage point factored into the mortgage.

2.6 INSURANCE AND MORTGAGES

There are two precluding issues as relates to mortgages and insurance which often are misunderstood and confused to mean the same thing. In the industry, we have homeowners insurance and mortgage insurance, two very distinct provisions. *Homeowners insurance* essentially provides coverage to the homeowner's property or dwelling. This is coverage that protects the homeowner's stake against losses from things such as fires, natural disasters, theft and so forth, the underlying point being "protection to the home owner". Mortgage insurance on the other hand provides protection to the lender in the event the borrower defaults on their loan commitment and is no longer able to make payments and satisfy contractual obligations.

2.7 BANKRUPTCY & FORECLOSURE

It would be remiss for me not to talk about the subject of bankruptcy and foreclosure as in many cases this is one of the many unintended consequences of an economic slowdown visa vie "recession". Consumers inevitably reach the breaking point with their resources exhausted and their back literally against the wall. At this stage things are beyond the "one pay-check away from disaster" mantra, this is basically dire straits and destitution. Confronted with such overwhelming odds, the options are two-fold, give up your house and dreams in many cases or try to salvage one's dignity with last straw bankruptcy reorganization.

Many consumers unfortunately misunderstand the notion of bankruptcy, indeed many people feel this is the parachute that will rescue their descent when it may not be necessarily the case. Filing bankruptcy does not mean the deed changes hands and thus extrapolating ones responsibility, in many cases if the bankruptcy is not filed accordingly, the foreclosure proceedings will still proceed and the homeowner still liable for all associated costs and attorney fees. Most homeowner's overlook the fact that they are still bearers of the title deed until the bankruptcy is declared discharged. In addition any surbodinate or junior liens against the property have to be cleaned up. Consumers in this circumstance need be sure an "Automatic Stay" has been issued which is basically an injunction prohibiting any creditors from any collection attempts.

CHAPTER 13 BANKRUPTCIES

This is the most common type of bankruptcy filed by consumers. The intent and objective of chapter 13 bankruptcy was designed to allow distressed consumers to "reorganize their debts". Reorganization in this case been achieved by paying of the secured debts first before any unsecured debts such as credit card bills are settled, it's not uncommon for unsecured debts to be completely forgiven under chapter 13.

CHAPTER 7 BANKRUPTCY

This is the second most common bankruptcy filled, in this case, the borrower is essentially asking for "liquidation", I can't deal with it, take the house, take the car, take it all, I don't care, its beyond my control is essentially what this translates to.

BANKRUPTCY DISCHARGE

A bankruptcy discharge is mandated under the federal bankruptcy statutes, in practice and principle, the debtor is discharged or released by law from any owed debt stipulated in the discharge document. Debt collectors in essence are forbidden to pursue any further collection action on debts owed.

2.8 MORTGAGE INDUSTRY REGULATION

Fair Debt Collections Practices Act: This by far is the most comprehensive and punitive regulation put in place to ensure debt collectors do not engage in abusive and unbecoming conduct in their efforts to collect owed debt. Commonly referred to as the FDCPA, it is a federal act enacted March 20, 1978 and has mandate over federal and state jurisdictions. In general it prohibits collectors from essentially harassing consumers that owe a debt, debtors are prohibited from calling debtor at awkward hours, making or insinuating threats, calling at ones work place, basically common sense is what this legislation implies.

Real Estate settlement Procedures Act: Commonly called RESPA, the law was enacted on June 20, 1975. The principle objective of the legislation calls for lenders to provide borrowers with timely advance notices of any costs associated with settlements, the law further stipulates detailed itemization of the process including issues related to escrow analysis.

2.9 COMMON MORTGAGE TERMS

AQUISATION

Purchase of an asset, such as a mortgage where the ownership rights are transferable to the owner.

ACT OF GOD

A consequence which is manifested by nature such as a tornado, a flood, an earthquake, a hurricane, etc.

ADJUSTABLE RATE MORTGAGE

This is a mortgage instrument with a fluctuating interest rate, the rate can increase or decline based on a number of factors. The rate is usually calculated against a monetary index such as a six-month Treasury Bill.

AMMORTIZATION SCHEDULLE

This is typically a table detailing the number of payments due, amount of installment payment due, due dates and the length of time to pay-off debt.

ANNUAL PERCENTAGE RATE

This the cost for obtaining credit, it is expressed in percentage terms per annum.

APPRAISAL

This is a written estimate of the value of the property by a qualified/certified appraiser. The appraisal is or can be based on replacement costs, sales of comparable properties or future anticipated income from the property.

ARREARS

Debt or unpaid loan payment, past due amounts, delinquent balances after allowable grace period.

ASSET

Anything tangible or intangible rightfully owned with monetary or economic value.

ASSIGNMENT

Signing over title rights or deeds to another party

ASSUMABLE MORTGAGE

This is a mortgage which allows for the borrower the right to assign the unpaid balance of the mortgage to another person upon sale without incurring a pre-payment penalty, it is important to understand that this provision must be spelled out in the original document to have merit.

AUTHORIZATION

This is commonly referred to as certification and basically means giving a third-party approval to make transaction on the borrower's behalf and could include things such as making routine payments or account inquiries.

BANKRUPTCY

Formal legal proceedings entered into for the purpose of reorganizing/ adjusting borrower's debts where obligations to creditors cannot be made and or honored.

BILLING NOTICE

A summary of transaction activity during the billing cycle period, also called a billing statement, invoice, coupon, etc. The billing notice will have the following staples, amount due, minimum due, past due amount if any, late fees if applicable and due date.

COLLATERAL

Asset pledged as security to secure a debt such as a loan. The collateral in essence acts as a buffer or insurance to the lender in the event the borrower negates on the arrangement, to recoup their investment, lenders can secure the collateral and liquidate the asset.

COLLECTION

Attempts by lenders to collect outstanding delinquent monies owed to them by a borrower.

CONVENTIONAL MORTGAGE

Fixed or adjustable rate mortgage not backed by federal insurance or guarantee. Typically these mortgages are fixed term loans and are not insured by the Federal Housing Administration or the Veterans Administration.

CONVERTIBLE ARM

This is an adjustable rate mortgage that offers the borrower an option to switch to a fixed rate mortgage, the borrower would pay a conversion or change fee premium. The upside of this type of loan instrument is that it is cheaper than refinancing, therefore the borrower can take advantage of a low adjustable APR and bolt to a fixed rate if variable rates are on the rise.

CREDIT REPORT

This is a report that lists available credit and a person's payment history. It also tracks a person's delinquencies, foreclosures, liens, bankruptcies and so forth. Lenders will request a copy of the report of the person seeking credit, they review the summary and make a determination whether the person is creditworthy. In the U.S. three main reporting agencies keep track of this date; Equifax, Experian and Transunion.

DEED IN LIEU OF FORECLOSURE

Process of a borrower giving up the property to the lenders without going through foreclosure proceedings.

DEED OP TRUST

Substitute of a mortgage document in some states, title to the property passes from the seller to a trustee who holds the property until the mortgage is fully paid at which point it releases the title to the customer. It is worth noting that the trustee has the authority to sell the property in the event of a default.

DEFAULT

Failure to meet payment obligations per agreement.

DEFICIENCY JUDGEMENT

Court order that authorizes the lender to recoup part of an outstanding debt by means of foreclosure and sale of the property.

DELINQUENCY

Past due balances

DISPOSABLE INCOME

Net income remaining after payment of all taxes.

DISCRETIONARY INCOME

Income leftover after paying for all essential household expenses, necessities.

EFFECTIVE DATE

Date registered where an agreement becomes effective and binding, in some states this may be after the 3 day recession period have been met.

EQUITY

Market value of real property less (minus) outstanding mortgage (owed amount) including liens if any. Difference between what is owed minus what house is worth, for example:

Hse worth $250,000 & person owes $200,000, to calculate the equity $250-200 = $50,000, since equity is always expressed as a percentage: 50,000/250,000 = 20%, so in this illustration, the equity proportion is 20%.

FIRST MORTGAGE

Main mortgage which holds the lien against the property, it supercedes and takes priority over any other subsequent mortgages commonly called junior mortgages. In the event of a default, the First mortgage takes precedence and is paid off first when the house is sold with the remaining proceeds if any going to the junior or subordinate mortgages.

FIXED RATE LOAN

A loan with an interest rate that does not fluctuate over the life of the loan

FORECLOSURE

Legal proceedings undertaken by creditor to take possession of property in the event the borrower defaults on agreement and fails to meet the spelled out stipulations.

GENERAL WARRANTY DEED

A deed where the grantor agrees to protect the grantee against any claims.

GRACE PERIOD

Forgivable period after due date where no late fees are assessed, typically within 10-15 day window, all depends on the agreement, some stipulations will charge a late fee a day after the due date.

HOME EQUITY LINE OF CREDIT

A loan a home owner takes out as a second mortgage using the house as collateral.

INSURED LOAN

A residential mortgage loan insured by the Federal Housing Authority (FHA), Veterans Affairs (VA) or via private mortgage insurance.

INTEREST RATE

Cost of borrowing money, expressed as a percentage rate on an annual basis.

INTEREST ARREARAGE

Amount of interest in arrears.

JUNIOR MORTGAGE

Surbodinate mortgage taken out after prior mortgages, it could be a second or third mortgage. People take out these loans for home improvements or for emergency funds access.

LATE CHARGES

Penalty assessed to borrower for not making payment on time as stipulated in loan agreement. Late fees are generally calculated as a percentage of the outstanding balance.

LIEN

This is a claim placed against the property by the lender to recoup owed monies, it is a legally binding means of collecting a debt.

LOAN TO VALUE RATIO (LTV)

Percentage coefficient detailing the loan amount when measured against the value of the property or in simple terms: Loan Amt/Value of House, for example:
Amount of Mortgage is $200,000, Current Value is $400,000. The Loan to Value rate is 50% (200000/400000) the higher the LTV, the better position.

MARKET VALUE

Highest price that an asset will command on the open free market, the highest price buyers are willing to offer and the lowest price a buyer will accept.

MATURITY DATE

Due date when principle amount of loan is due.

MODIFICATION

Changes made to original loan document.

MORTGAGE

This is a debt instrument that offers conditional ownership of an asset, typically a home or building, the asset is financed and the conditional ownership is contingent on the loan agreement terms with the conditional ownership becoming permanent when the payment obligations are fully satisfied.

NET INCOME

Gross monthly income less all taxes (federal, state, local) and social security.

PAYOFF STATEMENT

This is a document offered by the lender when a borrower wants to pay off the loan, a payoff statement will what's called a "good through date" before interest charges start accruing and the payoff amount is no longer valid.

PITI

Principal, interests, taxes and insurances.

POWER OF ATTORNEY

A legal document giving authority to another party to act as an authorized agent.

PRINCIPLE

Face value of loan less interest.

PRIVATE MORTGAGE INSURANCE (PMI)

This is insurance that protects lenders against borrower default.

QUIT CLAIM DEED

Document stipulating relinquinshment of ownership of property to another party.

SATISFACTION OF MORTGAGE

Documenting the release of a mortgage lien, essentially a document confirming that the borrower has paid or settled the debt in full. This release is also recorded as a public document and anyone can access it from the state public records.

SECURITIZATION

Conversion of bank loans and other assets into securities for sale to investors (such as bonds that manifested the sub-prime market)

SHERRIFS SALE

Public auction of a borrower's property seized during a foreclosure warranted by court order.

SKIP

Delinquent customer in limbo, missing in action, lenders have to hire someone to track down the debtor through skip tracing techniques.

TAX LIEN

Claim on real estate for not paying income or property taxes, tax liens supersede any other liens and are naturally compensated first

TAX SALE

Sale of property due to non payment of taxes, purchaser of taxes receives the tax deed.

TITLE

Document that gives legal valid claim visa a vie , ownership to property.

TITLE SEARCH

Process of identifying rightful owner of property.

TRUST DEED

Real estate designated to a third party for an interim period.

VERIFICATION OF MORTGAGE

This is form a lender provides upon request detailing original terms of loan and current status.

WORKOUT AGREEMENT

An agreement of mutual accord between the lender and borrower for a payment plan in lie of foreclosure proceedings.

REFERENCE NOTES

1. Federal Housing Administration
2. Fannie Mae
3. Freddie Mac
4. *http://mortgage-x.com/library/loans.htm*
5. http://www.fha.gov

CHAPTER III

U.S. LENDING REGULATION

3.0 BACKGROUND PERSPECTIVE

In America, banking institutions and credit card lenders are regulated by Federal agencies through established Acts. In this chapter, I look at the various legislative acts, examining their very nature, enforcement practices and subsequent intentions. The industry today is saturated by a host of lending institutions all grappling at gaining a bite of the pie, it is an extremely competitive arena and as a consequence, the need to gain a competitive edge can result in unscrupulous practices by a few rogue lenders, thus the need of federal regulatory agencies to ensure unsuspecting consumers are not compromised and abused. It is important to emphasize that the bulk of lenders out there are very responsible and ethical, but as always the case, there are a few bad eggs that warrant scrutiny.

This section as earlier pointed out is more concerned with presenting an overview of the various regulatory tools and their application. By the same token, consumers who decide to take up the burden of accepting or seeking credit need to be cognizant of the responsibilities of managing credit. So often than not, consumers are quick to take on credit beyond their means and typically end up overwhelmed and subsequently fail to meet the terms of their loan agreements. Failure to maintain the loan agreements will in turn lead to default and a derogatory credit standing, the lending establishments are then left with these negative returns and burden. So, the word to the wise, when taking up credit, be careful to bite only what you can chew and remember, the burden of responsibility is a 50-50 proposition between lenders and borrowers alike.

3.1 THE FEDERAL TRADE COMMISSION

The agency tasked to regulating lending institutions and protecting consumers from deceptive practices, fraud, predatory lenders, unfair practices within the market place is known as the "Federal Trade Commission". This body undertakes regulatory responsibilities as well as enforcement of laws. The Commission is also responsible for dealing with various antitrust and consumer protection laws. Aside from merely acting as an enforcement overseer, the agency by the nature of its function in essence contributes to efficiency in the free market system. Consumers who feel unfairly treated or abused by lenders can file a complaint with this agency outlining their grievances. The Commission strongly encourages consumers to feel free in contacting them. In this age of heightened fraud practices, identity theft, predatory lenders and so forth, the Commission is at the center stage in fighting and eliminating these social ills. The Commission makes filing a complaint a very transparent and painless experience, some of the common consumer complaints include but are not limited to: Identity theft, price gauging, unethical predatory lending practices and so forth.

The process of filing a complaint is fairly straight forward, one can file a complaint via mail correspondence, telephone or through electronic means via their website. Electronic filing is the most practical and efficient way of filing. Other specific complaint forms are made available as well on the Commission website. The Office of the General Council is the unit within the body that is tasked with representing the Commission in federal court & legal proceedings.

3.2 THE FEDERAL DEPOSIT INSURANCE CORPORATION

The Federal Deposit Insurance Corporation or FDIC as it is commonly referred to is an independent body of the United States of America federal government. The FDIC was created in 1933 mainly as a result of the prevalent bank failures and collapses that transpired in the 1920s and 1930s. [1] Learning from these catastrophic collapses, the United States government saw the need for an agency that would protect the U.S. financial system from uncertain failures. The 1920s and 1930s financial turmoil thus was responsible for the birth of the FDIC. The agency insures deposits in banks and financial institutions for at least $100,000 [2] Since the FDIC is an independent body, it does not receive government funding or appropriations, therefore it has to sustain its own operating budget, the agency is able to do this by relying on revenue it receives from premiums banks and financial institutions pay for deposit insurance. To its credit, the FDIC claims an impeccable record to the effect that since the start of this program, no single bank with insured funds has ever lost a cent as a result of bank or market failure.

3.3 OFFICE OF THRIFT SUPERVISION

The office of Thrift Supervision is a federal agency within the United States Department of the Treasury. Its main function is to regulate all Federal and State chartered savings institutions. OTS was established by congress on August 9, 1989 under the Financial Institutions Reform Recovery and Enforcement Act of 1989 (FIRREA). Like many congressional Act's, the creation of OTS was borne out of the savings and loan fiasco in the 1980s. During the late 1970s and early part of the 1980s, the United States economy was experiencing high inflation tendencies which in turn resulted in high interest rates that proved fatal for the Savings and Loans (S & Ls) institutions. Many of the S & Ls had most of their assets devoted to long term mortgage loans that were underwritten on fixed interest rate paper. Therefore, as the interest rates skyrocketed, the S&L banks were stuck with fixed rate paper, the net-worth of the S&Ls plummeted and thus the collapse of thousands of Savings banks, the crash cost the industry billions of dollars. In reaction to this debacle, the Office of Thrift Supervision was borne.

3.4 THE TRUTH IN LENDING ACT

The Truth in Lending Act was enacted by congress on May 29, 1969 as Title 1 of the Consumer Credit Protection Act. The Title was implemented by "Regulation Z" and became effective July 1, 1969. Like many legislative Acts, the TILA has had many amendments since its inception to accommodate the changing arena of the financial industry. The Act in brief calls for creditors to provide clear concise disclosures to consumers, in essence the legislations mandates that creditors disclose all credit terms in a transparent manner. This allows for consumers to be able to easily examine the credit terms at hand, make a comparison if need be and ultimately make a clear informed decision. The Act also calls for all creditors to use uniform terms when quoting interest rates, annual percentage rates, etc. Prior to the enactment of this Act, creditors did not have a uniform code and this brought about a lack of understanding & miscommunication on the consumer side. The main highlights of the Act are as follows [3]

- Shield consumers from incorrect and unfair credit card practices
- Gives consumers rescission rights, usually applies to home equity loans, commonly referred to as the 3-day cooling period allowing a consumer to rescind and opt out of agreement within 3 business days.
- Allows consumers to have a cap on variable rate loans, i.e. creditors have to disclose maximum ceiling rates on APRs.
- The Act gives limitations on home equity lines of credit, therefore protecting consumers from being overextended.

Therefore, when a creditor is extending a credit offer, it is imperative that they disclose to the consumer the following details:

- Applicable annual percentage rate
- Applicable origination/initiation fees
- Finance charge terms, a very important disclosures as dictates in part how much the consumer will be paying for the loan
- Late fee, delinquency fee over limit fees & any other associated fees
- Availability limits
- All terms of loan agreement such as due dates etc
- If credit is extended and accepted, the creditor is required to provide the debtor with timely billing statements and it is contingent upon the lender to ensure statements are mailed at least 14 days prior to the due date.
- Total number of payments in installment loans
- Total Sale price or Cost of credit(down payment and payment amortization)

The lender is required to provide a final disclosure statement at the time of loan closing. This disclosure follows a specific format and will usually include the following information:

1. Name and address of creditor
2. Amount financed
3. Itemization of amount financed (optional, if Good Faith Estimate is provided)
4. Finance charge
5. Annual percentage rate (APR)
6. Variable rate information
7. Payment schedule
8. Total of payments
9. Demand feature

10. Total sales price
11. Prepayment procedures
12. Late payment policy
13. Security interest
14. Insurance requirements
15. Certain security interest charges
16. Contract reference
17. Assumption policy
18. Required deposit information

3.5 THE FAIR CREDIT BILLING ACT (FCBA)

The Fair Credit billing Act is found in chapter 4 of the Truth in Lending Act, it is a United States federal law which was enacted as an amendment to the aforementioned Truth in Lending Act. Its key provision is to protect consumers from unfair billing practices and also allow for consumers to have a right to contest/dispute billing discrepancies in "open end" accounts, typically credit cards. This legislation offers creditors detailed guidelines and procedural time frames for resolving billing disputes. The Act also stipulates that creditors may not engage in collection efforts on any items brought forward for dispute by consumer, similarly a creditor is prohibited from reporting to credit bureaus any items under dispute proceedings.

The FCBA settlement procedures apply only to disputes about "billing errors." such as the examples offered below::

- Unauthorized charges. Federal law limits your responsibility for unauthorized charges to $50;
- Charges that list the wrong date or amount;
- Charges for goods and services you didn't accept or weren't delivered as agreed;
- Mathematical discrepancies or errors
- Failure by creditor to post payments and other credits like returns
- Failure by creditor to send billing notices to your current address (provided the creditor receives your change of address, in writing, at least 20 days before the billing period ends)
- Failure by creditor to respond to request by consumer requesting explanation of charges. When a consumer initiates a dispute proceeding, the creditor by legal requirement is to send a written

letter of acknowledgement of the query brought forward within 30 days of receipt of the respective notice. The creditor, having received the billing dispute notice is required to resolve the billing discrepancy within a period of two full billing cycles.

3.6 THE FAIR CREDIT REPORTING ACT

This Act is enforced by the Federal Trade Commission, its main function is to make sure that information accuracy and privacy adherence are maintained by Consumer Reporting Agencies in the United States. Consumer Reporting Agencies (CRA) are companies who are in the business of buying consumer information which is then sold creditors and a variety of other businesses. The information they gather and sell is called a Consumer report, the most widely known Consumer Reporting Agency and probably the largest is the Credit bureau. Given the sensitive nature of this business, i.e. handling consumer personal information, companies engaged in selling this information and those who buy these consumer reports must follow guidelines spelled out in the Fair Credit Reporting Act. This ensures that consumers are protected and also allows consumers the opportunity to opt out of consumer sharing arrangements. Another important provision states that if a consumer is declined a loan, job, accommodation, etc due to a derogative item from a credit reporting agency, the creditor needs to disclose this to the consumer.

3.7 THE EQUAL CREDIT OPPORTUNITY ACT (ECOA)

The Equal Credit Opportunity Act is essentially designed to allow any credit worthy individual the opportunity to gain access to credit. Creditors are therefore prohibited from discriminating against credit applicants on the basis of race, color, religion, national origin, sex, marital status, age, or because an applicant receives income from a public assistance program. The process of applying for credit can be stressful and in some cases nerve wrecking, whether it's a mere credit card application, car loan or a life changing event like a mortgage application for a new home, consumers don't need the added stress thinking their loan application may be denied unjustly, thus the basis of the ECOA. The ECOA stipulates that credit issuing institutions consider all applications equally, any violations or improprieties could conceivably be met with a lawsuit from the Department of Justice. To stay in compliance, grantors of credit need to abide within the guidelines illustrated below:

- Credit issuers must consider an application on the basis of certain economic factors, such as your credit history, income, and current amount of debt.
- Credit issuers cannot consider an application on the basis of personal characteristics, including your race or national origin, religion, gender, marital status, or age.
- Credit issuers cannot deny you credit because your income is from public assistance, or because you exercised your rights under the Consumer Credit Protection Act.

3.8 THE FAIR DEBT COLLECTION PRACTICES ACT (FDCPA)

The brunt of this Act is centered on protecting debtors from abusive collection practices by debt collectors to collect a debt. Therefore a debt collection company may not threaten or harass a debtor in efforts to collect an outstanding or delinquent debt obligation. A debt collector may not call debtor repeatedly or at odd hours (before 8 am or after 9pm) of the day making demands or threats for payment. Thus said, debt collectors are given a strict set of guidelines to follow and abide to in their efforts to recoup funds owed to them. This Act is mainly pertinent to Debt Collection companies and Third party collectors.

3.9 FEDERAL TRADE COMMISSION ACT (FTC)

The FTC is an independent federal agency tasked with protecting various consumer rights and also regulating unfair market practices that hamper or discourage fair competition within the marketplace. The agency has in place consumer protection laws and antitrust laws as a mechanism to enforce its jurisdiction powers.

REFERENCE NOTES

1. Federal Deposit Insurance Corporation website
2. Federal Deposit Insurance Corporation website
3. Comptrollers Handbook, 2006

CHAPTER IV

U.S. LABOR LAW RELATIONS

4.1 EARLY DEVELOPMENTS IN LABOR LAW

CONSPIRACY THEORY

The Conspiracy Theory was borne in the early 1800's as a tool by employer's to curb the activities of shoemaker unions. Employing this doctrine, employers utilized the court's to enforce the law on guilty conspirators, by subjecting violator's with imprisonment and fines. The stem of the theory lies in determining harm by a group of two or more people inflicted on other people or society as a whole. To support this theory, employers argued that unions by the very nature of their activities raised wages thereby harming the general public. They further argued that the resulting wage manipulation by union activity was unnatural and therefore taking advantage of the public. The resulting wage increases were also said to be responsible for higher prices of commodities, which in turn created greater harm to productivity as a whole, caused unemployment, damaged trade and ultimately infringed on the rights of all worker's.

Current Applicability of conspiracy theory: conditions to allow for this theory are as follows,

- There has to be an agreement of two or more parties engaged in illegal means.
- The second condition stipulates, conspirator's can be punished for acts even if acting in a co-conspirator role.

INJUNCTIONS

The widespread use of injunctions as relates to early union activities can be attributed to two primary factors. The first being the 1895 U.S. Supreme court ruling that upheld the injunction as a constitutional tool to stop union activities (Deb's case). The second factor argued that injunctions could be used to protect property against irreparable damage. The damage to property notion was widely used to include an array of union activities, which were viewed as a hindrance to free access of the labor pool and market's therefore constituting damage to property. To a large extent, the failure & decline of the conspiracy theory contributed to the labor injunction, as the conspiracy theory became less effective, employer's felt they needed a more effective tool to curb worker's engaged in union activity. In addition, employer's realized conspiracy trials were long, complicated, cumbersome and took too long to resolve, thus the birth of the labor injunction.

Unlike its predecessor, the labor injunction proved to be quick, simple and precise. Injunctions are issued by Judges in absence of juries and once issued must be obeyed immediately. They come in three forms:

1. Temporary restraining order
2. Temporary injunction
3. Permanent injunction

The popularity of injunctions brought about a tremendous amount of abuses. Some of the more common abuses included the indiscriminant manner by which judges employed this tool under the umbrella of damage to property. Other issues that arose as a result of injunctions included the notion of judges also acting as legislators. Current Applicability: all three types are used today in both labor and non-labor cases.

YELLOW DOG CONTRACTS

This is a tool that was employed by antiunion employers to eliminate the union movement. The principle trait of this tool was the promise made to prospective employees during the hiring process not to engage in union activity. The widespread use of this tool was further enhanced by the passage of the Hitchman-Decision that upheld the use of labor injunctions to enforce yellow-dog contracts.

Current Applicability: Yellow Dog contracts were made illegal with the passage of the Norris-La Guardia Act, this legislation effectively voided the

Hitchman decision. The Norris La Guardia Act denied courts the authority to enforce yellow dog contract's pointing out the conflict of interest. Subsequently, the NLRB would state that employer's attempting yellow dog tactics were engaging in unfair labor practices. It is important to note that yellow dog contracts were in use for 15yrs plus.

ANTITRUST STATUTES

These statutes were passed by congress to protect unions from being prosecuted. The Norris-La Guardia Act with its antitrust laws shielded unions, which was not the case with the Clayton Act. The Norris La Guardia Act was also a message the Supreme Court stated in reaction to the Bedford Cut Stone case.

Current Applicability: Unions still protected from prosecution by antitrust statutes as long as they do not hamper trade.

4.2 PROCEDURE FOR FILING AN UNFAIR LABOR PRACTICE COMPLAINT

Unfair Labor Practices Procedures:

- Step 1. Formal charge initiated (Parties fail to reach compromise)
- Step 2. Investigation (Field examination conducted)
- Step 3. Regional Director complaint (at this level, the following three outcomes can derail charge):

A) Withdrawal—case can be withdrawn
B) Settlement—a settlement can be reached between parties
C) No Merit—case could be disposed as having no merit to advance

* if case is derailed by any one of these factors, appeal could be made to General Counsel whose decision is final and non-review able.

- Step 4. Hearing (presided by administrative law judge)
- Step 5. NLRB (20 day window to appeal)
- Step 6. Court of Appeals (if warranted)
- Step 7. Supreme Court (if warranted).

4.3 NLRB (NATIONAL LABOR RELATIONS BOARD) JURISDICTION

The Wagner Act provided the NLRB authority to have jurisdiction over unfair labor practices and other arising questions related to interstate commerce. Due to the broad mandate offered to the NLRB, the Supreme Court allows for congress to play a role in certain matters. The NLRB essentially operates at its discretion regarding which cases to pursue and in what manner to operate. Given such a broad mandate resulted in some complications for the board. One such problem in the NLRB earlier days was that of case selection due to the heavy workloads and budget constraints, the board would overlook cases that tended to have minimal impact on commerce and invariably took up cases where the impact to commerce was substantial. Another concern relating to jurisdiction was the issue of federal v. state jurisdiction, the Wagner Act and Taft-Hartley amendments sought to clearly define the role and jurisdiction of the NLRB, most issues relating to unfair labor practices were deferred to the NLRB with the federal courts available for ultimate decisions if warranted. Another product of these amendments was the establishment of uniform application of NLRB policy. Landrum-Griffin: title vii addressed the issue of "no man's land" in response to the cases not picked up by the NLRB being left in void as states would not deal with them.

Under the NLRA, public employees at federal, state & local levels are excluded, others include federal contractors, domestic servants, agriculture workers, etc. Some notable expansions of groups covered by the board include sports professional teams, private colleges/universities, charitable institutions, undocumented aliens etc.

The NLRB has not fully exercised its potential jurisdiction in a variety of fashions. The primary failure lies in the bureaucratic delay in resolving cases. Another source of failure relates to fact that the NLRB may only hear cases referred to it by the general counsel, thereby making the board somewhat weak. The board also has no recourse in challenging cases derailed by the general counsel. The changing make up of NLRB board members also results in constant shifting views.

The role of states in labor relations seems uncertain and hazy; the issue of "no man's land "seems particularly disturbing. Supreme Court decisions take an unfavorable view over state mandate in labor disputes, which leaves states with an undefined role in labor relations.

4.4 Collective Bargaining

The NLRB determines whether all employees of a plant are to be included as a single bargaining unit on a case-by-case basis. Each defined group of worker's is examined in view of the circumstances at play, below is a synopsis of each group:

- Craft workers essentially are considered on a case-by-case basis. Current policy follows the "Mallinckrodt Doctrine" Board outlined six basic guidelines:

  1. Status of employees
  2. Existing bargaining trends
  3. Distinctive identities of general workforce
  4. Bargaining history in industry
  5. Integration & interdependency
  6. Qualification & experience of union

- Supervisors may organize but have no protection
- Managers are excluded from being part of a single collective bargaining unit, this policy is as a result of the Supreme Court ruling in the Bell Aerospace case, which stated managers not covered by law.
- Plant guards may not be part of a single collective bargaining unit as stipulated in Taft-Hartley, they may however bargain with fellow guards but are prohibited from organizing with other workers. In order for professionals to be part of a collective bargaining unit, the board has to allow these employees to vote in a special election. Confidential employees are excluded.

Procedure for processing representation elections

1. Petition (recognition)
2. Investigation conducted
3. Regional Director level (could issue withdrawal or stipulated election at this stage)
4. Hearing (by field examiner) *Can be appealed after this stage before decision
5. Certify/decertify/no cert (Regional director)
6. NLRB need not review
7. Court of appeals (if warranted)
8. Supreme court (if warranted)

4.5. EXPLAINING THE "GENERAL SHOE DOCTRINE

NLRB can reject or place aside election results in the absence of unfair labor practices if it deems either party involved have engaged in behavior capable of swaying employees from making a free choice during an election. The pivotal aspect of this doctrine focuses on the impediment of an atmosphere conducive to free choice during an election. Behavior such as visiting employees at their homes and pressuring them to reject the union or a manager conspiring with employees in his/her office to shoot down the union is certain to have the NLRB apply the Shoe Doctrine. In applying the shoe doctrine, the board conducts a thorough investigation of the circumstances at play.

Employer Do's and Don'ts in interfering with employees

An employer may:

1.) Call a captive audience staff meeting for all employees without affording the union equal time to reply.
2.) Make economic predictions based on a factual basis of what they believe will be the resulting effects of unionization, in making such predictions, the employer needs to be cautious from making suggestive innuendos bashing unions.
3.) An employer also has a lawful right to express their opinions provided no threats or coercion are part of such opinions.

An employer may not:

1.) Make threats to employees
2.) Assert coercion tactics
3.) Make promises to sway employees voting decision
4.) Visit employee homes for purpose discouraging them from voting for union
5.) Lie or Misrepresent facts
6.) Single out or harass employees

When can an employer petition the NLRB to conduct an election?

The Taft-Hartley legislation allows an employer to petition the board for new elections in the event the employer is confronted with two unions both looking for recognition within the same bargaining unit. This stipulation allows the employer to petition for elections even if only one of the two unions is demanding overall collective bargaining. Recognition status of the union has to exist before an employer can proceed with such a petition. Once a petition is filed, the board conducts a careful investigation of all factors prior to making a final determination.

Gissell Doctrine Explained

Under this doctrine, the NLRB can give union's bargaining recognition even if the union loses representation elections provided there is existing evidence of an employer practicing unfair labor practices during an election campaign. The logic of this doctrine follows that by allowing a new election in light of unfair labor practices carried out, employees are likely to follow the same voting pattern given another opportunity. Majority support for the union as a bargaining representative prior to the election has to be evident in the form of signed authorization cards (75% practical). Two conditions exist for unions to obtain certification without an election:

1.) **Jay silk type:** unfair labor practices taking place & employer refusing to allow employer requests to bargain, no election held, union must show majority cards.
2.) **Bernel foam type:** similar to above except election held.

Types of Gissell Doctrines

A.) Atrocious/pervasive: can issue bargaining order regardless of election or majority status.
B.) Serious: UFLP, requires evidence of card majority
C.) Minor: minimal impact, no bargaining order, but general shoe applies.

This is a seemingly reasonable policy because in its absence, unethical employers could continue to curtail employee's freedom of choice by continuously using unfair labor practices such as threats and coercion. Without measures to stop or discourage such practices, you end-up with situations like sweatshops or certain nations where employee's rights are non-existent. It is only fair that employers obey the law therefore avoid being caught up in such a predicament.

Issue of Closed Shops and right to work states

Unions and employers may not negotiate for the closed shop. The closed shop was outlawed by congress through the passage of the Taft-Hartley legislation. Unions and employers in some states may negotiate for a union shop, this is contingent on each individual state and its stance on union shops. They may not negotiate for union shops in right to work states as this practice of union shops has been eliminated under their state legislation. Such states have statutes within their constitutions that ban the pre-requisite union membership as a condition for employment.

4.6 SUCCESSOR EMPLOYER OBLIGATIONS

The U.S. Supreme Court decision in "Burns Protective Agency" is still the legal binding framework for employers in matters relating to the successor employer. The Burns decision stipulates a successor employer must recognize a predecessor's bargaining unit, but is not obligated to accept the labor agreement negotiated with the previous employer. This decision was further enhanced in 1987 when the U.S. Supreme Court upheld the NLRB use of the "Burns" doctrine. The U.S. Supreme Court was careful in pointing out that the NLRB and the courts deal with Successor problems on a case-by-case basis.

In summary, the criteria in successor employer issues is as follows:

1) An employer is required to recognize a predecessor union and has duty to bargain if the following conditions are satisfied:

A). Company retains the same structure
B). The majority of old employees are hired or retained. (If the successor employer is in doubt of this stipulation, the employer may raise a good faith doubt, however they need to present object evidence supporting their doubts).

2) A successor employer is not required to abide by the prior bargaining agreement.

4.7 REINSTATEMENT RIGHTS IN VARYING CIRCUMSTANCES

The issue of reinstatement rights of strikers varies depending on the nature of the strike, before further discussing this issue; a brief synopsis of each type of strike is essential.

Economic Strike: encompasses strikes that typically call for higher wages, call for better working conditions, working hour issues, better benefits etc.

Unfair Labor Practice Strike: this is a strike that results from an employer deemed to be engaging in conduct declared unlawful by the NLRB policy. Usually involves things such as union recognition matters, impediment of the collective bargaining process, employer interference in union organization or elections, and so forth.

Jurisdiction Strike: relates to dispute between two or more unions over the delegation of work assignments. (Illegal under Taft-Hartley)
Other types include:
Wildcat strikes
Certification/minority strikes
Sympathy strikes.

REINSTATEMENT UNDER ECONOMIC STRIKES

Employees engaging in economic strikes have very limited rights in terms of reinstatement. Such employees are not required to be reinstated and may be permanently replaced, unless employer engages in unfair labor practices in the process. The NLRB may order immediate reinstatement of such workers only if the employer does not fill their jobs with permanent replacements. The legal stance of employers being able to replace economic strikers with permanent replacements was borne out of the U.S. Supreme Court ruling in NLRB v. Mackay Radio & Telegraph. The courts further revisited this matter in 1986 where it reaffirmed its initial position. An employer is not required to reinstate economic strikers and may permanently replace economic strikers unless there is evidence of unfair labor practice.

Right to vote unless:

a.   Find new permanent job
b.   Job has been eliminated
c.   Evidence of misconduct.

REINSTATEMENT UNDER UNFAIR LABOR STRIKE

Employees that fall into this category have unlimited rights regarding reinstatement, striking workers are required to be reinstated regardless of whether an employer has replaced them. The NLRB has the overwhelming mandate not only to order reinstatement but may also instruct the employer to pay back wages & other lost benefits. Notable cases asserting this position include the Mastro Plastics case where the U.S. Supreme Court held that employees were entitled to reinstatement even if the strike was in violation of the no-strike clause in a labor agreement, contingent on the strike having stemmed from employer unfair labor practice conduct. One important aspect to note is the forfeiture of reinstatement rights if any violence is involved.

REINSTATEMENT UNDER JURISDICTION STRIKES

As earlier pointed out, such strikes are illegal as stipulated in Taft-Hartley. When jurisdiction disputes arise, the NLRB (as instructed in the 1961 U.S. Supreme Court case of Columbia Broadcasting System) is to hear arguments presented by both parties involved and make a decision, provided the parties involved have not established a mechanism to resolve such issues within 10 days. In 1971, the U.S. Supreme Court under "Plasterers Local 79" clarified its stand giving the NLRB mandate to settle jurisdictional disputes if the employer refuses or fails to submit dispute to an outside party for a resolution.

REINSTATEMENT RIGHTS UNDER RECOGNITION STRIKES

These are sometimes referred to as strikes against certifications or minority strikes. Congress outlawed such strikes for recognition when there is an existing NLRB certified union. Anyone engaging in such a strike where a certified NLRB union is present in essence is practicing an unfair labor practice as defined in section 8(b). If such a strike proceeds, the NLRB under section 10(1) is given authority to seek injunctions against strikers. In summation, recognition strikes are:

- Illegal
- No reinstatement
- No Voting.

UNIONS AND HAND BILLING PRACTICES

A Union may use such a tactic as long as they are not physically harassing consumers or causing disruptions such as blocking traffic, or any other acts constituting disorderly conduct. This issue was bought to the forefront in the 1998 case involving the De Bartolo Corporation at one of its shopping malls in Tampa, Florida. The U.S. Supreme Court unanimously voted that the practice of hand billing was lawful, effectively reversing the earlier position taken by the

NLRB. The court stated unions could handbill a shopping mall in order to try to get the owner to unionized workers.

CONTROL MECHANISMS REGARDING DUES AND FEES

As regards dues, initiation fees and assessments, different requirements apply based upon the type of union. Local unions can raise dues, initiation fees or assessments via secret ballots in two ways listed below:

1.) Vote taken at membership meeting with a reasonable notice having been allowed detailing that the issue will be put forward to members for a vote
2.) Membership referendum, posted notices as well as announcements may be utilized to satisfy the reasonable notice requirement.

STATUS OF NATIONAL UNIONS

Follow the criteria outlined below:

1.) Majority of delegates at regular convention (delegates selected by secret vote plus 30 days notice)
2.) Majority, secret vote by referendum
3.) Majority of vote of executive board if given authority in by-laws

Fiduciary Responsibility:

- Loans to members limited
- May not pay fines for unlawful conduct of officials.

DUE PROCESS PROTECTIONS FOR UNION MEMBERS & DISCIPLINARY ACTION

Union members may not be fined, expelled, or disciplined without due process protocol being followed. Landrum-Griffin in its "bill of rights" outlined the following procedures to be followed when union are to be reprimanded.

A.) Union member must be served in writing with specific charges.
B.) Union member should be given reasonable time to prepare their defense.
C.) Member should be given a full and fair hearing.

If a union violates any of these procedural standards, the union member in question has the right to initiate a court challenge of the action levied. The U.S. Supreme Court made it clear that the courts in such matters were limited to procedural determinations and not to be embroiled in specific union rules [1971 ruling & 1992 Chicago Federal appeals court case]. The burden of enforcement of the purported violations of bill of rights is placed upon the union member suing unions or its officers in civil court.

DISCRIMINATION BASED ON SEX, RACE OR RELIGION

The passage of Title VII made it illegal for an employer as well as unions to discriminate based on sex, race, religion, disability or age. Congress formed the Equal Employment Opportunity Commission to administer the broad legislation. Clearly, the legal framework is in place to deal with discriminatory issues, however it is notable to address some oddities. The first issue pertains to sexual orientation, such preferences are not governed by any federal statues but rather left to the state statutes. The second odd exception involves the notion of BFOQ where out of business necessity, the employee make up is comprised of a certain gender, and the business necessity is job related and carries non-discriminatory intent or consequence.

SHOULD FEDERAL EMPLOYEES BE ALLOWED TO COLLECTIVELY BARGAIN?

Federal employees should be allowed to engage in collective bargaining as long as their position does not compromise national security or civil law & order. By allowing bargaining in the federal realms, this would not only satisfy the wishes of those federal employees who desire to do so but may also force some government agencies in being run more efficiently as they realize that they are being held to the same standards as the private sector in employee related matters. The critical issue goes back to maintaining a balance between protecting the greater good of society or allowing for bargaining to satisfy federal employees who may desire bargaining, until that balance is quantifiable in terms of opportunity cost, the logistics are still gray.

CURRENT LABOR LAW: PRO LABOR OR PRO EMPLOYER?

The current labor law status has come a long way, and through its journey has bestowed a great deal of progress to worker rights. However, the current environment seems rather edged towards the employer, not necessarily by design in my viewpoint but rather as a result of changing times and the free-market system at hand. The changing climate of labor law can be seen in the rising number of work free states particularly the Sun Belt states where their state statutes are overwhelmingly pro-business. I honestly see this trend intensifying and spreading as the success in some of these pro-business states begin to manifest themselves. My opinion is not solely as a result of the declining membership numbers of NLRB even though that in itself gives credence to my observation. I do not think this trend, i.e. pro-business environment is such a bad thing, and I think it will take a while for society to adjust their skills to cope with this new order of business.

4.8 THE DEMISE OF U.S. UNIONS IN THE GLOBALIZATION ERA:

The U.S. labor movement has undoubtedly had a tremendous impact on labor relations over decades acting as a voice and guardian for worker's rights. Along the way, the labor movement has confronted obstacles from employer's and other anti-union forces but has always exhibited a tenacity to forge ahead in achieving its goals. Despite various pitfalls and sustained criticism of the movement, many positives for workers have resulted due to the labor campaign, one need only look at the various legislations and amendments passed over the years ensuring the protection of workers rights. Unions today and for a while as a matter of fact are at a pivotal crossroad, their membership numbers have dwindled to all time lows, collective bargaining has been marginalized, and most troubling for the labor movement is the continued erosion of union jobs as they are relocated elsewhere.

The relocation of production facilities and the shift in the workforce is the cornerstone of this assessment. The subject of globalization is obviously very extensive and all encompassing, thus focus is drawn on two specific subject matters as relates to the globalization environment. The first part lays emphasis on the mobility of production facilities and the latter part of the review examines the dilemma of the changing workforce of immigrant conducive states. In each case, I examine the scope and nature of the issue from the perspective of unions and employers. Applicable law, if any will be addressed as well as other factors at play. Naturally, both parties, that is unions and employers have varying views on this subject matter, which will be addressed, in the latter part of this section.

LABOR & EMPLOYER RELATIONS OVERVIEW

A brief perspective of labor relations and unions is essential in setting the stage for the issues at hand. The development of labor relations is an interesting journey dating back to the pre 1930's to its current state. This relationship has evolved with times and undergone a variety of changes. The first part of the relationship saw a dominant judicial system playing a heavy hand in regulation. [1]. Unionism saw it's rise in the 1930's with its membership reaching astonishing numbers, this dramatic rise was fostered by the passage of the Norris-La Guardia and Wagner legislation which promoted unionism and collective bargaining.[2] During this period, federal and state courts made it difficult and in some cases impossible to form unions. Prior to the Norris-La Guardia era, the environment for the labor movement was very hostile and unpleasant, employers utilized tactics such as the "conspiracy theory", injunctions, yellow-dog contracts, and so forth. Such tactics ran out of steam and simply faded away with time or were nullified by Norris-La Guardia as was the case with Yellow-Dog contracts. The Wagner act under section 8(a)(1) made it an unfair labor practice for an employer to use tactics that undermined employee's rights [3]. As such, the Wagner act provided the NLRB authority to have jurisdiction over unfair labor practices and other arising questions involving interstate commerce.

The current environment enjoys an array of legal protection for workers, however the dynamic is constantly evolving and changing. Unions today are faced with new challenges under the global environment, unlike some of the earlier battles waged on home turf, unions now have to contend with crafty employers who have found a new weapon in their arsenal. Whereas unions had relied on collective bargaining and strikes as negotiating tools with employers, such tools have been marginalized by employers as they simply move their production facilities elsewhere to avoid dealing with unions. Employers are also effectively using loopholes in shifting traditional workforce patterns. As earlier pointed out, unions by their very nature are and have always been a very tenacious group which has put up a commendable fight over the years, however, this fight with globalization is daunting &perhaps their biggest , the very survival of unions may come down to this battle ground. The labor movement has taken some heavy blows from the manifestations of globalization and they will need all the muscle they can garner for this battle.

MOBILITY OF PRODUCTION FACILITIES

This is perhaps one of the biggest threats looming on the very existence of American unions as we know them. The continued relocation of American production facilities to various locales across the globe which in most cases are developing countries has reached epic proportions. Ironically, the very basic rights unions evolved out of, i.e., fighting for employee rights is at the pinnacle of this trend. The very lack of such employee rights in developing countries is actually fostering this movement. Since labor costs are significantly much lower in such developing nations, compounded with the absence of enforceable labor protection laws & other factors such as corruption, poverty etc, the rapid disappearance of union jobs has continued. As this trend has steadily risen, the effect on American jobs lost is astounding; "between 1969 to 1976, 1.2 million jobs lost, 1980 to 1985, 2.3 million jobs lost". [4] The main beneficiaries to this trend have been Mexico and south East Asia. To put this in perspective, consider this phenomenon, 40% of IBM's total workforce resides in foreign countries and the largest private employer in Singapore is General Electric, which just finished building a $150 million Hungarian light bulb factory. [5]

Politicians in developing countries strapped for foreign currency & often poverty ridden are aware of this trend and are standing in line to coax & entice western companies by promising them the lowest labor costs(1996 comparative average compensation for production workers in manufacturing between Mexico & the United States, $17.70 U.S. $1.54 Mexico) [6] and offering corporations virtual tax havens. The governments in developing countries usually assure the western companies protection from union activity through special immunity provisions, or may simply squash any noisemakers by any means necessary. In many of these countries, protection laws for employees are essentially non-existent. The first dilemma borne out of this trend for unions relates to collective bargaining, considering the ease at which corporate owners can relocate production facilities, union organizers are faced to ask themselves how do they effectively engage in collective bargaining with an employer who has at their disposal the option of just closing shop and relocating to a new locale offering enticing capital returns. In some cases, an employer may just be waiting for any labor dispute as an excuse for relocating operations, in fact it is common practice nowadays for companies to openly state their intentions of moving operations. Unions in industrial states with labor intensive manufacturing economic bases & the largest concentrations of unions have been particularly hit hard as illustrated below (selected economic levels from study on effects globalization on U.S. workers).

Share of Total Private Sector Employment in Goods—Producing (%)

Year	US	Indiana	Michigan	Kokomo	South Bend	Jackson
1969	49.5	58.4	57.0	71.8	50.3	60.6
1979	42.85	50.8	49.7	64.6	42.2	52.4
1989	34.0	41.5	38.1	54.8	32.0	41.9
1994	30.7	34.3	30.6	48.2	25.7	30.5

Source: U.S. Census Bureau, Annual Report of County Business Patterns. [7]

Labor & Corporate Response

As the table above illustrates, states that traditionally relied on industrial manufacturing jobs have shown a trend of declining numbers as has the U.S. as a whole. As unions continue to cry foul play on the part of corporate owners who engage in this practice, the owners counter-act stating this is the only way they can survive in this new order of business. They argue that they are simply allocating their capital and resources where they can maximize their returns while following ethical business protocol. Business owners feel the business environment has become so inter-twined and relocation of the production unit comes with the territory in order to stay competitive. Supporters of the global trend utilize the economics 101 theory of "comparative advantage", asserting that resources will be allocated where they are best utilized & productive.

Unionists on the other hand view such reasoning as simply rhetorical nonsense and see the real motive of the business owners as taking advantage of the cheap labor while lining their pockets. They contend, the owners are irresponsible and lack corporate morality for abandoning communities that made them what they are and are simply driven by maximizing profits at any cost. Faced with this dilemma, unions have sought creative ways to fight this force despite the lack of legal recourse in most matters of transcontinental commerce. The AFL-CIO union leadership for instance, recognizing the challenges of the global era implemented some new initiatives & policies. it's new policies centered on international competition, which emphasized cross-border union alliances and protections of all workers across the board all over the globe[8]. Some notable cross-border alliances include, the AFL-CIO, Hotel Employees and Restaurant Employees International Union, International Federation of Chemical, Energy, Mine and General

Workers, World's Pulp and Paper (represents workers in 21 countries, six continents), all these unions have a common objective of uniting all employees across borders employed by the same multinational parent companies. The effectiveness of cross-border unions however is somewhat limited, besides serving as a solidarity reaffirmation of workers, companies are still engaging in business as usual. Unions have also employed campaign messages such as "Buy American", union leadership has also employed lobbying campaigns to law makers calling for protectionism in some core industries. The AFL-CIO under the leadership of Sweeney has followed a pro-active strategy by bringing the issue of low wages to the national debate, Sweeney's campaign was instrumental in getting congress to raise the minimum wage. [9] Clearly, the labor movement is not staying put, but rather, taking some initiatives; if anything, to at least slow down this onslaught. As for its success, that remains to be seen over time. Unions are further constrained and hampered by the absence of any applicable current law with jurisdiction of cross-border commerce and worker rights.

Changing Workforce Dynamics

In the first part of this analysis, I looked at the issue pertaining to U.S. production facilities being shut down and being transplanted in foreign countries, usually developing countries. The ramifications of this trend are clearly evident, this next section is however dedicated to an equally important facet of globalization manifestations, which is often overlooked. The point of reference is the issue relating to the changing workforce make-up of employees particularly in high density immigrant states such as California, Texas, Florida and Arizona, also commonly referred to as border states. The stem of the problem centers on "new immigrants", essentially referring to recent foreign arrivals with intent to make a new living. The influx of this group in such large urban metro cities such as Las Angeles, Houston, Miami, Phoenix, etc. has been viewed as a blessing or a curse depending on who you talk to. Since this group of "new immigrants" are often from less developed economies and very often find themselves in desperate situations attempting to maintain a daily existence, they are compelled to take up any available position to get income, in most cases they take jobs that are low paying and typically undesirable to the general public. Such jobs include, taxi drivers, landscapers, janitors, hotel housekeeping, fast-food attendants and the likes.

This unusual relationship eventually takes on a domino effect and soon transcends industries as employers realize that they can lower their cost by hiring such employees and boosting their profit margins in the process. Due to this dynamic, union employees become vulnerable as inevitably they consequently face layoffs and things of that nature. It comes as no surprise that the recent trend indicates a sizeable segment of new production facilities seem to favor the sunbelt geographic regions to set up shop, naturally this may also have to do with the "work free" statutes that most of these states follow. The statistics on the following page put into perspective the magnitude of this phenomenal in the S. Florida metropolitan area of Miami-Dade County.

Percentage of Foreign-Born Residents in the Miami Standard Metropolitan Statistical Area (SMSA), Selected Years

- 1940 (9.7 %)
- 1950 (12.1 %)
- 1960 (16.9 %)
- 1970 (41.8 %)
- 1980 (53.7 %)
- 1990 (59.7 %)
- 1998 (53.6 %)

Current Population Survey, March 1999.

Percent Immigrant Labor in Various Industries, Miami-Dade County, 1980, 1980, and 1998

- **1980:** Eating & Drinking (29.9), Hotel & Lodging(39.8), Apparel(82.6), Nursing Home (19.5)
- **1990:**Eating & Drinking (51.3), Hotel & Lodging(65.7), Apparel(85.7), Nursing Home (54.0)
- **1998:** Eating & Drinking (67.3), Hotel & Lodging(67.4), Apparel(85-95*), Nursing Home (75-85*)

Sources: For 1980: U.S. Census Bureau 1981, table 227, pp. 941, 942; for 1990: 1990 Census, analysis of Public Use Micro data Sample (PUMS) data; for 1998: Current Population Survey; March 1999, excerpt for apparel and nursing home industries, which are authors' estimates. [10]

H1-B and L-1 dilemma

Another troubling aspect for unions involves the practice of employers attracting foreign workers through the H1-B and L-1 visa programs. This practice became especially widespread in the 1990s following the economic boom and the dot.com explosion.[11] Under this program, U.S. corporations lobbied congress to raise the cap issued on H1-B visas from 65,000 to 195,000 [12]. This move caused extreme outrage and debate all the way to presidential candidates as well as union leadership who contended that this drive was taking away jobs from skilled American workers. The corporations however in their main argument stated there was a shortage of such skilled workers and thus the necessity for foreign workers. It is indeed ironic that the worlds wealthiest economy would lack highly skilled labor, but such was the reasoning presented. The bulk of such foreign workers would come from India, which raised red flags for union activists who viewed this as simply a plot for corporations to get away with hiring cheap skilled labor. It is important to note that the widespread outcry by unions and anti-immigrant right wing groups did payoff as congress did introduce legislation to reduce H1-B numbers to about 80,000 as of 2002 [13].

It is evident to see that the issue of U.S. unions and globalization as relating to job relocation and changing dynamics is a very critical matter. Throughout the section, valid concerns and arguments from both parties were raised. The object however is not to pick sides on who is right or wrong but rather to present the issue at hand and look at both vantage points of the parties involved. On the first issue of job relocation, after careful review of all factual background materials, I draw the conclusion business corporations by nature are driven by maximizing returns and thus relocating production facilities fits into the business plan of utilizing the cheapest available labor thereby ensuring maximum profits. One would also say the same logic & reasoning applies to the latter dilemma. As for the outlook on unions fighting this trend, my research leads me to believe the picture is not a bright one, particularly in the absence of legal recourse for unions when it comes to dealing with such issues. It is an unfortunate situation, but one, which unions have to deal with by applying, continued pressure on congress and anyone willing to listen.

REFERENCE NOTES

1. Witney, Fred & Taylor, Benjamin J., Labor Relations Law, 1996. Pg1
2. Witney, Fred & Taylor, Benjamin J., Labor Relations Law, 1996. Pg1
3. Witney, Fred & Taylor, Benjamin J., Labor Relations Law, 1996. Pg23
4. Craver, Charles B., Can Unions Survive,pg45
5. Craver, Charles B., Can Unions Survive,pg45
6. Table1, U.S. Census Bureau
7. U.S. Census Bureau, Annual Report of County Business Patterns
8. Nissen, Bruce. Unions In A Globalize Environment. P212,213
9. Tillman, Ray M., The Transformation of U.S. Unions, 1999. P17
10. Table 2 & 3
11. http:www.atimes.com, Indian IT professionals targeted in US
12. http:www.atimes.com, Indian IT professionals targeted in US
13. http:www.atimes.com, Indian IT professionals targeted in US

CHAPTER V

ZAMBIAN HUMANISM IDEOLOGY IN THE POST INDEPENDENCE PERIOD

Humanism was an ideology expounded after the onset of independence as the national philosophy of Zambia. It was to be the core basis of all the policies and programs of the Party and Government. As such, all development efforts in Zambia were to follow the principles and guidelines of humanism which emphasizes the importance of "MAN" as the center of all activity. (MAN used as a metaphor to collectively encompass all humanity)

Zambian humanism provides the moral basis for all human activity in the country whether it be political, economical or social. The philosophy is the social cement that holds together and inspires the young and varied nation that is Zambia. The framers of this philosophy sought to distinguish "Zambian Humanism" from other forms of humanism, they emphasized that "Zambian Humanism" is not like that shirt or that dress that we wear for special occasions but rather, humanism is our dress for all occasions. It is like the skin we wear on our bodies. It is our way of life for all time. As earlier pointed out, the movement and subsequent declaration of humanism as the national philosophy of Zambia was borne out of the struggle for independence by Zambia's founding fathers & freedom fighters. These freedom fighters suffered from an oppressive British colonial regime which denied them their very basic right to exist as a man, hence the emphasis of man at the center as the underlying principle of the philosophy.

Principles of Humanism

1. **Man at the center**
   "This man is not defined according to his color, nation, religion, creed, political leanings, material contribution or any matter . . ."
2. **The dignity of Man**
   "Humanism teaches U.S. to be considerate to our fellow men in all we say and do . . ."
3. **Non-exploitation of Man by Man**
   "Humanism abhors every form of exploitation of man by man."
4. **Equal opportunities for all**
   "Humanism seeks to create an egalitarian society—that is, society in which there is equal opportunity for self-development for all . . ."
5. **Hard work and Self-reliance**
   "Humanism declares that a willingness to work hard is of prime importance without it nothing can be done anywhere . . ."
6. **Working together**
   "The national productivity drive must involve a communal approach to all development programs. This calls for a community and team spirit . . ."
7. **The extended family**
   ". . . under extended family system; no old person is thrown to the dogs or to the institutions like old people's homes . . ."
8. **Loyalty and Patriotism**
   ". . . It is only in dedication and loyalty can unity subsist."

CONTRIBUTING PERSPECTIVE: HUMANISM: ISSUES OF IMPLIMENTATION SINCE 1968

5.0 HISTORICAL PERSPECTIVES

In order to understand the circumstances out of which Zambian Humanism has grown, there is need to know some historical perspectives of Zambia.

Zambia became independent on October 24, 1964 and she is a product of a bitter freedom struggle born out of a Cha-Cha-Cha (master plan) fervent Cha-Cha-Cha spirit mooted at the Mulungushi Rock of Authority intensified massive resistance against the hated colonial and racial minority rule.

In colonial Northern Rhodesia, racial discrimination was rife and exploitative capitalist tendencies held away in all spheres of life. Settler society in Northern Rhodesia had its own ideology which was built on the myth of

European racial superiority which was nurtured to justify the minority racial group. The country was divided into watertight compartments of Europeans, Asians, Coloreds and blacks. Blacks were also compartmentalized into tribal groups and disorganized through tactics of indirect rule. Racial inequality flowed as natural corollaries from this unjust and abominable system.

At independence, Zambia inherited a colonial structure which had been designed to serve foreign interests. The policy makers & advisors were foreign and so were the executors.

Before independence, UNIP (United National Independence party) under the leadership of President Kaunda had well laid out objectives set out in the pre-independence UNIP consistitution regarding the nature and form of government nationalists wanted to replace the colonial government or nature of society they wanted to establish. Two amongst such objectives were:

- To achieve African democratic socialism for Zambia, raise the standard of living of the people and generally strive to make the people of Zambia happy and content.
- To ensure acceptance of the principles of equal opportunity for all people in all aspects of life including wages of workers, social, health and educational facilities (pages 9-11 of humanism in Zambia; Part 1 deals with pre-independence objectives)

The tone was set in the pre-independence party objectives and the leaders were quite clear in their minds of what they desired for the new country. Immediately after independence, Dr. Kaunda and his cabinet team started giving the new country firm direction and image of a sovereign and independent state.

5.1 ROOTS OF ZAMBIAN HUMANISM

Zambian Humanism was launched by President Kaunda at the UNIP National Council on 26th April, 1967 and finally accepted by the whole country at the party's annual conference on 14th August, 1967. Humanism which was known in 14th Centaury Italy and popularized by Francesco Petrarch as a subject of intellectual thought and study is different from Zambian Humanism. This definition related to the Church and state relations in Italy in that centaury. In our context, Zambian Humanism is a formulation and systematization of the values and social principles which existed in pre-colonial Zambia—absence of exploiting classes, leading communal lives, existence of self-reliance and mutual aid society. In short, it is an ideology which governs an all round development on MAN in Zambia. It is a process which establishes a social, economic and political order that is man-centered and exploitation free.

Zambia removed a colonialist, oppressive and foreign racial power in order to bring about a new social, economic and political order based on the noble principles of egalitarianism. The ideology of Zambia humanism is intended to re-organize the Zambian economy from a basically capitalistic one to an essentially humanist one—free of exploitation of man by another. Zambian humanism provides the moral basis for all human activity in the country whether it is political, economic or social. The philosophy is the SOCIAL CEMENT that holds together and inspires the nation of Zambia under the grand MOTTO of ONE ZAMBIA—ONE NATION. The challenges of national unity demanded that all people be treated on the basis of equality.

Zambian humanism rests on the social values of the Zambian traditional society as it was before it was distorted by capitalist influences of Western imperialism and colonialism. Traditionally, MAN—whatever his station in life—had a place in society. Everyone regarded himself/herself as a subordinate to the community and not above it.

5.2 PRINCIPLES OF ZAMBIAN HUMANISM

- Man at the center (man centeredness)
- The dignity of Man (respect of human dignity, respect for the aged and inferior)
- Non exploitation of man by man
- Equal opportunity for all (egalitarianism inclusiveness)
- Hard work and self-reliance
- Working together (co-operative effort, communalism and mutual aid)
- Communalism and mutual aid
- Patriotism and respect for authority
- Reciprocal obligation

Zambian Humanism is not a duplicate of the European humanism movement. It is instead a moral philosophical and ideological process that is seeking to guide a new nation of Zambia. In a complex web of socio-economic realities that have characterized the capitalist epoch. Zambian humanism shares one central principle with the European humanism and that is, it upholds the centrality of man in all activities. But it also sharply differs with European humanism in that Zambian Humanism recognizes the spiritual divine and abstract supernatural existence.

Consequently, while the cultural teachings of European humanism aimed at liberating man and his society from the Vatican oppression. Zambian Humanism has adopted the cultural teachings on the basis of the traditional Zambian society which was based on some kind of communal systems of production.

5.3 WHY HUMANISM

Zambia is basically a Christian society and the majority of Zambians believe that MAN is the creation of God. As humanists, we accept the equality of MAN before God our creator as well as before the law of the land. Zambians therefore have an idea of what is needed or have a mental impression or opinion of the nature and form of what their society should be. A man-centered society seems to satisfy an idea of what Zambians perceive to be perfect for their society—the Zambian society.

Universally, man wants love, to be loved, to seek the truth and to create. He also wants peace, stability and progress I.e. good food, good shelter, clean clothes, clean water and he wants these things on the basis of freedom and justice. Yet, man's cherished goals are hampered by the powerful forces against humanity. These are:

A). Divisions based on race, color, creed, tribe, religion:

B). Problems of poverty, hunger, ignorance, disease, crime and exploitation of man by man:

C). Problems of isolationism of nation states and the false confidence giving boundaries

D). problems of competing and often mutually exclusive ideologies within the nation states:

E). Problems of population increase:

F). Problems of pollution:

G). Problems of leadership.

Faced with such powerful forces against every society, need arises to decide and chart the course of direction a country wants. Zambia has chosen HUMANISM because MAN must be central in all that we decide to do. Since NO SOCIETY CANNOT BE WHAT ITS INDIVIDUALS ARE NOT, the party UNIP has planned the Zambian society in such a way that all forms of exploitation by man are fought and eliminated. In many walks of life, we have planned our society in such a way as to introduce equality both in theory and practice. The mentally and physically strong should not prey over the weak and helpless.

5.4 ISSUES OF IMPLEMENTATION SINCE 1968

The road to implementation of Zambian Humanism is a long one. Zambia has had to learn to walk before it could run. Besides, its geo-political position played some part in slowing the pace of the implementation process. This notwithstanding, a lot has been achieved in the five spheres of human endeavor.

Like most ex-colonial territories, Zambia at independence took the reins of government with a scanty high-level manpower. Seriously, the economic sector at independence remained entirely in the hands of non-citizens particularly Europeans and Asians. This was a deliberate and direct result of the colonial policy of denying economic opportunities to local/indigenous citizens. This policy was implemented to the worst degree in Zambia which was not only dominated by the colonial administration but by the Boer breed and their South African apartheid influences, so much so that exclusion from economic activity and opportunity for the Zambian entrepreneurship was obsolete. The Zambian leadership realized in very good time that political independence without participatory democracy and economic independence were handicaps which needed to be put right early enough. Humanism has therefore been a good guiding star in Zambia because it places MAN at the center of all activities.

POLITICAL SPHERE

A). The challenges of National Unity in consonance with Zambia's Motto of ONE

ZAMBIA—ONE NATION have been addressed. In March 1972, president Kaunda appointed a National Commission on the establishment of One-Party Participatory Democracy in Zambia. By early December, the UNIP National Council approved Government decisions and Parliament enacted the necessary legislation to give effect to the decision. On 13th December, 1972 Zambia became a ONE-Party Participatory democracy while also Parliament became a One Party parliament though ANC members continued sitting in Parliament as independents until their elected term expired at the end of 1973. These measures were designed by the Party in order to bring unity in Zambia to achieve humanist goals.

On June 27, 1973 Mr. Harry Nkumbula accepted the new political system of One-Party Participatory Democracy when he merged his ANC with president Kaunda's UNIP during the now famous Choma Declaration. From that time henceforth peace and unity prevail and clashes between party supporters ended. Under the principle of Participatory Democracy, members of the same party UNIP contest elections at the Section/ Village, Branch, Ward, District, Constituency, etc under the philosophy of Humanism. Having attained independence, people have proclaimed participatory democracy as a political system to safeguard it. They have devised a system of electing leaders.

B). Decentralization of Party and Government

Power to the people has been achieved. Decision making in the party and government have been decentralized to local levels and Provincial members of Central Committee, Provincial permanent Secretaries, District Governors and District Executive Secretaries head provinces and districts. Decentralization is direct involvement in decision-making at local level. It has been discovered that decentralization of Party and government has the following advantages.

I).   Local people get accustomed to handling their own affairs
II). Local people acquire more experience which in turn reduces clamoring for experts from the center.
III). Leads to greater efficiency since the power to solve problems is closer to the people.
IV). Central government ceases to be cop heavy
V).   local people learn to appreciate the art of government

The objective of decentralization is to distribute the power of decision making to the local people. Humanism in terms of policies implies that the only safe repository to power are the people themselves. Humanists believe that political stability can only come about if there is a full and unfettered system of participatory democracy both in theory as well as in practice. Participatory democracy is an advancement or improvement on representative democracy. You elect people and then keep them on their toes by making them participate in the day to day decision making process.

They make decisions on those things which affect lives, i.e. The Basic Needs

The Civil Service has been oriented and politicized and the president's Citizenship College was established in Kabwe to accelerate the orientation programme for public officers. This had to be done because of widespread complaints of the menace of bureaucracy which does not implement the reform program quickly and effectively. The problem lay in the fact that the colonial civil service initially consisted of law enforcement cadres, i.e. police, prisons, provincial and district officers whose fundamental functions were limited to the maintenance of law and order to pacify Africans so that they do not disturb, let alone acquire and enjoy the privileges of the European settlers. Secondly, the colonial bureaucracy concentrated on the collection of revenue from various forms of tax. Development planning was not considered important. It is also important to realize that the colonial civil service was racial in character. Recruitment of senior officers was confined to European expatriates. Very few Africans were given senior civil service posts.

C). Party committee and Works Committees
Party and Work committees at places of work were established to facilitate productivity in various institutions and to encourage industrial Participatory Democracy.

D). Trade unions
Trade Unions have been strengthened in industry and government service to enhance relations between employers and employees and also to obviate exploitative tendencies.

5.6 ECONOMIC SPHERE

One of the demands of Zambian Humanism is to work relentlessly to rid the world of the evils of capitalism, imperialism, colonialism, neo-colonialism, fascism and racism on one hand, while fighting poverty, hunger, ignorance, disease, crime and exploitation of man by another man. Independence was therefore not meant to be a mere change of guard but rather it was a liberation of the oppressed from foreign domination, racial domination, deprivation and segregation which institutionalized the forces of exploitation.

Since one of UNIP's objectives during the pre-independence period was: "to secure the most equitable production and distribution of wealth of the country in the best interests of the people". President Kaunda in his wisdom ushered in the now famous Mulungushi reform of 1968 and the Matero reforms of 1969 in order to secure the most equitable production and distribution of wealth in Zambia to benefit all Zambians irrespective of color, race, creed, religion or station in life. Indeed the objective was to bridge the gap between the haves and the have-nots. The Party and the government had adopted the Mulungushi and Matero reforms and other subsequent ones to prevent the rise of a group of exploiters. The economic measures include:

A). The promotion of Zambian companies rather than individual ones.
The growth and expansion of the Zambian private sector enhances greater participation of Zambians in the growth of the private sector as a whole.

B). the promotion, consolidation and expansion of co-operatives
A ministry of Co-operatives has been created to consolidate the work of co-operatives in the country. This is because co-operatives are viewed as the best guarantee for the spread of benefits of economic prosperity and social improvement to the majority of the people in the country.

C). the widening of opportunities for co-operatives and Zambian entrepreneurs to participate in government programs.
The Matero reform of 1969 included a declaration of government policy designed to award building contracts below a certain level in value to co-operatives and Zambian contractors for example. This was a deliberate act of policy to encourage as many Zambian building contractors as possible to take advantage of the benefits of the economic reforms.

D). Workers Councils
The establishment of workers councils and the acceptance of the concept of co-determination. This ensures greater participation of workers in the direction of growth of the national economy and bring about a new way to constructive partnerships between management and the workers. Their interests would be intertwined.

E). Credit Extension
Credit facilities for Zambian businesses were made available in order to create a mechanism for transferring the economy into Zambian hands.

112

F). Limit Expropriation of funds

Limiting local borrowing by resident expatriates as a measure to control expropriation of funds by foreign controlled companies. Application for loans by no—Zambians had to be approved by exchange control authorities.

G). Small Markets

Establishments of small markets in towns to provide better services to the communities. In this way people would not have to walk long distances for their shopping. Smaller markets are also easier to maintain and also generate employment on a local level.

H). Granting road service licenses to Zambians to enable indigenous Zambians to operate transport services (taxis, buses, trucks, etc)

I). Sub-contractors to large companies should be Zambians. Small jobs such as digging trenches, painting houses, building walls, etc should be given to Zambians.

J). Establishment of restaurants, tearooms and cafes in towns and cities.

K). State participation in major enterprises and industries—Government nationalized the:

Mining industry—Zambia Consolidated Copper Mines (ZCCM)

Major industries—Zambia Industrial and Mining Corporation (ZIMCO)

The government introduced Economic Participatory Democracy in all economic activities in order to curb exploitation of man by another. Participatory democracy in the Zambian economic life means that all major means of production and distribution are placed in a safe repository of power which is the people themselves. To do this effectively is to put economic and financial power in the hands of the indigenous people. This way we shall remove those evils that degrade man such as poverty, hunger, ignorance, disease and crime. This also motivates hard work and promotes the spirit of self-reliance.

In President Kaunda's watershed speech of the 30th June, 1975 land reform was announced. From the 1st of July 1975, all freehold titles to land were abolished and all land held by commercial farmers under freehold titles was converted from that date to leasehold by present title holders. This decision was in fulfillment of the requirement of Humanism in Zambia part 1 which states that "land obviously must remain the property of the state".

The 1968 Mulungushi Economic reforms which ushered in Zambia's economic revolution also gave top priority to RURAL DEVELOPMENT—Assistance to small farmers was created. Credit organizations for small scale farmers was pledged. Credit facilities were improved and eased for a lot of ordinary people, Producer prices are increased every season. Subsidies have been paid to farmers and co-operatives to help them increase their productive capacity and to make them self-reliant.

5.7 SOCIAL SPHERE

Humanism is a way of organizing society in such a way as to remove, in the final analysis, all forms of exploitation of man by the other. After independence, the Party and the Government have adopted measures intended to eliminate anti-social forms of behavior such as greed, envy, oppression, self-indulgence, laziness, theft, plunder and murder etc all of which are forms of exploitation of one man by another. To this end and in order to create a MAN centered society, the following measures have been taken:

- Education from primary to university is free, technical education and vocational training institutions have been established, adult education through an extensive and intensive literacy program by the Community Development services is being carried out.
- Educational reforms giving emphasis on vocational skills has been introduced to provide opportunities for all.
- Medical care and public health services have been improved tremendously. Hospital fees have been abolished to provide access to all.
- Flying Doctor service has been established for emergency cases catering for outlying areas.
- Free agriculture extension is provided
- Prices for essential commodities and foodstuffs are subsidized
- Rates of commuter transport have been subsidized
- Abolition of racial compartmentalized medical and educational institutions
- Low-income groups, who are in the majority already enjoy exemption free income tax and abolishment of the Bicycle Tax as well as similar taxes.
- The National Provident fund was established in order to serve the interests of all the populous.
- Anti-Corruption Commission has been established to expose cases and incidents of corruption.
- Commission for investigations has been established to protect the interests of all people against injustice and unfair action.

- Leadership Code regulates the behavior of those holding public office.
- An Ideological College has been established—the President's Citizenship College to train public officers.
- Department of Participatory Democracy which is intended to democratize the industries has been established.

* A great deal has been achieved in the sphere of defense, security, scientific and technological sectors.

5.8 IMPLEMENTATION CONSTRAINTS

Internal factors

- Relaxed political education for propagating the philosophy.
- Crises of expectation—the lazy use the philosophy to exploit relatives and the state.
- Push & Pull factors accelerating the urban drift.
- Lack of resources to back up decisions.
- Lack of commitment by some decision makers and implementers.

External Factors

- Geo-political position of Zambia has necessitated outstretching of resources.
- Resistance by donor countries
- Lack of surplus investments
- Diversity of foreign ideologies

Natural Factors (Drought)

5.9 CONCLUSION

On balance, Zambia has done very well. A lot has been achieved in all the five areas of human endeavor. The quality of life of the people has improved. Most people have the basic needs of food, shelter, clothing, water, within reach of a rural health care center, and a good level of literacy. The Social services have improved. The road network is very remarkable. Racism and segregation were buried on independence day. Zambia is firmly united under President

Kaunda and UNIP and enjoys peace under ONE ZAMBIA—ONE NATION motto. Although the Zambian society is well away from reaching the socialist stage, the gap between the haves and have-nots has been greatly narrowed. The methods and tactics of the goal for creating a man-centered society have been introduced and despite some lapses in implementing the set methods and tactics, more has been achieved. The latest economic measures adopted by the Party and Government after the break with the IMF clearly show the spirit of determination that exists in Zambia about the welfare of MAN. With goodwill and concerted efforts by all Zambians, the stage has been set for achieving Humanism in Zambia.

CHAPTER VI

ZAMBIAN ECONOMIC OVERVIEW & KEY INDICATORS

6.0 BACKGROUND & GOVERNANCE

Zambia is a relatively small country in population numbers (10-11 million) and geographic proportions (752,614 sq. kilometers). This landlocked nation is located in Southern Africa, it. is bordered and engulfed by eight countries therefore making it a very diverse cultural and ethnic hub. Zambia unlike the plight and demise of many African nations has maintained a peaceful and harmonious existence through it's young existence, one indeed can in retrospect attribute this in large measure due to the diverse background of each citizen. The "One Zambia, One Nation" motto reinforces the need to embrace the differences and build on the common shared beliefs and principles

Liberation & post-independence era: (1964-1991)

The country has experienced many timelines beginning with the pre-colonial era, followed by the British colonial period transitioning to the post colonial independence period and culminating to the current period of multi-party liberalized environment. Founding President Kenneth Kaunda took office in 1964 after gaining independence from the British colonial administration. They were faced with immense challenges and a lack of firsthand experience in general management capacity which to a degree was inevitable and expected under the circumstances. The Kaunda era had a plate full, from dealing with the freedom struggle and being thrust into an arena where they had to build and manage a brand new independent nation, no easy task by any measure. The administration in brief embarked on a Socialist economic model approach which was perhaps good at the time and indeed many benefited from all the social programs implemented. In tune with what was transpiring in that era & the quest for self identity, massive nationalization of industry especially in mining followed independence. Kaunda was also very instrumental in the liberation struggle throughout the region particularly in the independence of Zimbabwe & South Africa. As a result of these efforts, the country exhausted many resources and faced punishing retaliation from the Apartheid regimes. Kaunda adopted a one party-rule system, in hindsight and reflection, Kaunda echoed these sentiments in an interview with the BBC [1]. "It would have been disastrous for Zambia if we had gone multi-party because these parties would have been used by those opposed to Zambia's participation in the freedom struggle," This approach run its course and diminishing returns started to set in mainly due to mismanagement and the slump in commodity copper prices The heavy reliance on copper revenues accounting for more than 80 percent of revenues was a double edged sword, diversification of the economy and national revenue savings would have been prudent. The low commodity prices meant the economy was stagnant from the 1980s to the early 1990s, the nationalized parastatal companies were struggling and underperforming, beset with all these underlying forces and cries for democracy, the Kaunda era relented and came to an end after 27 years of rule.

Multiparty democracy period: (1991-2002).

These widespread calls for change brought about the era of a former charismatic trade unionist called Frederick Chiluba in 1991. After almost three decades of the Kaunda legacy, Zambia was among the first African countries to peacefully transition to multiparty government. The Chiluba administration opened up the economy by selling and disposing the previously nationalized companies in a swift manner, some argue perhaps too eagerly. His efforts paved the way for a new dawn of democracy and open market liberalization during the two terms served. This administration was hampered by issues of mismanagement and bad policy which resulted in many adverse consequences on the country. Chiluba's legacy continues to be dogged by corruption allegations and the former leader has had ongoing litigation. The Chiluba era concluded after serving two five year terms.

The "New Deal" third republic (2002-2008)

The "New Deal" administration under the leadership of president Mwanawasa took the helm in 2002 after narrowly winning a heavily contested election in 2001. Mwanawasa immediately committed himself to building a free market economy, fighting corruption and reducing poverty. This administration has been very diligent in tackling economic issues confronting this country and demonstrated candid commitment in its social-economic policies, granted the country still has a long way to go but it has certainly made strides in leaps and bound. Prudent fiscal and economic sound policies on a macro level have yielded favorable returns. Sadly, the Mwanawas presidency was short-ended by the death of Mr Mwanawasa in August 2008.

Ruphia Banda Era: 2008—

Mr. Ruphia Banda who was the sitting vice president under the Mwanawasa administration won a narrow hotly contested run-off election to finish of the remaining term until 2011. Many expect him to carry on with the previous administration policies focusing on inward investment growth, poverty reduction & transforming the country into a middle income nation. The global economic slowdown will create some challenges as commodity prices decline and inflation creeps up. In response to the global economic slowdown, the government authorities revised the earlier projection of 7% economic growth forecast for 2009. The inflation mark was also revised upwards of 5 percentage points for 2009. The finance ministry outlined its immediate priorities centering on finding investors for major power generation projects, copper mining, agriculture and manufacturing. The authorities singled out finding developers for the Kafue Lower Gorge project which they expect to generate more than 750 megawatts of power as priority number one, the cost of this project is pegged at $1.5 billion. This is very critical as the country is facing power shortages due to increased demand and aging unreliable power plants.

6.1 ECONOMIC ENVIRONMENT & GAINS REALIZED (2002-2007)

The predominant economic activity and lifeline of the Zambian economy is mining. Zambia is Africa's largest producer of copper it is mineral rich and fortunate to be endowed with large mineral reserves, the industry alone accounts for over 70% of Zambia's exports. Other prominent economic sectors are Agriculture, Manufacturing and Tourism. The Zambian economy over the last several years has sustained robust growth and resilience, the economy has experienced growth rates in excess of 6% and single digit inflation rates for the first time in many years have been attained. The country has also experienced massive direct foreign investment particularly in the Copperbelt mining district and the Northwestern province where new copper and uranium reserves are in progress to be mined under what will be Africa's largest copper mine. ([2]. The sustained favorable copper prices on the commodity markets has fueled this large-scale investment drive and resurgence of copper mining in Zambia. These direct investment inputs have naturally infused a lot of foreign liquidity into the market place and due to the ease of access to foreign exchange and open markets, the economy has continued to perform well in terms of output. The continued upward growth rate expansion in effect has been fostered by the favorable copper prices on the external market, reduction of the external debt burden Zambia had to contend with (many of Zambia's debt was written off) and also in large measure good governance & macroeconomic policy as I mentioned earlier played a critical role. Many experts and observers expect this growth to sustain for a number of years barring a drastic collapse in world copper prices.

FIGURE 6.1 COPPER GRADE A CASH PRICES ON GLOBAL MARKET

Source: London Metal Exchange

6.2 INVESTMENT OUTLOOK

The investment environment in Zambia currently is robust and thriving, the return on investment on the dollar is extremely competitive. This market segment is a high growth economy with little to no saturation market shares, this compounded with the current high liquidity levels circulating in the economy make this market a top notch investment destination. As I alluded to in the prior section, one positive in this market has been the positive government effort, the excellent governance exhibited and the liberalized trade atmosphere. The country enacted the "1993 Investment ACT" This act in principle assures investors that at no time would their business interests be taken over without fair due compensation.

The Zambian economy is wide open and the push to privatization and direct foreign investment has been in full swing. The autonomous government body tasked with facilitating this transition is the Zambian Privatization Agency, the government established this agency in 1992 under the Privatization Act. This body seeks and identifies the most suitable investors both financially and more importantly, those companies that would offer a mutual beneficial relationship to the greater society of Zambia. The strong dedication in attracting foreign investment firms is articulated in the motto of the Zambia Privatization Agency which states *"To privatize identified state owned enterprises in a transparent, efficient and effective manner, thus contributing to the :*

- *stimulation of economic growth*
- *acceleration of development*
- *facilitation of transformation of the economy with broad participation*
- *generation of capital for the government and longterm potential for employment*

We will provide a stimulating and learning experience for our staff, thus equipping them for a future role in the business community whilst rewarding them with attractive remuneration.

We will be perceived as a forward looking organization dedicated to the economic success of the country".

Other related legislation enacted to boost investment include, The Securities Act of 1993, The Privatization Act of 1992, The Companies Act of 1994 and the Zambia Revenue Authority Act enacted in 1994. All these regulations and laws are a testament of the commitment of the Zambian authorities. Over 150 government owned companies have been gutted and put on the auction blocks all in the name of forward thinking development, the results of all these drastic measures will of course manifest in due course.

Zambia and the whole SADDC region is very robust and attractive for investments. The confidence and potential this market segment presents is daunting, this is the new growth frontier with high returns on investments, below are a few examples of developments on the ground:

BANKING INDUSTRY

The banking industry in Zambia is fairly liberalized, transparent and flow of capital is transparent with no constraints or restrictions. Foreign capital is available on the open market and operates on a floating mechanism. The principal monetary institution is the central bank called the Bank of Zambia, the bank overseas & implements overall fiscal monetary policy and monitors commercial banking activity. There are currently over 12 commercial banking institutions, 8 foreign owned and 4 locally owned. In addition to these institutions are an increasing number of non-traditional lending institutions mainly involved in micro-lending operations, savings banking, development banking and currency exchange provisions. The bank of Zambia regulates all these entities through the Banking and Financial Services Act of 2000. The market also recently saw the entry of Capital trading markets in the form of the Lusaka Stock Exchange (LUSE), the stock exchange has been relatively progressing well and has seen an increasing number of listed companies

Liberalization and opening of the banking sector has naturally fostered competition in the industry as the lending institutions vie for the same customer base, this has manifested in reduced borrowing interest rates, while the rates are still comparably high from a regional standpoint, the rates have been declining which is a good indication of confidence and optimism in the market as a whole. Current borrowing interest rates range between 20-30 % which is still on the high end especially when compared or pegged against inflation rates which register between 8-9 %. The gap between inflation rates and bank borrowing rates is obviously still too wide and the gap needs to be bridged to materialize meaningful economic growth within the middle 70% population group, an ideal or target rate differential generally should be about 5%. This baseline differential provides for a capacity of borrowers to achieve reasonable savings while paying back interest and principal payments on their loans

AGRICULTURE SECTOR

The agriculture sector in Zambia to my disappointment is grossly under appreciated and not fully capitalized, according to available statistics, only 15% of the 60 million hectors of arable land is under cultivation. Whichever way one looks at this picture, the reality is painful. This in my estimation is the biggest underutilized sector with windfall potential, export commodity oriented farming commodities are readily welcome to global markets and potential foreign inflows are merely sitting ideal and going to waste.

TOURISM SECTOR

The tourism industry is on the rise with a lot more unexplored potential still at hand. At last check, Zambia had some 19 National Parks and over 34 game reserves, clearly, this goes without saying, the tourist industry is ripe. While commendable developments have taken place in southern province, a lot is left do desire. The developments in Livingstone, Zambia's self proclaimed tourist capital destination should be looked at as a blueprint model. What has happened and continues to happen in Livingstone is a true testament to commitment and partnership between stakeholders involved. Of course, the story in Livingstone is somewhat of an unfair comparison considering the destination is home to one of the world seven wonders in the Victoria Falls or Mosi-O-tunya. The significance of the developments in Livingstone reflect how an untapped and underutilized resource can be transformed into a major attraction through competent marketing and financial strategies.

MANUFACTURING

Despite making some positive strides over the past few years, the manufacturing sector is also untapped and underutilized. According to government reports, the sector has registered a positive growth for five consecutive years. In 2008, the growth rate was 3.6% compared to 3% in 2007. Zambia is well positioned to become a regional entity in Southern and possibly Eastern Africa. The manufacturing industry compliments well with mining industry which is a capital intensive area relying on tertiary supply components. This is where an opening exists, the industrial base in Zambia is actually quite good despite the many years of neglect and deterioration. The Copperbelt in particular is poised for resurgence as a manufacturing regional base, this development is inevitable contingent of mining activities in the region. Another recent measures by the government to establish commercial trading zones are a testament to the potential, other initiatives such as the Multi-Facility Economic Zones (MFEZ), Duty Drawback Schemes (DDS) and so forth have been implemented.

6.3 ECONOMIC INDICATORS

FIGURE 6.2 ZAMBIAN ANNUAL INFLATION RATE

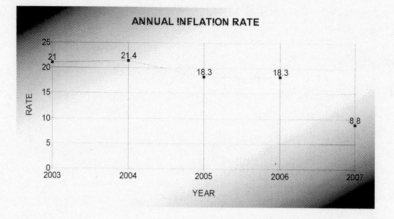

Data source: Central Statistical Office of Zambia [3]

The government authorities have done a very good job in managing liquidity, The Bank of Zambia which is the central bank and the Ministry of Finance which are the two primary agencies tasked with monetary and fiscal policy have shown prudent macro-economic planning and strategy. Over a five year period, the annual inflation has gone from a double digit high of 21% in 2003 to a record single digit low of 8.8% in 2007. The main components in the Consumer Price Index (CPI) that create great volatility are food and energy prices fluctuations. The food inflation rate in January 2005 was 17.9% where as in January 2008, the rate fell to 6.9%, in contrast, non-food rates registered 18.7% to 11.7%. The government is aiming to keep the inflation rate in single digits for the third consecutive year in 2008. The Bank of Zambia anticipates better food harvests will help ease the inflation, the high unpredictable energy and water prices are a concern. The Central Banks main overriding objective of monetary policy in 2008 is to consolidate the gains made in establishing price stability.

Growth output in the economy has continued an upward trend and is expected to stay on course in 2007 and 2008. The growth rate in 2008 is projected to be between 6-7% range as long as copper prices on the London Metal Exchange remain fairly stable with no shocks or drastic price collapse. The strong growth performance was also triggered by continued increased capital investments in the copper belt as well as modest increases in the construction and telecommunications industry. Good macro-economic policies played a role in this positive trend as well.

FIGURE 6.3 ZAMBIA ANNUAL GDP

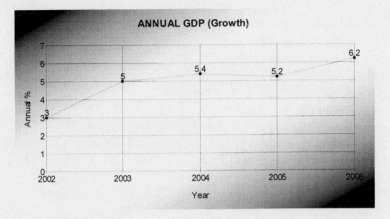

Data Source: Central Statistical Office of Zambia [4]

FIGURE 6.4 ZAMBIA DIRECT FOREIGN NET INFLOWS

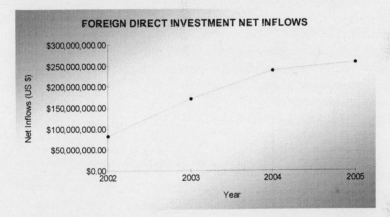

Source: World Development Indicators (World Bank Group) [5]

The cash inflows have followed growth rate trends and as earlier mentioned, the growth in inflows is directly a correlation of the massive capital investment in the mining industry. This will level off but inflows should remain positive with newly revised tax revenues from the mining royalties, therefore as the mines boost production capacities, the shift should align toward positive tax income inflows. Production efficiencies and huge demand from rapidly expanding China should mitigate any short-term price shocks on the external metals exchange market.

125

Investment confidence in the Southern African region remains very strong and robust. Invested Asset Management Ltd which manages $65 billion in assets and is the second biggest money manager in Africa plans to invest $5 billion in the region. The Cape Town based outfit has total holdings in the SADDC region of about $30 billion, The company's $240 million Africa Fund which invests in African stocks outside South Africa returned 39 percent in six months boosted from holdings in Zambia, Ivory Coast and Botswana according to the company in a report. Growth in sub-Saharan Africa is expected to reach 6.8 percent, the fastest in more than 30 years according to the international Monetary Fund. The growth in part is being fueled by debt cancellations and Chinas ferocious demand appetite for raw materials.

The confidence in the market is sound, Illovo Sugar Ltd., which is Africa's largest producer of sugar plans to increase its output on the continent by 37 percent by 2012, the company states it plans on expanding output in Zambia by 80 percent by April 2009 to 450,000 tons and is considering producing ethanol at a Zambia plant to be used in a 10 percent blend with gasoline according to company CEO Don Macleod. The company is 51 percent owned by Associated British Foods Plc. The company's strategy is to become a major European supplier after 2009

The Central Bank states foreign reserves rose 56 percent from the previous year to $1.1 billion directly as a result of debt cancellation and increased direct foreign investment

FIGURE 6.5 ZAMBIAN KWACHA V. U.S. DOLLAR

Source of exchange rate data: Oanda.com [6]

The exchange rate in Zambia operates on the open market and the rate is determined via the inter-bank foreign exchange market, this system has been in place since July 2003. The central banking authority, Bank of Zambia maintains a hands free approach but may intervene to mitigate any potential unstable market positions, the bank may also use this fiscal policy approach to manage foreign reserve requirements, but for the most part, the market is self-sustaining based on monetary demand and supply forces. Zambia's Kwacha (local currency) is expected to rise a second year straight against the U.S. dollar, the currency ended 2007 with a 15 percent appreciation. Experts predict the continued appreciation to be fueled by the newly incepted government mining taxes and royalty structures, observers point to the rationale that the increased tax base will inherently reduce foreign capital outflows. The Kwacha has fared well and remained sound and stable, a few bumps have followed the metal market fluctuations but nothing of concern, the currency has also appreciated when pegged against the U.S. dollar as the U.S. dollar has continued to struggle and decline, this is noteworthy because the Kwacha has shown resilience & stability rather than mirror the downward trend of the U.S. dollar. Many currency experts expect the Kwacha to remain buoyant and gain slight appreciation particularly if the U.S. dollar continues sliding. The Bank of Zambia has managed liquidity and the financial markets very well showing exceptional monetary and fiscal policy. This good monetary management in part has also kept inflationary tendencies contained as liquidity levels are in the right margins and balance.

FIGURE 6.6 ZAMBIAN CENTRAL BANK DISCOUNT AND PRIME RATES

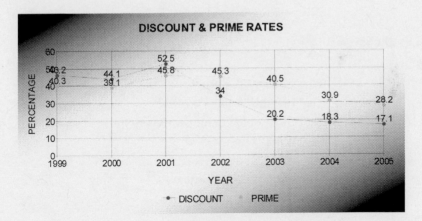

Source: Bank of Zambia [7]

Although still relatively high, both the discount and prime rates are definitely trending in the right direction, if this trend continues, it will in turn stimulate economic activity as borrowers are able to borrow funds at reasonable rates. The rates need to further come down and almost align with inflation rates or at least within a 5% differential margin, the narrower the gap between inflation and interest rates the higher the propensity for greater savings and reinvestment back into the economy.

MELLINIUM DEVELOPNET GOALS ASSESSMENT

1. Eradicate extreme poverty and hunger
2. Achieve universal primary education
3. Promote gender equality and empower women
4. Reduce child mortality
5. Improve maternal health
6. Combat HIV/AIDS, malaria and other diseases
7. Ensure environmental sustainability
8. Develop a global partnership for development

The eight Millennium Development Goals (MDGs), which 189 heads of state agreed to at the UN Millennium Summit in September 2000, are the most clear-cut and widely accepted set of development priorities the world has ever known.

TABLE 6.7 HOW ATTAINABLE THE MDGS ARE FOR ZAMBIA:

Goals and targets	Will target be met?	State of national support
Extreme Poverty: Reduce by half the proportion of people living on less than a dollar a day (Goal 1)	Likely	Strong
Hunger: Reduce by half the proportion of people who suffer from hunger (Goal 1)	Likely	Good
Universal Primary Education: Ensure that all boys and girls complete a full course of primary schooling (Goal 2)	Likely	Strong
Gender Equality and Women Empowerment: Eliminate gender disparity in primary and secondary education preferably by 2005, and at all levels by 2015 (Goal 3)	Likely	Good

Child Mortality: Reduce by two thirds the mortality rate among children under five **(Goal 4)**	Potentially	Good
Maternal Mortality: Reduce by three quarters the maternal mortality ratio **(Goal 5)**	Unlikely	Weak
HIV/AIDS: Halt and begin to reverse the spread of HIV/AIDS **(Goal 6)**	Likely	Good
Malaria and other major diseases: Halt and begin to reverse the incidence of malaria and other major diseases **(Goal 6)**	Potentially	Good
Environmental Sustainability: Integrate the principles of sustainable development into country policies and programmes; reverse loss of environmental resources **(Goal 7)**	Unlikely	Good
Water and Sanitation: Reduce by half the proportion of people without sustainable access to safe drinking water **(Goal 8)**	Potentially	Good

Source: undp.org [8]

6.4 OBSERVATIONS & IMPACT OF THE GLOBAL ECONOMIC SLOWDOWN

A brief look at developments on the economic sphere in Zambia within the past few years presents one with an optimistic disposition, indeed noteworthy strides have been made and the government authorities deserve to be commended on their efforts and diligence. Examining the economic indicators from a detached outlook and simply zoning in on the economic indicators, the picture looks sharp, but as any artist will testify, all images have gray areas and I will address those areas shortly. Back to the key indicators, my assessment is the trend is obviously in the right direction, the single digit inflation in over a decade is a milestone, to sustain this trend, the government needs to proactively develop strategies that promote the agriculture sector because food prices are the overriding factor in the overall inflation rate. Initiatives to promote the agriculture sector would also fall in line with intended objectives of diversification of the economy. Export oriented farming is an area of opportunity not fully being utilized, to cite an example, Zambia earned $60 million from exports of flowers and vegetables in 2007 [9]. Clearly,

Zambia, a country with so much underutilized fertile land resources could earn significantly more in this sector.

The Zambian government authorities also need to make sure the recent economic gains are sipping down to the common man and not only benefiting the investor community. As a policy immediate objective, the Zambian government authorities need to formulate income opportunities for the poor population base which by all accounts has been left out of this new economy. History is a great teacher as the saying goes, commodity prices are often cyclical and unpredictable, after all Zambia witnessed first hand the devastating effects of the copper price declines of the 1970s. It is therefore imperative that the natural wealth and wind full profits being made by mining companies are shared across the board and every Zambian who is entitled to their countries natural wealth benefits. I welcome the new mining tax reforms as not only required particularly when you look at comparable mining tax rates industry wide, whether in Chile or the U.S., so why should it be any different in Zambia, it's the right approach and simply stated an ethical issue, a country's God given wealth should benefit everyone and contribute towards the development of a developing country such as Zambia. Copper accounts for about 70 percent of Zambia's export income, copper prices have been on the rise in recent years, mining companies operating in Zambia posted sales of $4.7 billion year ending March 31, 2006 and only paid a shocking $142 million in taxes, however one looks at this picture, its insane, it does not make any sense, it is ludicrous, it's criminal, it's daylight robbery, thus said, the new mining taxes are long overdue. The new mining tax measures raise the effective tax rate from 31 percent to 47 percent. Miners will be charged a sales tax if the price rises above $2.50 per pound, a charge of 25 percent will apply to the surplus amount above $2.50 to a maximum of $3.00 per pound and the rate is staggered to increase to 50 percent for prices between $3.00 and $3.50, the rate is 75 percent once the price surpasses $3.50. The new measures also stipulate a 3 percent royalty on sales. All in all, this is a forward looking initiative and an equitable one for the foreign mining companies, it is still much competitive compared to industry standards, so companies should accept it or make room for other stakeholders, it's not a bargaining issue, it's the law. I pay my taxes as much as I may despise them, so why should private companies bargain over taxes or be afforded a free pass.

The recent electrical energy supply problems in Zambia and the whole Southern Africa region are a major area of concern, this inadequacy is adversely affecting productivity in the economy, the governing authorities will need to swiftly deal with this obstacle and create a more efficient energy supply. Talks of rehabilitating the existing power sources and development of new power stations have been in the pipelines for too long, words need to be implemented into action for Zambia to better position it's self as a favorable investment hub.

The broader global economic downturn will invariably impede and undermine many of these goals and objectives. As the global economic meltdown spreads its tentacles, the effects will be far reaching, while the common themes of the global recession such as rising inflation rates, unemployment rise, tight credit availability and so forth will be evident, a more hard hitting and devastating impact will be on the country's mining sector. The inflationary pressures are already starting to manifest as consumer prices have been steadily rising under the heals of high food and oil prices. The government authorities are cognizant of this development and such, the inflation projection for 2008 was revised upward. The closing inflation rate for 2008 was 16.6%, far above the initial projection of 7% before the global recession took its stranglehold. The mining sector is feeling the pinch from the global slowdown in the form of lower copper prices on the global market. Copper prices were recorded at a peak high of $8985.00 per tonne in July 2008 and by December 2008, the price slumped to around $2900.00 per tonne. [11] The lower prices will translate in the mining sector cutting back costs and future investments. The mines might employ measures such as layoffs to curtail the immediate effects. The global economic slowdown will also be apparent in direct foreign investments, as most investors in recessionary times stay put to weather the storm. The reduction in foreign cash inflows will cause upward pressure on the Kwacha (Zambian currency). As the supply of foreign currency tightens, the exchange rate will likely rise, this is already starting to manifest its self. The immediate effect of the kwacha depreciation will translate in higher costs to import goods & services. The country has fared relatively well, as the global economic slowdown hits full stride, the Zambian economy will be put to the ultimate test. Despite the diminished global growth rate, the Zambian economy was still able to realize a 6% growth rate during 2008 [10], a slight drop from 6.2% recorded for 2007 & short of the 7% projection before the global economic meltdown. This is a good measure perhaps indicating that growth in other sectors aside from the traditional copper exports remains robust. I expect all economic indicators to be pushed upwards naturally, to what extent the indicators are stretched is the key question. What happens in the western economies will be mirrored and transposed in the Zambian economy, the red flag will occur when the changes in the Zambian indicators start to exceedingly outpace the global indicators.

REFERENCE NOTES

1. BBC website
2. Financial Times
3. Central Statistical Office of Zambia
4. Central Statistical Office of Zambia
5. World development Indicators (World Bank)
6. Oanda.com
7. Bank of Zambia
8. UNDP
9. Zambia Export Growers Association
10. Central Statistics Office of Zambia, Ministry of Finance report
11. Ministry Of Finance 2008 report

CHAPTER VII

GLOBAL MANAGEMENT STRATEGY

7.1 MNCS AND CHANGES IN THE GLOBAL ENVIRONMENT

Changes in the international operating environment have had a drastic effect on MNCs and consequently a shift in global management strategy and general approach by MNC managers. These external changes have involved political, social, economic and technological forces. On the political front, many host governments have increased their level of restrictions and demands on MNCs. In many instances, host governments have applied pressure on MNCs to invest and transfer technology locally, required greater local management involvement and in some rare cases insisted on part ownership arrangements. Adding to this constraint for MNCs, local customers at times have looked at global products with disdain and their calls for national products have increased.

In view of such political & government forces, MNCs have recognized the importance of responding to such local forces. MNCs have realized that the need to respond to local forces was synonymous with their goals to remain globally competitive and efficient. This observation resulted in many MNCs following what's referred to as the "transnational" strategic mentality. This approach allowed companies to shift their main activities from a centralized base and instead focus on each international market, as it's own self-sustaining operation performing its functions on a localized basis. By employing such an approach, the MNC to a certain degree is able to respond to growing government and local forces while also maintaining its global competitiveness. Since the transnational approach lays heavy emphasis on domestic level operations unlike some of the earlier global strategy, managers of MNCs have been able to deal with other environmental factors such as social and cultural differences.

The impact of globalization particularly in the 1990s meant MNCs had to re-evaluate their operations to ensure optimal global integration and coordination. Some of the forces driving this phenomenon included factors such as economies of scale, economies of scope, factor costs and a liberal global trading environment. As such, MNCs had to respond to each force appropriately to remain competitive, for instance, the resulting economies of scale in many cases drove companies to outside markets in order to remain competitive. Collectively, all the above-mentioned forces in large part contributed to MNCs enhancing their global coordination so as to optimize their global competitiveness. However the biggest influence to the globalization drive could be attributed to the liberal environment for global trade, NAFTA for instance is good case in point. Technological advances also played a role in driving globalization forces, the product life cycle was reduced due to these resulting technological advances, which meant that only those companies adapting to worldwide innovation could gain a global edge. In response to all these forces, MNCs enhanced their global operations by specializing their production process, standardizing parts design, specializing the manufacturing operations and other measures. MNCs also increased their research and development budgets for developing products on a global scale.

7.2 MNCS AND STRUCTURAL FIT

The first part of this section devoted attention to the changes within the international operating environment and how these very changes made MNCs adjust their global efficiency structures, responded to localized forces and engaged in worldwide learning. Naturally, all these responses and adjustments are channeled through the MNC management structure. The second part examines the assertion that the basic problem underlying a company's search for a structural fit was that it focused on only formal structure and that this proved to be unequal to the task of capturing the true complexity of the strategic task facing most MNCs. Indeed this notion of finding a "structure fit" consumed managers in the earlier years and in fact for most managers, this way of thinking became the norm rather than actually implementing a strategy. As most managers would come to learn, paying attention exclusively to the formal structure presented colossal failures in many organizations. The reality of the matter was that by exerting such a one-dimensional focus, managers did not pay attention to other external influences, instead they were consumed on choices based on product or geography. Another negative trait of this approach was its effect on the organization structure as most realignment's were implemented briskly and this sudden change in many cases created chaos. Finally, the obsessive focus on structure created stagnation within the organization while the environment was ever changing calling for fresh multidimensional strategies. As such, the notion of structural fit is rarely relied upon and is a dying strategy as most organizations opt for multidimensional flexible strategies in tune with time changes.

7.3 MNC HISTORY & DEFINATION

The first inclines of multinational companies spawned from the vast empires held by Britain, France, Holland and Germany. This period in the 17th and 18th centauries manifested vast British and Dutch companies

An MNC is an entity that has substantial direct investment in foreign countries and actively manages such holdings as an integral part of the company.

7.4 TRADITIONAL MOTIVATIONS FOR MNC's

1. Secure key supplies particularly raw materials such as Aluminum, Copper, Rubber, Oil, etc.
2. Market seeking behavior in order to expand brands to larger markets and exploit economies of scale.
3. Internationalization, acquire low-cost factors of production, capitalize on lower tariffs and government subsidies.

7.5 RISK OF COLLABORATION

TACIT VS EXPLICIT COMPETENCES

Given the ever changing and evolving international arena, inherent risks and costs were inevitable. We therefore turn our attention to this very issue of risk and cost. The underlying risk in this situation is the vulnerability one partner may face in terms of their core competences. This situation could take the form where two companies decide to form a strategic alliance in order to compliment skills and resources. Given, these two companies are rival competitors outside this collaboration, the true motives of the parties involved may be to actually gain a competitive edge over the other partner. The potential risk in this collaboration is that one of the partners core competencies and skills could be highly engrained in the larger organizational structure and thus out of reach, where as the other partner's competencies could be explicitly displayed therefore making this partner vulnerable. The greater risk is that once the predatory partner has gained the skills and competencies of the other partner, the collaboration could deteriorate and subsequently collapse as was the situation with the General Foods & Ajinimoto alliance.

CAPTURING INVESTMENT INITIATIVE

This is also a predatory tactic where the motive is to take advantage of the partnership so as to eliminate the partner's competitive position. In this situation one of the partner's ensures that they are the primary beneficiaries of critical investments by being the aggressor. The danger here lies in the fact that weaker partner could eventually be stripped of its independent decision making thus making it dependant on the aggressive partner.

COSTS OF COLLABORATION

The biggest and ultimately the most significant cost of a collaboration relate to the opportunity cost the partnership presents to organization as a whole, meaning, are the risks and rewards entailed in the partnership justified and ultimately beneficial to the organization. A comprehensive cost benefit analysis would in part offer an answer to this question. Another inherent cost of collaborations lies in the uncertainties such arrangements present. Since such costs for the most part cannot be predicted or quantified, such uncertainties could present unforeseen additional costs. Internal strife's & conflicts that may result due to the combination of two organizations that have different corporate cultures could create redundancies and unhealthy environment, which in turn creates additional, costs because of inefficiencies within the collaborating structures. Conversely, national background, cultural differences and local political forces often bring about suspicion and in extreme cases resentment of whichever partner is viewed as the outsider, such bias similar to other examples pointed out ultimately is costly to the collaboration in its entirety.

In closing, as we have seen, operating in an international arena presents the MNC management with a very unique set of obstacles and challenges while at the same time offering many potential rewards. The key area the management of an MNC organization needs to focus on is not just a one-dimensional approach but a rather a flexible approach reacting to each situation with a tailor made initiative. The international arena is ever changing and cultural, environmental, and technological factors compound the task. Thus said, an effective MNC manager operating in the international arena has to operate like a fox and pay great emphasis to learning the internal environmental forces at play. Employing a flexible localized organizational structure could have dividends for the organization as well. The international arena is a difficult market but one that not be tamed.

7.6 COPPER MINING OPERATIONS IN ZAMBIA; THE ROLE AND CHALLENGES EXPERIENCED BY MULTINATIONAL COMPANIES

Zambia is a landlocked nation located in central southern Africa, eight countries namely, Tanzania, DRC, Malawi, Namibia, Angola, Mozambique, Botswana and Zimbabwe border it. The land area covers 752,614 square kilometers. The most recent census figures put the population figures at about 11 million. Zambia has one of the highest urbanized population rates in the Sub-Saharan region with the figure estimated to be at 46%. [1]. The principal city and commercial capital is Lusaka (pop 1.5 million). Other major cities include, Ndola, Kitwe and Livingstone. Copper and Cobalt exports account for 77% of export earnings and the remaining primarily agriculture and tourism. Average daytime temperatures are 15-27 Celsius. Zambia is a country with an enormous amount of mineral resources with copper dominating, other minerals include, zinc, lead nickel, uranium, coal, gemstones, gold, etc. Zambia is however internationally recognized as a major copper and cobalt producer. Since the 1920s when copper production began, the social and economic fabric has heavily relied on this industry.

The primary purpose of this chapter is to explore and examine the copper mining industry in Zambia and how the Multinational Companies have been part of this industry. The chapter will address some of the strategies employed by the MNCs and point to some successes as well as failures. The opening part of the chapter presents an overview of the beginning of the copper mining activities in the 1920s Colonial period. The following section looks at the 2nd phase in mining activities, what is described in this chapter as the post-independence era. The third section examines the decline of the 1970s as world copper prices slumped. Section four gives an incite of the privatization of the Zambian mining industry in the1990s, this section will also give a detailed look at the MNCs that are active players in the privatization efforts. As each chapter unfolds, the review will also look at other pertinent issues. The final segment offers closing remarks and observations.

ZAMBIA COPPER MINING INDUSTRY BACKGROUND

Mining activities in Zambia began in the 1920s in what at the time was called Northern Rhodesia. At that time, the country was under colonial rule under the British government. The British South African Company, a vast conglomerate with mining interests in the African region, first undertook copper exploration and development in the early 1920s spearheaded by Cecil Rhodes who founded the company. [2]. It wasn't until the 1930s that large scale commercialized mining begun. Financing of this operation was undertaken by two of the biggest investors in mining during that period, Alfred Chester Beatty and Ernest Oppenheimer. Chester Beatty formed the Rhodesian Selection Trust (RST), which was under the control of an American company called American Metal Climax (AMAX) while Ernest Oppenheimer helped create the Rhodesian Anglo-American group of companies. [3].

Mining activities were concentrated in the Northern part of the country, this area would later come to be called the Copperbelt province due to the dominant copper mining activities. The first large-scale commercial mine was Roan Antelope mine opened in 1931 in the town of Luanshya. Nkana mine was the second large-scale mine in Mufulira opened in 1932. Nchanga was opened in 1939. [4]. These three expansive mines would form the basic backbone of the mining sector, the "big 3". Production from the three operations was over 400,000 tones per year and during its peak reached 720,000 tones in 1969 making the Zambia the largest copper producer in the developing world and the world's third largest copper producer behind the United States and the former U.S.S.R. It's copper production accounted for 12.2% of total world production. [5]. This period was the best productive period the Zambian copper industry saw, this early success can be attributed to the high copper prices on the world commodities market. The Zambian economy became a one dimensional economy heavily dependent on foreign exchange derived from copper exports, at the very peak of the copper boom, over 80% of the foreign exchange was from copper export revenues. During this colonial period, British South Africa Company's motive from a global management perspective followed Traditional Motivations, which present companies with "Push and Pull" factors to internationalize. The First recognizable such motivation that drove the company to invest in the Zambian Copper industry relates to the need to secure key supplies, in this case resources. In fact it could be argued that the British South Africa company fits in the mold of early emerging MNCs. Market seeking behavior in this case seems to have played no factor and thus not a motivating pull factor. Availability of lower-cost capital also played no part & no government subsidy enticements were present. Therefore, the motives that were the driving force behind the overseas expansion of the British South African Company into Zambia could be narrowed down to resource seeking behavior. The British South Africa (operating under the two companies mentioned earlier, Rhodesian Selection trust and Rhodesian Anglo-American) company had a significant advantage in its international expansion into Zambia in that the competition aspect was virtually non-existent as it was the pioneering company within this industry and therefore enjoyed exclusive mineral rights with agreements drawn up with the British government. Another advantage the company enjoyed was its experience it had in the mining industry in South Africa, though not particularly in Copper Mining but rather mining in general, this meant the company had a certain level of existing expertise and competencies engrained within its organizational framework. This is a very important observation because scholars of transnational management will agree that a company cannot succeed in the international environment unless that company possesses a given set of core competences that allow it to flourish and overcome the barriers the international arena comes with. [6].

The issue of Factor Costs is also worth pointing out, during the colonial era the British Empire was stretching it's reach all across the globe particularly in Africa, Factor Costs clearly played a significant role with the British South Africa Company. Demand for copper was very high in Europe and other parts of the western world but it's availability and ease of access was not readily available and perhaps to some extent not as cost effective, therefore it's abundant availability in Zambia and relatively easy access facilitated the investment decision. We can rule out some of the more recent forces such as global liberal environment, globalization and so forth for obvious reasons i.e., these forces were not on the playing field yet. The British South Africa Company enjoyed enormous success as the paper pointed out earlier, however the fortunes of the British South Africa Company would prove to be short-lived. The early sixties would see a wave of newly emerging independent countries rising from the grips of colonialism, indeed Zambia was not spared from this manifestation and October 24, 1964, the country formally known as Northern Rhodesia formally became an independent sovereign state. Naturally, this new environment had to be somewhat concerning for the British South Africa Company, after all the company had poured substantial capital investments in the Copper Mining industry and it's revenues were at their peek. The tensions and anxieties surrounding the independence movement would pass and operations continued with rising outputs peeking in the late 1960s. However, drastic political economic changes in the early 1970s would change the fortunes of the British South Africa Company when then president Dr Kenneth Kaunda nationalized the mining industry. The industry was consolidated into what was called the Zambia Consolidated Copper Mines Ltd (ZCCM). This effectively ended the era of the British South Africa Company.

POST INDEPENDENCE DECLINING COPPER PRICES

After Zambia became an independent state in 1964, the British government addressed the issue of mineral rights, which up to this point had been exclusively held by the British South Africa Companies. An agreement was reached and the newly formed Zambian government was given the so critical mineral rights. The Zambian government progressively increased their stake into the mining companies and by the early 1970s announced the government's intent to nationalize all critical industries including the mining sector. The government began by purchasing a controlling share into the mining giant MNCs and effectively became the majority owner with 51% ownership. The government would go on to consolidate the copper mining industry into a huge company called the Zambia Consolidated Copper Mines creating one of the largest copper mining companies in the world. [Table 7] This nationalization drive was replicated in all major industries and was not just confined to the mining industry, however the mining industry drew the most attention because of the huge revenues and profits.

Table 7 World's 10 biggest mining companies ('000t)

Rank	Company Name	Production
1.	Codelco (Chile)	1227
2.	BHP (Australia)	860
3.	Phelps Dodge (USA)	699
4.	Rio Tinto (UK)	648
5.	Freeport (USA)	436
6.	KGHM (Poland)	425
7.	Norilsk (Russia)	360
8.	Cyprus Amax (USA)	341
9.	ZCCM (Zambia)	314
10.	SPCC (USA)	308

Source: Mining Journal, 1997

The Internal political forces within the newly formed country also became interesting as then president Kenneth Kaunda adopted a one-party state with socialist overtures and thus moving away from multi-party democracy. At the same time all these events were unfolding, a new set of external forces were also becoming apparent and these forces would have devastating consequences on the Copper Mining industry in Zambia. World commodity prices for copper, which had always been favorable and consistent, began to plunge. The declining global Copper prices inevitably started to be felt at home and the once prosperous mining industry started lagging. Another set-back for mining industry was lack of reinvestment in the mining infrastructure which on turn meant plants were deteriorating and production being hampered, in fact production levels dropped from the 600,000 levels down to the 400,000 plus mark. [Table 7.1.] Even though the Zambia Consolidated Copper Mines was still by far the single largest employer in the country, inefficiencies due to its large size made it very difficult to efficiently run all the various mining operations and divisions.

Table 7.1 Exports of Principal Commodities 1965-1993

	Copper	Zinc	Lead	Cobalt	Tobacco
1966	683	45153	15645	1433	9716
1970	684	50334	22079	1814	4041
1975	641	41265	19349	1344	5394
1980	600	30787	8749	1924	1218
1985	474	19024	5122	1924	2604
1990	441	9489	40	4931	2026

Source: Central Statistics Office, Zambia

By the early 1990s, twenty years of decline, decay and record low copper prices on the world commodities market had clearly taken its toll on the Zambian copper industry. Production reached an all time low in 1995 at 307,000 tonnes. It was during this period that the political dynamics in Zambia also started taking a different direction. After enduring one-party state politics, voices calling for multi-party democracy were being echoed across the landscape. The political change would eventually be realized as the long time president since independence was defeated in the countries first ever multi-party elections. With the new democratic administration in office, there were renewed calls to resurrect the ailing copper mining industry and bring it back to it's old glory days. These calls would eventually turn to talk of privatizing the entire copper mining industry, the privatization wave was sweeping the whole country with nationalized industries being sold off to private investors but the big question was when and how the mines could be privatized. It was a huge task that would take several years with endless consultations with investors, the World Bank, the IMF and every other conceivable entity. In the mid 1990s, the Zambian government began a full-scale drive to privatize the Zambian Copper mining industry. Bids and tenders were formally put out to the public and major mining companies began to line up and submit bids, the process as one might expect was long and drawn out with a lot of red tape and bureaucracy. In 2000, the Zambian government had completed the comprehensive privatization of the Zambian copper industry. The next section presents an overview of the new companies that entered the Zambian copper industry following privatization.

PRIVATIZATION OF THE ZAMBIAN COPPER INDUSTRY

A.) GLENCORE INTERNATIONAL AG

Glencore is a Swiss company with its primary operational offices in Baar, Switzerland, Stamford, CT, London, England and Singapore. The company has 60 global offices and independent agents in over 50 countries. Its copper mining operations in Zambia began in 2000 and involve a 73% ownership stake in Mopani Copper Mine in the Copperbelt region of Zambia. The mine facility includes 4 underground mines, a concentrator, and cobalt plant with a capacity of 450,000 tons. This is being rebuilt to boost capacity to 650,000 tons [7] the mine facility employs over 7400 employees. Primary export markets are USA, Europe, Asia and the Middle East. The company announced in February 2010 it plans on sinking a new shaft at Nkana mine at a cost of $100 which would extend the mine life by 25 years.

B). KONKOLA COPPER MINES

This is a Zambian registered company with its head office in Chingola, Zambia. 65% of the ownership is by the Zambia Copper Investments Limited of which 51.9% is held by Anglo-American (has since sold controlling interest to Vedanta). Konkola Copper Mines (KCM) is a subsidiary of Vendata Resources PLC a London based Metals Company. The remaining ownership is split between minority stakeholders. KCM is Zambia's largest Mining and

Metals Company. The company employs 10,549 employees at its mining operation with over 100 expatriates. The company structure is segmented into five business units or operations listed below:

1. Nchanga—comprised of Nchanga open pit, Nchanga Underground, Nchanga concentrators, Tailings Leach plant & support services.
2. Konkola—Shaft #1, Shaft# 3, Concentrator & support services.
3. Nampundwe—Underground Mine, Concentrator & support services.
4. KCM / Nkana—Smelter, Refinery, Acid Plant & support services.
5. Corporate office

Anglo-America primarily focuses on the smelting, refinery and acid operations. Anglo American has committed $82million in operational costs and contributed an additional $30million in cash. [8]

C). FIRST QUANTUM MINERALS

This is an integrated mining and metals company specializing in copper, cobalt and gold. The company is based in Canada and listed on the Toronto Stock Exchange in Canada. It lists its primary activities as mineral exploration, development and mining. In the Zambian market, it has 100% ownership in the Bwana Mukubwa mine and has an 80% stake ownership in the Kansanshi open pit copper & gold mine. It also has a 16.9% share in the Nkana underground mine as well as 16.9% in the Mufulira mine and smelter operations. The company also holds a18.6% stake in the Australian mining company, Anvil. The company seems well positioned for the Zambian copper industry with its strong diversity strategy.

D.) NFC AFRICA MINING PLC (Chambeshi Copper Mine)

This is a Chinese company controlled by the Chinese parastatal, China Nonferrous Materials Industry Engineering and Construction Group.) It bought a closed mine from ZCCM in 1998 for $20million and this was followed by repairs and investments of $200 million[9]. The company has an 85% ownership in the Chambeshi mine. Chambeshi Mine began operation in 1965 and was closed in July 1987. The Zambian government issued bidding for the mine in September 1996 with the tender being awarded to NFC in 1988. Operations began in 2002 and the company anticipates production levels of 40,000 to 45,000 ton/year. In 2009 NFC Africa also acquired an 85% stake in Luanshya Copper Mine.

E). AVMIN (ANGLOVAAL MINING LIMITED)

Avmin a South African mining company got into the industry with two ventures. The first venture was an 80% stake in the Konkola North project while the second venture was a 90% stake in the Chanbeshi cobalt plant. Avmin presents an interesting case study, because it entered the market with very ambitious objectives and pumped a reported $100 million in the investments [10]. Despite these huge investments and commitments, Avmin would later announce that it was disinvesting and getting out of the Zambian copper industry due to overwhelming constraints and failing to break even.

F). LUMWANA COPPER MINE

This is one of the world's largest new mines which 100% owned by Equinox Minerals of Canada. Project development of Lumwana began in 1999 with commissioning occurring in December of 2008. The mine is located in Solwezi, a town lying in North-Western Zambia. The company has a target projection of 135,000 tonnes in 2010 according to the company website.

G). OTHER NOTABLE PLAYERS

1. BINANI GROUP—Indian company with 85% ownership in Luanshya underground mine.
2. VANTAGE ENTERPRISES CORP—Canadian company involved mainly in Amethyst gemstones.
3. Cyprus Amax Kansanshi plc—U.S. Company with 80% stake in Kansanshi mine
4. Adastra Minerals—Canadian company involved in exploratory ventures.
5. Quasim Mining(Colossal recourses corp.)—Canadian company, 60% of Kabwe cobalt trails.

CONCLUDING REMARKS

The Zambian copper industry seems to have gone full circle, from the early discoveries and commercial production of copper deposits by the pioneering Cecil Rhodes, the British South Africa Company involvement, the nationalization efforts post independence and ironically back to what is seemingly like the starting point, copper production back in the private sector. One thing is clear, the nationalization efforts with seeming good intentions of self-sufficiency were perhaps too bold and flawed from the onset. To begin with, the Zambian government lacked the foresight to consider just how important the expertise to run such large-scale operations entailed. Secondly, the government run nationalized company had so many inefficiencies and overlooked reinvestment back into the operations and thus the facilities continued to deteriorate and produce below par. Given the low commodity copper prices were depressed, the production levels could still have been better. The new privatization quest is a very positive step in resurrecting this industry, the vibrant environment within the industry and the large capital investments by international companies is already paying dividends as not only are production levels rising, but more importantly, the world copper market price is slowly climbing as well. There is a glimmer of hope and I anticipate a very positive outcome for the Zambian copper industry and economy overall.

REFERENCE NOTES

1. *http://usembassy.state.gov/zambia/cguide.html*
2. *United Nations Environment Programme* report by Grijp,Nicoliene; Mupimpila,Christoper. pg15
3. *United Nations Environment Programme* report by Grijp,Nicoliene; Mupimpila,Christoper.
4. *www.zambiamining.com*
5. Bostock & Harvey, 1972
6. Bartlett,Birkinshaw, Ghoshal, S. 2004 *Transnational Management.* Pg7
7. *www.glencore.com*
8. Anglo American Fact Sheet
9. US Geological Society
10. *www.mining.co.za/copperbelt*
    Table 2: Mining Journal, 1997

Chapter VIII

BOTSWANA: EXEMPLARY ECONOMIC & DEVELOPMENT POLICY

The tale of Botswana is indeed one of a kind in the confines of the African continent, a continent beset with an endless trail of economic and political failures that are mind boggling and heart breaking. And yet, against this backdrop of gloom and despair, a little landlocked unknown nation outside of Africa is defying the odds and quietly sparkling like a bright gem. Quite fittingly, "the Gem of Africa". How then is this "miracle" for lack of a better word possible when for a long time the odds have always been against many that have undertaken this quest in this majestic and magical continent. It's a question many have pondered upon and at the very least requires some scrutiny, that is my quest as such, simply take a sneak peak at Botswana's playbook and blueprint, a road less traveled. How has Botswana been able to succeed where many others have failed? The story of Botswana is truly a tale of contradictions in the African economic development paradigm, consider this scenario for a brief moment: Zambia at independence in 1964 was the second richest country in Africa, its GDP in 1970 was $440, by 1996 the GDP was down to $360, today Zambia is one of the poorest countries in the world. In contrast, Botswana at independence in 1966 was in the bottom 20 poorest countries in the world with a GDP of $70, fast-forward to 1996, GDP was at $3210, today Botswana is one of the few middle income countries in Africa. I point to this contrast because unfortunately, this is the story that has been played out time and time again, a trend of countries actually regressing rather than progressing. The examples are endless, Zimbabwe once the bread basket and envy of Southern Africa with excellent infrastructure and a well developed economy, where is the country today, literally in a free fall with it's populous being harbored as refugees in diaspora, a diminished currency with billion dollar notes, such transgressions sadly seems to be the norm. It is worth noting that despite the remarkable progress made in Botswana, not all is utopia, unemployment is still high, wide income disparities are the norm and the effects of AIDS have been ravaging. Some go as far to argue that the economic success professed by Botswana in index measures such as per capita GDP is superficial and does not paint a true picture of developments on the ground which present a contrast of inequality.

8.0 HISTORICAL PERSPECTIVE

Botswana was not spared from the rush for Africa under the British empire, it became a British protectorate of Bechuanaland in 1885 until its independence in 1966 It's status as a British protectorate prevented the Boers in the South and the Germans from the South West to push in and inhabit the land. Botswana is located in Southern Africa just north of South Africa. It is a landlocked country sharing borders with Zambia, Zimbabwe, South Africa and Namibia. It covers a total area of 581,730 sq km (224,607 sq miles), roughly the size of the state of Texas. It has a semiarid climate and the terrain is mostly flat tableland with the northwest occupied by the Kalahari Desert. Botswana is very sparsely populated with a population of approximately 1.8 million with the greatest concentration in the principal city of Gaborone (224, 286 pop.). Roughly 80% of the population is of the Setswana ethnic group with the remaining groups representing splintered minority ethnicities. The principal economic activity by far is diamond mining accounting for close to 80% of GDP earnings. Botswana it the world's largest producer of diamonds. It has a GNI per capita of $5,180 (World Bank 2006). The dominant language is Setswana with English as the official language. Republic of Botswana follows a British parliamentary form of government and has a peaceful democracy since independence

FIGURE 8 BOTSWANA

Source: Botswana Export Development and investment Authority

8.1 HUMBLE BEGINNINGS

The tale of Botswana from the naked eye seems very simplistic and straight forward, an improvised country that was fortunate to discover diamonds and got rich overnight, however nothing could be further from the truth than such a narrow summation. One need only look at the many African countries fortunate to have vast natural or mineral wealth reserves but are essentially failing impoverished nations mainly due to senseless wars, widespread gross corruption and overall incompetence. Botswana unlike many former colonies has had the most unorthodox path since it's independence, where as most African countries at independence inherited a reasonable or considerable level of infrastructure, Botswana was essentially a barren arid waste land at independence since it had little practical importance to the objectives of the British empire. Where as countries such as Zimbabwe, Kenya, Zambia had well built up functioning cities and reasonable commercial manufacturing, Botswana had virtually no meaningful infrastructure. During the colonialization period, minerals and natural resources were being extracted in places like Zambia (Northern Rhodesia), Congo, Zimbabwe (Southern Rhodesia), Nigeria & South Africa, therefore, there was an incentive for colonial forces to facilitate infrastructure investment, however Botswana was left out of this mix because diamonds were not discovered until after independence

8.2 ECONOMIC ACHIEVEMENT SNAPSHOT

At the time of independence in 1966, Botswana was one of the world's poorest countries with an annual per capita income of barely $80, fast forward today:

- Between 1966 to 1997, Botswana averaged an annual growth rate of 9.2% which according to the World Bank [2] was the fastest growing economy in the world. Botswana is one of the few handful middle income countries in Africa with a per capita income of about $15,000 and is considered the richest non-oil producing country in Africa, it's real per capita income averaged more than 7% growth over three decades, a growth matched to the Asian Tigers such as Thailand and Korea.
- Primary school enrollment went from 66,100 in 1966 to about 320,000 by 1995 representing an increase of 5.4% per year.
- Poverty reduction from 59 to 47 percent between 1985-1994
- Access to portable water increased from 56 to 83 percent from 1981-1994
- It's currency the "pula" is strongest currency in Africa
- Since independence, Botswana has had the fastest growth in per capita income in the world. Economic growth between 1967-2005 has averaged 9% per year. The gross domestic product at independence was about 37 million pula and by 2000, GDP was over 15 billion pula. During a 35 year period, Botswana did something the bulk of African countries have failed to do, it transformed itself from a low income country to a middle income country, quite a remarkable feat.
- Botswana has consistently registered one of the highest human development index in Africa.
- As an investment destination, Botswana is at the top of the class, Standard and Poor's (S&P) and Moody's Investors Service have both

ranked Botswana with an "A" rating, the highest sovereign rating in Africa, essentially making it the best credit risk.

- Transparency international rated Botswana as the least corrupt country in Africa. The World Economic Forum lists Botswana among the top 2 countries to conduct business in, the country has also consistently recorded the highest human development index in Africa. The accolades are numerous and undoubtedly, Botswana continues to win praise as the "darling of Africa" in terms of economic management. A beacon of hope and a poster child of what can indeed be achieved with the right policies.

8.3 EARLY POST INDEPENDENCE PERIOD: "Bottoms up approach"

The incoming administration of Sir Seretse Khama in 1966 at independence had a lot to contend with, how to move forward a country which under the British rule had essentially been neglected. The country had insignificant infrastructure or a viable functioning economy, GDP was between $70-$80 and a largely uneducated workforce. Against such a backdrop, not to mention, dry arid barren terrain, no minerals, the odds were stacked against this young nation by all accounts. Almost in sync with the independence euphoria going on was a more subdued development in the sidelines, DeBeers prospectors from the huge South African mining giant were actively prospecting for minerals. Their persistence and tenacity would shortly be rewarded in 1967 when diamond and copper reserves were discovered at the Orapa fields, actual mining activity would not commence until 1971. This single event would forever change the fortunes and future of Botswana. It would be a while before these minefields could be developed and made viable, so in the mean-time the authorities of Botswana forged along. British subsidy direct payments and other international aid supplemented the governments meager earnings. The late 1960's and early 1970's saw the massive growth in beef production which was driven by high beef demand on the world market. According to the Botswana meat commission [3], cattle production grew from 127,000 heads in 1970 to 209,000 in 1974. This provided a boost to much needed foreign reserves for the country. Botswana also successfully renegotiated the 1910 "Customs Union Agreement" with South Africa, this placed the country in a better strategic position and boosted revenue inflows.

8.4 DIAMOND MINING AGREEMENTS & CONCESSIONS

At the very on-set of the discovery of diamonds in 1967, Botswana quickly came to the realization how much of an impact these gems would play in shaping the course of this young country. The government authorities immediately knew what they were dealing with was a very valuable commodity, recognizing the reality that they knew nothing about diamond mining & the industry as a whole, the authorities knew that their only bargaining chip was to present the mining foreign prospectors with a viable arrangement that would be mutually beneficial to all parties involved. This in essence was the birth of Botswana's mineral policy, borne out of the realization that mineral resources, diamonds to be specific would be the base and back bone of all future economic development. Given the prospect of such a one sided dependent economy, the first order of business for the Botswana government was to ensure they negotiated and entered into a solid and air-tight agreement with the foreign mining investors who had the capital resource base. The authorities knew kicking out these foreign investment mining companies would not be a wise direction but rather a self inflicted wound, so rather than prematurely go with a take all strategy, the government sought to find common ground, it established a mineral policy which emphasized and called for mutual benefits to all parties involved. In 1969, it is reported that the Botswana government was paid $20 million for a diamond concession which in turn paid back $60 million in profits a year, i.e. four month pay-back period [4] This indeed was an eye-opener for Botswana, it realized going forward, any such deals and agreements were to be approached with extreme caution with the right expertise that understood fully the complexity of contract negotiation. The government sought independent outstanding contract lawyers rather than exclusively listen to suggestions from World Bank & IMF specialists who perhaps had other motivations not necessarily suitable for Botswana.

Henceforth, when new larger diamond fields were discovered, Botswana after having learnt it's lessons earlier was able to aggressively enter into meaningful and equitable agreements in the 1980s, issues of ownership and royalties were renegotiated resulting in an equal partnership between the government and South Africa's DeBeers mining company to form the largest diamond mining company in Botswana called Debswana. [5]. Since the 1980's, Botswana has been the world's largest producer of diamond gems, in 1989, diamond export earnings totaled $1.4 billion [6] Another lesson was learnt after the successful mining renegotiation deals: The use of outside advisors from independent experts rather than bureaucratic NGO & IGO body's like the IMF & the World Bank was prudent and effective In fact, Botswana rarely sought advise from the likes of the IMF but rather utilized its own contracted independent experts from a broad international spectrum, the key to employing such professionals lay in the fact these people did not answer to any organization or body with its own motives, but rather, these advisors were experts by profession hired to simply take care of business. Ironically, when IMF mission teams would visit Botswana in the 1980s, they were surprised to find that what they were coming to propose was dead upon arrival because Botswana had already established and put into place such mechanisms using their own experts. [7] These very early policy implementations played a critical role in the development of the country, policy frame work had a basis and a blue print to implement policy into tangible results. This was true with the education plan, health plan, and infrastructure plan. Shying away from IMF and World Bank recommendations to an extent played a pivotal role in the country having very low debt obligations, the need to borrow money at exorbitant rates with a noose around the neck was circumvented by brilliant economic and fiscal policies. Botswana today has one of the lowest comparative debt obligations of $0.7 billion, with debt servicing accounting for about 4% of exports and huge foreign earnings. [8]

8.5 HUMAN DEVELOPMENT

The early years were dominated by developmental plans intended to set the course of Botswana's future and this resulted in two important initiatives being implemented. The first commitment was to advance the nation of Botswana as a free market economy. The second initiative was borne out of circumstance, with very few skilled people at time of independence, the authorities foresaw the need to invest in human and social capacity as a path from the bottom to the top. While it's very obvious, Botswana's economic expansion and sustained economic growth was fueled by diamond export revenues, what's remarkable is how well planned policies were able to facilitate and channel these revenues into the developmental sector. Botswana in essence entered into an informal "contract with it's people" by pledging to use the new found wealth for the betterment of each Botswana citizen. Many countries, and I emphasize "not just African nations" have vast natural resources that have earned billions and billions of dollars, but the sad reality is how these countries have mismanaged or misappropriated these revenues with little or nothing going to the common man. All one needs to do is sit back and see all these impoverished countries having food aid or grain dropped down from aid agency planes and it's citizenry scrounging like animals and yet to the dismay of many, these very same governments begging for aid have been embroiled in counter active wars and conflicts that have drained their financial vaults, a sad reality by all accounts. Although Botswana maintains a liberalized economy, it was careful not to neglect the social fabric of society in essentials such as education, transportation, healthcare and so forth.

8.6 EDUCATION PLANNING

Since it's early modest beginnings, the government authorities set out to put educational planning on the front burner as a priority of the overall national development plan. This agenda fell in line with a quest for the country to attain an educated workforce which was mainly driven by the newly independent country starting out with an uneducated population and practically no educational system in place. The core of the educational plan was detailed under the National Policy on Education (NPE) of 1977. This policy initiative was the blueprint for today's education system in Botswana. The policy was fairly straight forward with little nuances but rather simply calling for policy planners to map out and implement a strategy that ensured access to education to all citizenry. Policy makers were also tasked with formulating mechanisms of training educators as well. Unlike many developing countries where priorities are skewed with large expenditures allocated to defense appropriations, the Botswana government in its budget allocation channeled large resources to education.[9] The initial emphasis of the plan focused on universal free access to primary education, these early efforts did result in increased enrollments and also new schools being constructed during the early 80's. During these years, the government also recruited foreign skilled professionals from neighboring nations such as Zambia & South Africa particularly in higher education and medical fields.

In the mid 90s, the policy was refurbished and retooled under the auspices of 10 year plan implemented in 1995, this was done in line with the changing demographics and needs. The Revised National Policy of Education of 1995 had the hallmarks and staples of the original plan but also added emphasis to providing universal access not only to primary education, but to secondary and auxiliary levels. This goal according to government sources was fully realized in 2005. [10] The government did not stop there, a new initiative called Vision 2016 pillar of "An Educated and informed Nation" is the new Revised National Policy on Education (RNPE) which came into play in 1995 and builds on earlier protocols while adding enhancements with the changing environment. Vision 2006 is part of the broader 20 year development plan that calls for economic diversification as well. Clearly, the education policy has been managed brilliantly by the authorities; over 90% of children today are enrolled in primary school [11] and Botswana's standard of public education is comparable to international standards Government spending allocations on education have been increasing at an annual rate of 4% over the past decade, in 2005 education was recipient of 8% of the total development budget [12]

8.7 HEALTHCARE

No mention of Botswana goes without addressing the AIDS catastrophe that has ravaged this nation, by far the greatest challenge the country has faced. The HIV epidemic confronted Botswana in the late 80's and early 90's, projections for the impact on the population were dire in the early days with some calling for almost 1.78 million of the population being infected by 2010. [13] To the credit of Botswana's government campaign, the numbers were not realized. Today, the infection rate is approximately 17.1% of the population. The Botswana authorities took this scrooge head on, government committed itself politically, emotionally and financially. The government devoted a large share of GDP in fighting this challenge, in fact, many contend the country mounted one of the world's most sophisticated and aggressive fights against AIDS. The efforts involved political will & ambition and a massive educational campaign. Nationwide testing and free antiretroviral (ART) treatment, prevention of mother child transmission (PMTCT) were also commissioned, all these efforts immensely paid off and greatly reduced infection rates. As in the case with the education policy, the government devoted huge budget allocations to the healthcare sector and also set out concrete policy plans and strategy. Today, practically all urban residents are within a medical care facility and 80% of the rural population has access as well.

8.8 POLITICAL STABILITY

As I briefly mentioned earlier on, one of the hallmarks of Botswana is its political stability since independence in 1966, some have made the argument that this stability is skewed as the country has been ruled the same political party (Botswana Democratic Party) despite having three different presidents. It's a fair and reasonable argument, but I think the more important observation is how this political picture has played out. Botswana politics are transparent by all reasonable accounts with no reports of intimidation or harassment. In fact a government media source reported participation of over 10 political parties in contested elections. Perhaps a more compelling rationale for the dominance exhibited by the Botswana Democratic Party is an observation raised by many scholars regarding the role and backdrop of the traditional hierarchy in Botswana society. As in practically all African societies pre-colonial period, society was centered on the traditional model of chiefs and tribalism, two very important fundamentals in this context [14].[Daron Acemoglu, Simon Johnson and James A. Robinson in the research paper "An African Success Story" brilliantly narrate these sentiments and further expound on the notion of "tribal institutions that encouraged broad based participation and constraints on political leaders during the pre-colonial period; only limited effect of British colonialzation on these pre-colonial institutions because of the peripheral nature of Botswana to the British empire" Botswana by virtue of geography and fate was spared the unfortunate tribal decimation many African counties faced as colonial powers divided and redrew natural traditional boundaries based on economic ownership or resources. So in effect, when many of these countries gained independence, they were composed of non homogeneous ethnic groups lumped together as one nation. This as one would expect created tribal tensions from past animosities or unresolved conflicts, as such many of such tensions carried on and perpetuated ethnic conflicts which have beset many African nations. Examples include the Rwanda conflict between the Hutus and Tusi's, Kenya's squabbles between the Kikuyu's and Luo's, Ivory Coast war between North & South groups, the Sudan Dafur conflicts between the Arabs and Africans and so the list goes on.

8.9 MONETARY POLICY

Having a mineral based economy can mean being vulnerable to price shocks and external up and down forces, fortunately for Botswana, diamonds have remained strong on the commodity markets with few contraction periods. Single commodity dependent economies as is Botswana where this sector accounts for 90 per cent of foreign income need to employ very stringent macroeconomic policies to withhold and mitigate inflationary pull & push factors. Botswana's economy has remained robust and has been very stable. The main thrust of government monetary policy is geared on reducing inflation and avoiding erratic price shifts. The authorities have effectively managed this metric and in 1997 the inflation rate reached a 10 year low point of 7.8%. [15] Maintaining low inflation and a stable currency are the key macroeconomic policy objectives for Botswana, by keeping these variables in check, the authorities hope this will drive the overall objects of economic diversification and sustained growth. The authorities have had a good conservative exchange rate policy and have avoided an artificially overvalued currency.

FIGURE 8.1 Botswana Inflation Rate 2000-2005

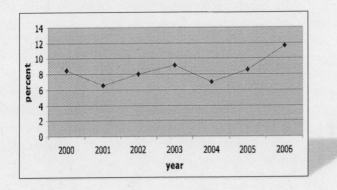

Source: Botswana Central Statistics Office

8.10 TRADE POLICY

Botswana's trade policy is in line with true market economy principles and is very transparent, good sound effective fiscal and monetary policies have facilitated an open market environment. Naturally, export of diamonds dominates the trade policy and overall balance of trade, however the framework and focus of the countries mid and long term policy is geared on attracting foreign investors in order to counteract the over dependency on diamonds. To achieve the objective of long-term diversification, the country is aggressively courting investors by offering a number of incentives.

Tax Incentives [source: BEDIA]

- Botswana maintains a low corporate tax rate of 15 per cent compared to many countries, this is deliberately marked down to foster investment. The 15 per cent rate is in place until 2020
- Exemption from withholding taxes in Botswana
- Credits for taxes withheld in other jurisdictions
- Access to double taxation treaties
- Tax exemptions for collective investment undertakings

Custom Incentives

- Industrial Rebate concessions allow for exempt custom duty payments on select raw materials used in manufacturing goods.

- General rebates for export oriented manufacturers.
- Schedule 470.03 allows for duty free import of inputs to be used in production of goods exclusively for export.

Zero tolerance for corruption

The Botswana authorities have made corruption eradication a priority, their efforts have resulted in low levels of corruption which is critical in fostering a healthy business environment. According to a 2002 Transparency international report, Botswana was ranked 24th out of 102 countries, the highest rating of all African countries surveyed.

8.11 FISCAL POLICY

- The government authorities have maintained an active fiscal approach but have also been very deliberate and disciplined. The government has orchestrated a nyrid of carefully crafted development plans which to an extent have driven fiscal policy and by the same token kept it in check. The bulk of the fiscal approach has been balancing budgetary expenditures against balancing foreign reserve accumulations. The government has huge foreign reserves at its disposal enough to overcome any nuisance shocks, they authorities clearly recognize their predicament on having an economy dependent on diamond prices and because of the volatility of minerals, they have made it a priority to hoarde as much reserves to offset any down-turns or when the gravy train leaves the station. Some, particularly the likes of the IMF & World Bank view this fiscal approach with skeptic eyes and too conservative, they on the other hand would suggest Botswana be a little more daring with the huge reserves and take up on some investment ventures that could yield favorable returns, I suppose the jury is out on this one. Revenue streams will continue to be sound and the government has made long-range strategic plans for expenditures while maintaining desired saving levels.

REFERENCE NOTES

1. Source: Botswana Export Development and investment Authority
2. World Bank
3. Botswana Meat Commission
4. Joseph E. Stiglitz, Botswana, A Development Success
5. Botswana.gov data
6. [www.gov.bw
7. [Joseph E. Stiglitz, Botswana, A Development Success]
8. [Osei Hwedi, African studies Quarterly]
9. [Africafiles, 2005]
10. [Africafiles, 2005]
11. [Africa Studies Quarterly].[
12. Botswana Export Development and Investment Authority
13. AIDSMAP
14. [Daron Acemoglu, Simon Johnson and James A. Robinson in the research paper "An African Success Story"
15. BOTSWANA GOVERNMENT SOURCE
16. Botswana Central Statistics Office
17. : BEDIA

CHAPTER IX

EMMERGING "BRIC" NATIONS

The world today is experiencing an economic shake-up and power shift, the days of economic power being concentrated in few familiar players is fading fast as new players are entering into the mix at a very rapid pace. Traditionally, when talking economic wealth, Western Europe, Japan, Australia and North America immediately jump to most people's mind, fast forward to today's new global economy and one finds that paradigm completely gutted and reconfigured. In today's world, wealth is being created in every nook and crevice across the globe at the fastest rate we have ever seen. The traditional power house economies are being forced to move to the slow lane as hungry rapidly emerging economies with cash on hand to spend wheeze by in the fast lane. The G8, a fraternity which represents the interests of the traditional wealthy nations more and more is becoming irrelevant and out of touch. Gone are the days when countries had to go on their knees to Europe and America begging for handouts, in fact the opposite is happening in some instances, look around and see who holds the vast concentration of sovereign wealth funds which have bailed out the U.S. economy on a number of occasions and you find names like Malaysia, Singapore, Dubai, China, Saudi Arabia and so forth holding billions of dollars in these funds Citigroup in November 2007 was bailed out by the Arab nation of Abu Dhabi with a cash capital infusion of $7.5 billion. Merrill Lynch also received a capital bailout of over $7 billion from Singapore. UBS has also sought the help of Singapore for a life-line. Morgan Stanley was reeled in by China. The Chinese have deep pockets and are keen on heavy foreign investments. China has a sovereign wealth fund of $200 billion which is managed by China Investment Corporation. The Arab-Gulf nations with billions of dollars dripping from their coffers are also jumping into the game, the main players in this region are Qatar, Kuwait and UAE.

Economic growth is not only confined to these specific countries but rather can be seen spread out across the globe In 2006 and 2007, over 124 countries grew economies at over 4% with 30 of these countries being in Africa, this according to a Newsweek article. When you travel to Africa, the face of investors is changing, the norm from the colonial period to the mid-nineties was dominated by western European multinationals. The post nineties era has seen a domination of Chinese and Indian investors. This perhaps one of the stronger indicators of where the money lies as we see a balance of power shift, it used to be when one looked at the Forbes listing of the world's wealthiest people, one would find the list dominated by your typical Middle east oil barons, American venture capitalists & industrialists and European tycoons, today you look at that list and you see a rather interesting mix, Mexicans, Russians, Indians and so forth Fareed Zakaria [1] in his Post American World excerpt made an interesting observation in that the world is going through the third great power shift in modern history, he contends the first rise occurred in the 15th century and saw the rise of the Western world and shaped today's world. He further points out that the second shift took place in the 19th century and saw the rise of United States as an economic and super power. Clearly, the U.S. is still the world's largest economy even though it's dominance is waning and not as prominent. As China surges, many observers agree it's not a question "if" China will become the new world superpower but rather "when" China becomes a superpower. As such, I present a brief synopsis of some of the new dominant players known by the acronym "BRIC Nations" (Brazil, Russia, India & China).

9.0 CHINA: Dawn of a new superpower

China is on a serious run, what began as a carefully crafted marathon is now a full fledged sprint in its quest to become the world's premier economic powerhouse. The signs are written everywhere and inevitable, anyone with the slightest vision can see it coming like a deranged locomotive full speed into the station. The Chinese are like a deprived child suddenly given a wad of cash and walks into a candy store buying everything in sight, venture to North America, you find Chinese money buying up real estate, capital ventures or anything they can get their hands on. Go to Africa and you find Chinese money in mining, oil and a host of other sectors, no one single country has embarked on such a massive buying spree in the modern era.

China's economic expansion has been dizzying and relentless, year ending 2005, it's economy grew 9.9% according to government statistics, this represented a third consecutive year of near 10% growth, this caught Western economies by surprise and it wasn't before long that cries were being echoed or circulated that Chinese authorities had previously been under reporting real growth rate numbers in order to lessen attention on what was really going on. I leave that to pundits and speculators. China went on to post an astounding 6 year marathon of 10% plus growth rate. Many analysts feel this growth will slow down in 2008 & 2009 as the economy reaches an overheat threshold. A hallmark in China's era was recorded in 2005 when national economic output reached $2.26 trillion, an astounding value by any measure, but more significantly, reaching this mark, China surpassed France, Britain and Italy to become the world's fourth largest economy. [2] Given such remarkable strides, China is well poised to leapfrog Japan and takes its place as the world's second-biggest economy.

China Vs Japan GDP

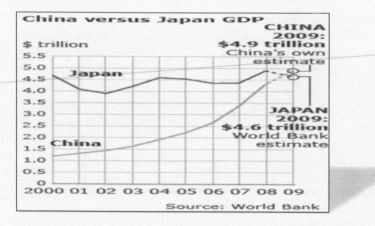

Source: World Bank

China is firmly planted as the factory to the world, all one needs to do is look around what's around them and see the country of origin, because of low labor costs and an unbelievably huge labor pool, China has mastered this low cost production game and very few can match them, China in contrast to the boom going on still has vast poverty and wide income disparities particularly in the rural areas, so much of the make up of factory workers that toil in the garment and electronic factories are uneducated rural impoverished folks as well migrant inferior workers. The fact that China has been able to exploit cheap labor costs and is often accused by the Western world of unfair practices has been a thorn to these economies particularly the U.S. which has been running enormous trading deficits for years now, in 2003, the U.S. had a $418 billion record deficit at the time. [3] While U.S. exports are slumping and in some cases in reverse mode, China's exports are in high gear.

Another interesting aspect in this power shift pertains to the numbers game, in this case population numbers. By the year 2020 China is expected to have a middle class population of over 650 million with an annual income exceeding $5000 [4]. This is a huge number considering in 2004 the number was 79 million. If these projections hold true, one can only imagine the marketing potential of such a vast middle class group. Foreign banks are already starting to gear up for this potential lucrative market especially with the recent opening up of the financial and banking sector by the Chinese government. According to reports, large bankers such as HSBC and Standard Chartered bank are planning large penetration into the market.

9.1 BRAZIL: Beast of Southern America

Brazil is on a mission with an economy on full throttle, the country has enjoyed a sustained period of growth over the last few years. It is one of the four countries dubbed "BRIC" countries, an abbreviation for Brazil, Russia, India & China which many observers tout as newly emerging economic powers of the future. Brazil is South America's largest economy and the world's 10th biggest economy is quietly making monumental economic strides. Brazil has a population of over 180 million, this is a huge market on the crisp of an economic rocket propulsion, traditionally, the mainstay of the economy was large scale commercial agriculture, manufacturing and mining, while these sectors still play a pivotal role, the economy is experiencing a rather interesting diversification. The interesting shift of economic activity is a function of a number of variables, firstly, the influence from a global perspective of the China surge has resulted in a demand market for Brazilian products, and secondly the onset of high commodity prices on the world market has propelled economic action. Brazil is the world's largest producer of sugar, soybean and coffee, which have both seen increased global demand. Brazil is also the world's largest producer of iron ore whose prices have also soured mainly due to high demand from China. Brazil has also made remarkable strides in the area of bio-fuels technology and today is a world leader in this field, more importantly, this investment has made Brazil energy independent since 2006. To add to this countries rich mineral base, two vast oil reserves were recently discovered off

Brazil's Atlantic coast which experts estimate will propel Brazil amongst the world's premier oil producers.

Brazil's economy has long been plagued with erratic up & downswings associated with commodity prices. Prior to World War II, Brazil's economy was tied to export commodities. The first phase was Brazil wood, followed by livestock, sugar, gold, rubber and coffee. Recognizing the pitfalls of relying on commodities, a strong push for diversification was made in the 1960s, this brought about the economic miracle period from the mid 1960s to early 70's, growth was rapid and exceeded 11% during this era. The early diversification efforts paid off and today, Brazil is the third most industrialized country in the Americas. with large scale automobile and aircraft plants. In the mid 1980's, Brazil was hit by high inflation rates past 100% The record inflation rates perpetuated a deep recession through the 90's with inflation at a dizzying rate of 2,700% in 1994 [5] Brazil sought the help of the IMF to be bailed out of this mess, the IMF intervention measures continued until about 2003, incidentally, the expiration of the IMF programs were just in time as the world global commodity prices and demand started to surge, which propelled exports from brazil and jump started the economic surge. The country survived the brutal financial crisis between 1999-2003 and exports have made a huge comeback due to increased global demand.

All this upsurge has brought a large infusion of foreign reserves circulating within the economy, in 2005 foreign reserves were pegged at $57 billion, in 2006, reserves were recorded at $85 billion and by 2007 foreign reserves had swelled to $200 billion.[6] Direct foreign investment has also been on the rise, in 2007 direct investment doubled to $34.6 billion [7] The rise in foreign inflows has trickled down to the masses meaning more Brazilians have disposable income to spend on goods and services. Brazil has seen it's middle class population swell and is now a middle income country. One of the phenomenon to the Brazilian economic transformation is the rise and prevalence of credit within the economy, traditionally, Brazil like most emerging economies was a cash dependent society where transactions relied on hard cash. However with the stability and sound economic management, financial lenders are finally confident in the market and are extending credit to more and more people. Middle income people now are purchasing cars, houses, household appliances, etc under credit terms Mortgage financed homes rose 72% in 2007, home appliances rose 17%, a record 2.46 million car sold and overall credit-card borrowing increased 20%.[8] The authorities have also managed the inflation rate well holding it at 4.5% in 2007. Middle class Brazilians are on a buying spree, total bank loans between 2003-2007 have more than doubled exceeding $530 billion, banks are making huge profits with assets in 2006 expanding by 19% representing more than $1.1 trillion [9] This market represents a huge growth opportunity as bank loans in Brazil account for 35% of GDP where as in the US, the rate is 80%. Observers expect the Brazilian economy to continue to grow at over 4% through 2012. The large expanding middle class via consumer demand will play a pivotal role in driving the growth as will the export revenues from manufactured goods and commodities.

9.2 INDIA: A nation poised for take off

While China is commonly referred to as the world's factory, India has been branded the dubious title as the world's back office in response to the prominent role of Business Process Outsourcing (BPS) India plays. Outsourcing has been very good to India, analysts expect the industry to mushroom to $130 billion by 2010 [10]. Today, Bangalore is the home to the world's second largest technology campus behind the Microsoft campus in Washington, USA. [11] Business Process Outsourcing essentially is the shift of company functions oversees for cost reduction reasons, the functions typically involve back end or back office clerical functions, even though this is changing as more prominent roles are now being off-shored as well. Why "outsource" one might wonder, well the plain simple answer is cost period, bottom line saving for corporations nothing more to it. Consider starting salaries in the U.S. for these types of jobs average $30,000, in places like India and the Philippines, the starting rate is usually $5,500, in addition to the bargain rate, the employees in these markets are usually university level educated unlike in the U.S. where such jobs are for high school leavers. Given the disparity in incomes, it is not surprising U.S. companies are not hesitating to relocate certain functions to cut costs and boost the bottom line. The BPO market in many respects has been an engine to the Indian market surge, however there is more than meets the eye as why this happened to India besides just low labor costs. While labor costs play a pivotal role in the BPO market, other considerations factor in as well, take for instance, India has been well known for churning out a lot of skilled personnel in science and technology. In fact one might argue it is probably an imminent global leader in that field. India is still largely a poor country and as such many of these highly skilled professionals are willing to take up these clerical back office jobs thus creating a win-win situation for both parties. The issue of "outsourcing" has been sensitive in the U.S. as many harbor resentment towards India and feel they are taking their jobs. The U.S. Bureau of Labor Statistics reported

The BPO and technology industry has put money into the common man's pocket and many have joined the ranks of the middle class and having a middle class demographic always translates into a population segment with buying parity. The middle class are always the driving catalyst's of any economy as they typically buy consumer good's and services which keep the economy performing. As such, GDP has been on the rise in India, in 1995 per capita incomes were approximately $1000, by 2005 the figure was up to $2500 a remarkable jump by all accounts. The disposable income infiltrating the Indian economy has boosted economic activity as more Indian citizens have purchasing power, experts anticipate the economy to continue to grow over 9% for a record third straight year. [12] Foreign investment in the telecommunications industry has also propelled India to become the world's third user of telecom services behind China and the U.S. The expansion is also being exhibited by indigenous Indian companies with Multinational operations who are making large notable global venture investments. Tata which is India's largest automobile maker recently staked ownership in Jaguar and Land Rover units. India is well positioned to becoming the first nation to lift its self from the ranks of developing nations to an economic power house by shear brain power as opposed to conventional minerals &natural resources.

9.3 RUSSIA: Reclaiming it's place in the world

Russia has refused to take a back seat and since the collapse of the Soviet Union in 1991, Russia is regaining its stature as a global powerhouse. After the break up of the Soviet Union, the country experienced a period of economic contraction for about six years. However, the opening and liberalization of markets around 1997 presented an opportunity for economic investment in the once tightly held communist structure. Between 1999 and 2005, the economy grew at an average rate of 6.7%, much of this marathon growth spurt was spurred by the high global commodity prices particularly oil and natural gas which are abundant in Russia. Today, the Russian economy is the 5th largest in Europe & 9th globally. The economic reforms in the early nineties under the Yelstin administration ushered in an open market economy with sound fiscal and monetary policy.

REFERENCE NOTES

1. Newsweek
2. New york Times, january 28, 2006
3. USA Today, July 25, 2003
4. business Line, India June 29, 2008
5. Nationsencyclopedia
6. www.independent.co.uk, 5/2/2008]
7. International Herald tribune, 5/13/2008
8. International Herald tribune, 5/13/2008
9. Charlotte Observer, 2/16/08
10. Christian Science monitor
11. National Post, Canada
12. LA Times

CHAPTER X

INTERNATIONAL LAW OVERVIEW

10.0 State Sovereignty in the Modern Context

State sovereignty in the modern context is essentially aligned with the 1933 Montevideo Convention on rights and Duties of states as provided in article 1 of the UN charter. In accordance with these provisions, the modern outlook on sovereignty follows four main criteria's listed below as a stipulation for state sovereignty.

a). Permanent population

This stipulation entails the physical permanent presence of human beings cohabiting in an established community regardless of their differences in terms of religion, beliefs, etc. The essence of this notion primarily calls for an established population group sustaining as one community regardless of any sub-cultures present within the larger group.

b). Defined territory:

This ideal calls for not only having and possessing a territory, but rather more important is the ability to have ownership and control of such territory, therefore just occupying a territory without valid ownership and control could be a disqualifier to the general doctrine of state sovereignty. (It is important to note that an occupied state within a state may exist, however whether or not such an entity is recognized as a sovereign state under international law is a different issue.)

c). Government Structure

A functional government with authority to effectively manage the population and the accompanying territory is the third stipulation. This condition calls for both internal stability and external cooperation with the international community, therefore a state cannot only expect to meet its internal governance and forego international established parameters. Exceptions could be raised when a state takes action based on what it perceives as a threat to its core existence as a sovereign state.

d). Capacity for agreements & negotiations

Relates to a nation being capable and able to carry out interactions with the international community through treaties, conventions, tribunals, and common good for all parties.

10.1 PRINCIPLE OF STATE RESPONSIBILITY

The principle of state responsibility allows for nations to act reasonably and within the accepted principals of international law. This includes but is not limited to honoring signed treaties, agreements, declarations and so forth. Deviating from compliance will put a state into a conceivable breach of international law. Actions against violators are not uniform and for the most part tend to be very cumbersome and bureaucratic, however the most common approach is associated with imposition of sanctions.

10.2 CONDITIONS MAKING A TREATY BINDING

The traditional framework calls for "conclusion and entry into force of treaties" as spelled out in Article 9 of the 1969 Vienna convention. Two principle provisions within the article articulate the following stipulations:

a). Adoption of a treaty will call for agreement by all parties or states putting forward the initiative, i.e. consent amongst the parties

b). Adoption of the treaty will follow a vote of two-thirds of the participating states.

Article 11 further expounds on this notion focusing on the expression of a treaty by means of signature, ratification and accession as the main stipulations. Also included in this reading as binding conditions are acceptance, approval or any other agreed upon criteria amongst the states. (goes to show how broad the criteria of binding a state to a treaty could be stretched.)

Modern practices have also utilized other mechanisms as pointed out below:

a). Exchange of correspondence between states
b). Open ended treaties (Article 83)
c). Acceptance or approval instead of ratification
d). Treaty drawn by international body.

Conditions making a treaty non-binding

a). Provisions for termination met by all parties involved
b). Mutual consent by parties
c). Breach by one of the parties involved
d). Treaty failure or collapse
e). Change in circumstances from those initially agreed upon
f). New customs or new view in international law framework (implies a change in worldview)

10.3 NATURE OF STATE SUCCESSION

Stems from the notion of change in sovereignty as regards to territory. Key considerations point to which rights and obligations of the precluding treaties are recognized or nullified. International law to begin with is very ambiguous in this area and therefore, this area of international law lacks clarity. Recent examples include the Yugoslavia disbanding and the disintegration of the USSR, which resulted in numerous, fragmented states having conflicting notions of which treaties to recognize.

What Motivates States to Establish IGOs?

- Enhancement of the states influence as a coalition building party.
- Security concerns
- Economic motives
- Increased economic interdependencies
- Capitalization of raw materials
- Humanitarian objectives
- Protection of human rights

- Environmental concerns, nuclear proliferation concerns, transportation and communication issues.

Legal status of IGOs in world affairs and legal rights and responsibilities

IGOs operate within the constraints and binding objectives of the respective member states, as such the legality of IGOs is a function of the member governments. IGOs in some instances are capable of proclaiming judgments.

10.4 PURPOSE OF THE UNITED NATIONS

a). Promote and maintain international peace and security across the globe.
b). Develop friendly relations among nations
c). Cooperate in solving international economic, social, cultural and humanitarian issues.
d) Promote respect for human rights and freedoms.

The UN carries out these functions through its six principal organs, namely the: General Assembly, Security Council, Economic & Social Council, Trusteeship Council, International Court of Justice and Secretariat.

Status of General Assembly Resolutions in International Law

Resolutions passed by the general assembly can have a quasi status of international law by serving as tribunal hearings for settlement of disputes, such decisions though binding lack the authority to bring an individual state before a court without it's consent.

UN operating as a collective security arrangement

The UN utilizes its various operational wings to achieve this goal. The General Assembly and the Security Council are the prominent tools in collective security. The General Assembly as body allows for all member states to convene and deliberate on motions of concern patterning to issues of threats, security, human rights etc. Members cast votes and can condemn a state as being in violation to agreed upon principles. In such a manner, the UN through the General Assembly exhibits a collective security arrangement.

Another means is through the Security Council where binding decisions can be made to states in the interest of international peace and stability. Actions can also include sanctions, embargos, military intervention and so forth. All these actions through the Security Council entail a collective security arrangement, as the ultimate goal is collective global security.

UN practice under Chapter VII of the Charter After the Cold War

After the Cold War, the UN has had more room and flexibility to engage in broader causes such as human-rights agendas. An increase in humanitarian engagements such as the Dafour & Somalia crisis have been undertaken by the UN. The UN has also been more actively involved in various peacekeeping missions. The UN role also took a turn after the 911 catastrophes in the US, the 911 attacks put the UN at the forefront as did the Iraq & Afghanistan conflicts. The post-90s have seen a greater role by the Security Council.

International law governing the use of force by nations

The simplistic notion for use of war today by states follows the premise of acting in self-defense or protecting a states territory, inhabitants, resources or interests. However, as we all know, the decision to use force is not a simple matter but rather a very complex decision requiring utmost thought. As such, international law through history has struggled with this issue; the last century has seen an attempt to translate customary rules into multilateral international agreements. Examples include The Geneva Convention (1864), The Paris Declaration (1856), The St. Petersburg Convention (1868) and The Hague Peace Conference (1899 & 1907). All these agreements combined form a framework in guiding the use of force by states today. Whether they are effective or not is a different matter altogether. As mentioned earlier, these agreements were early protocols, today's international law protocol relies mainly on post WW II initiatives embodied in the UN charter. The international community in concert seem to all agree upon these stipulations as detailed in the UN charter. The four cornerstone rules justifying use of force are outlined as follows:

1. Right to self-defense when attacked (armed attack)
2. UN Security Council enforcement
3. Enforcement actions by regional organizations authorized by the Security Council
4. Peacekeeping e.g. ECOWAS forces in West Africa

Is Terrorism a violation of international law?

The context of this question presents one with a two-fold answer, allow me to expound; "Attacks carried out on civilians who take no part in hostilities are prohibited by international humanitarian law" as spelled out in the 1949 & 1977 Geneva Convention protocols. Thus a terrorist act that follows such manifestations could conceivably constitute a violation of international law in theory and practice. Having said this, the dynamics of terrorism are always not this cut & dry. Terrorism by nature has been a tactic employed through history, as events would testify, a reference point could be made in the American colonist actions against the British where terror tactics were employed. The key underlying question and dilemma when discussing terrorism is the lack of consensus as to what constitutes terrorism. Often, terrorism and freedom fighting cross paths and in many cases mirror each other, each acting as means to an end to each other, indeed so often, one man's fight for freedom can be construed as another man's fight against terrorism. The issue of state sponsored terrorism across the globe as one might anticipate presents a distorted gray area, which is often overlooked by international law, and for that matter general law. Given the ambiguity involved, this question remains very convoluted.

State sovereignty's continued role in international law?

The relationship between state sovereignty and international law is clearly not a new phenomenon but rather one that dates back centuries. The dynamic though not new has seen several transformations over the different periods of time, one constant being that the two ideals are intertwined to varying degrees. Recent changes in the global structure particularly with the demise of the cold war and the onset of globalization has naturally changed the role each plays. This section will thus examine the modern role played by sovereignty in international law with primary emphasis on post-cold war influences, nation invasions, sanctions, failed states, human rights and NGO groups. However, before exploring the above-mentioned themes, a brief overview follows.

The theory of sovereignty dates back centuries with prominent theorists such as Machiavellian, Jean Bodin, Thomas Hobbes and John Austin at the forefront. In fact, John Austin defined law as the general commands of a sovereign state and went on to proclaim that international law was not law since it did not align with his theory [1]. Subsequent shifts in international law readings associated the notion of sovereignty generally as an independent state but not above the law. [2]. This theory continued to evolve over time through the classical era which saw the emergence of the basic principles in international law centered on territorial sovereignty, control over territory etc., however not included in these principles was the right for a state to go to war to protect it's sovereignty. [3]. Other developments relating to human rights protection would eventually follow as well as influence by international organizations such as the Hague peace conference of 1899 and 1907. [4]

POST COLD WAR INFLUENCE

The sudden collapse of the Soviet Union and effectively the diminishment of the cold war brought a whole new set of dynamics in the global arena as long established allegiances between east vs. west were crumbling. With effectively only one super-power left, that being the United States, the United Nations took on a bigger role in conflict resolution across the globe while the United States for the time being retreated and took a back seat. [5]. The permanent members of the Security Council took on a more prominent role in mediating and in some cases making demands over sovereign states. Clearly the prominent role taken by the UN showed a new shift in the relationship between sovereignty and international law given the UN as an instrument of international law. In many cases, fragile sovereign states on the brink of collapse non-the less still considered sovereign states worked in concert with the UN in resolving their conflicts thereby circumventing chaos and destruction. Such was the case in Africa where the withdrawal of Cuban troops was successfully negotiated between the parties and, as was the case with the withdrawal of soviet troops in Afghanistan. [6]. Other eventualities and mediations followed, however these two situations are just a few circumstances of sovereignty playing a role in international law and vice versa for that matter of fact.

IRAQ INVASION OF KUWAIT

The invasion of Kuwait by Iraq in 1990 is a classic example of sovereignty playing a dominant role in international law. Saddam Hussein, the leader of Iraq at the time felt it within his sovereign right to invade Kuwait as he deemed it a part of Iraq territory and therefore justifying his invasion of that nation. The international community through the auspices of the United Nations Security Council saw Saddam Hussein's action as unacceptable and lacking merit therefore calling for the immediate withdrawal of Iraqi forces from Kuwait. The tug of war went back and forth with a series of resolutions, which were ignored by Iraq. Subsequently, Iraq was given a deadline to pull its troops out of Kuwait or face consequences. In this instance, we see a state defying an international order in Resolution 67 and facing the consequences of the order spelled out under the international order.

IMPACT OF FAILED STATES

Somalia presents a scenario of a failing sovereign nation where the international community through the UN had to intervene due to catastrophic humanitarian concerns. The UN organized food aid through various agencies and a multinational coalition of over 37,000 was deployed to restore law and order. Other collapsing sovereign states such as Rwanda, Yugoslavia and so forth have also played a role in international law through international courts of justice to bring perpetuators of heinous human war crimes to trial. In these incidents, former accused leaders such as Milosevic and the former head of state of Rwanda were tried under international court tribunals. Haiti is another case of a crumbling sovereign state where in this situation the sitting president was actually forced out by the international community (mainly the U.S.) in order to restore law and order. Sovereign states that infringe on their subjects human rights also play a crucial role in international law. Such abuses are monitored by the International Law of human rights under the UN umbrella. [7]

As we draw to the end of this section, we have seen a few instances of sovereignty interacting with international law in a variety of ways. Indeed the scenarios examined just represent a fraction of the other various manifestations, however one can clearly see that the issue of sovereignty and international law can be very complex and uncertain. It's an ever evolving dynamic, as has been illustrated from the earlier periods of the classical international law era to the present where we see a wider role played by international coalition bodies such as the UN and the wider scope of treaties. I see this situation even taking a greater role as we dig deeper into this globalization era where the world is interconnected and thus sovereignty taking less significance going forward.

10.5 UN TOOLS FOR ACHIEVING SECURITY IN THE WORLD

The United Nations employs a variety of branches within its organizational body in achieving order and security across the globe. The nature and scope of influence exerted through such tools is the primary focus of the latter part of this section. Also addressed will be the different roles of the UN in the post-cold war as opposed to its role at its founding in the pre-World War II period. The concluding part of the section will look at the prospects of the UN serving as a vehicle for maintaining world order after the cold war.

The Security Council is a critical tool the United Nations has at its disposal for attaining world peace and order. The core function of the Security Council as spelled out in the Charter is to promote and maintain international peace and security. Other auxiliary functions of the Security Council include but are not limited to, investigating disputes, reconciling settlements, recommending & imposing sanctions, and military action against an aggressor state. Given such a broad realm of responsibilities, the United Nations inherently treads diplomatically and assumes an indirect approach. [8]. When such an approach proves futile, the UN begins to take a more forceful approach, as some examples later will show. Typically, the Security Council steps begin with a complaint brought forward concerning a perceived threat to peace, at this juncture the Security Council recommends to the parties involved trying to reach an agreement using peaceful means. [9]. If a peaceful truce appears unlikely, the UN can further utilize Chapter VII of the charter therefore binding the parties in question. When the UN takes such a decision, given an established link between human rights and security, then economic or military action is a possible consequence. [10]. This expression of influence by the UN was utilized in conflicts in Rwanda, Sierra Leone and the former Yugoslavia. The UN also uses non-binding measures in certain instances, as was the case with South Africa in the late 1970s. At that time, South Africa was in the grip of the Apartheid system and the Security Council in 1977 voted for an arms embargo against South Africa on the basis of people's denial of self-rule and majority rule [11]. This tool was earlier used in the case with Rhodesia (now Zimbabwe). The UN may also impose economic sanctions through the Security Council to deal with a state posing as a threat to peace as was the recent case in the 90s with the "Food for Oil" embargo against the Iraqi regime. When a conflict ensures, the Security Council can opt to send peacekeeping troops to bring the conflict to an end, this measure has been used recently in conflicts in Africa.

Another arm the UN relies upon in securing global peace and security is the General Assembly. This body consists of all member states representatives with each member having one vote. The primary function of the General Assembly is to deliberate and pass resolutions promoting international peace and stability. Included in this definition of responsibilities is the promotion of human rights, therefore the General Assembly also condemns acts that are in contrast to the promotion of basic human rights by casting up and down votes. This practice can be very embarrassing for the condemned state in violation therefore could result in such a violator making amends to their practices. The UN can also use The Office of the Secretary-General as a useful tool. Secretary-Generals may take an active role in an area that is of interest to them such as human rights or refugee issues and bring that to the forefront. By virtue of the stature of the office itself, the exposure a Secretary-General brings over an issue is an invaluable tool in itself. Koffi Annan has been an overwhelming crusader for the plight of human rights. [12]. The UN

High Commissioner for Refugees, The UN High Commissioner for Human Rights, The Human Rights Commission and other auxiliary bodies are also additional tools the UN utilizes in achieving order and security in the world. These bodies are particularly influential in creating stability and order in areas where human degradation can easily erupt into potential chaos and anarchy.

UN Mission Post Cold War

In today's Post-Cold war era, the role of the UN has evolved from its earlier mission following the World War II period. The Cold-War period was an era of enormous tensions between the East-West powers, which created a high degree of isolation with lesser emphasis on internationalized solutions to conflicts. Given the Cold-War tensions, the two main super-powers (USA & the Soviet Union) were consumed with maintaining and building their ideologies. This situation meant the UN played a lesser role in conflict resolution and pursuing it's set objectives. The end of the Cold War in turn created many fragmented states particularly in the former Soviet bloc and other nations that had allegiances and financial support from the USA & Soviet Union. This manifestation, particularly the Soviet collapse also resulted in new internal conflicts in the newly independent states such as Yugoslavia, Bosnia as well as other states such as Cambodia, Angola and so forth. The collapse of such states is also significant in the new emergent role of the UN in that; the Soviet Union for instance had expended a vast amount of resources sustaining the Cold-War to the extent that by the time the Cold-War ended, it's treasury and resource base was greatly diminished. Under the leadership of Mikhail Gorbachev, the Soviet Union sought to take a new direction and revamp it's economy and become more integrated into the world economy. In fact, Grobachev called for a renewed relationship with the UN at the General Assembly in 1988 in resolving global conflicts. [13]. This renewed world outlook in conflict management called for the UN to take a more active role in peacekeeping campaigns in failing states from the cold-war collapse. This view was not only echoed by the Soviet leadership but also shared by the U.S. Leadership. Both President Ronald Regan and later on President George Bush made similar sentiments calling for the UN to capitalize on this opportunity and play a bigger role in global conflict management. This renewed vigor toward the UN gave the organization new legs in the pursuit of new post Cold-War commitments. The biggest change in the post Cold-War period for the UN was its increased role in peacekeeping missions. Between 1988-1993 alone, the UN engaged in five military operations after a ten-year absence. [14]. With the vow and commitment from the U.S. and the Soviet Union to pay their dues to the UN, the organization was also able to engage and undertake in more humanitarian causes. The Gulf War in the early 1990s gave the UN a forum to play a very visible role on the world stage. The Security Council for the first time since 1950 unanimously condemned the invasion of Kuwait as violation to world peace. [15] The UN voted to use economic sanctions against Iraq and passed a critical resolution,"678" allowing for "all necessary means" to remove Iraq from Kuwait. The September 11 tragedy in the U.S. and the resulting invasion of Afghanistan and Iraq also thrust the UN again in addressing state sponsored terrorism and nuclear proliferation. In essence, the UN post Cold-War has seen a rise in Peacekeeping & humanitarian missions and has actively followed its objectives of creating norms against violence, create international stability, and pursue humanitarian concerns.

The prospects of the UN to serve as a vehicle for maintaining world order now that the Cold War is over offer mixed results. While the UN has clearly increased its role in this era, measuring the results of such efforts presents a challenging and complex dilemma, however one thing that seems clear is that with the world becoming so intertwined in this era of globalization, more challenges are inevitable. The global poverty disparity is widening in places with vast populations such as Africa, and given such poverty proportions, one can expect and foresee ethnic conflicts such as we have seen in Rwanda, Somalia, Liberia, Sierra Leone, and many other parts of the world. In summation, this section has illustrated that the UN evolves with times and as such, one can expect it to continue serving as a vehicle for world order, however the issue of success and failure of its pursuits remains an open ended matter with varying interpretations.

10.6 HUMAN RIGHTS AND INTERNATIONAL LAW.

The issue of human rights as relates to international relations have long being intertwined and the very notion of extending entitlements to legally protect individuals, minorities, & indigenous groups from state interference or abuse in many cases is in contradiction with the states concept of sovereignty. The origins of the concept of human rights has paralleled the development of today's modern state. One can look back at the early Western governments and find that human rights concerns were echoed in the American and French revolution. Such early intrusions of human rights concerns were very limited in scope and had little or no impact outside their immediate domain. The 19th century saw an explosion of human rights concerns on the scene with Karl Marx at the epicenter of this development. The 1890 Brussels signing by Western countries to abolish the slave trade was another landmark moment in the ever-developing concept of human rights with regard to international affairs.

However, the watershed turning point of human rights and international law took root after World War II. Prior to WW II the international community was more concerned with engrained ideals of maintaining their individual sovereignty and as a result, human rights issues were typically viewed as matters to be dealt with internally within each sovereign state. This mode of thinking and approach changed following the events that transpired in WW II. After the brutal holocaust events subjected on Jews by Nazi Germany, the global community realized they could not just sit and let such atrocities go by simply as an internal matter. This in essence brought the issue of human rights to the forefront and thus allowing for a new approach. Central to this new approach regarding human rights was the United Nations. The UN Charter under Article 1 elevated human rights as an issue of utmost importance. Article 55 spelled out this global respect for human rights and freedoms. Article 56 further reaffirmed this commitment calling for all members to pledge their support in achieving the goals stipulated in Article 55.

The commitments addressed in Article 55 and 56 are ideally supposed to bring international law in concert with human rights in protecting the vulnerable, and as earlier pointed out, there has indeed been an increased emphasis on matters pertaining to human rights which is in direct contrast to classical traditional international law, non the less that has been the trend. Also significant is the reaction and attention the pro human rights approach attracts, i.e. cries from governments of interference within their internal matters. The dilemma lies in the fact that most states still view issues pertaining to their own nationals as an internal matter and vehemently oppose any interjection by outside forces proclaiming existing human rights violation. Most states would seem to be more supportive of human rights pursuits as long as it does not apply to their internal circumstances therefore bringing another problematic issue of double standard. The nation of Zimbabwe recently has been internationally castigated as violating human rights with its demolition of squatters and political intimidation of opposition members.

Another troubling issue that crops up when dealing with human rights issues are engrained cultural, economic and political differences that exist across the globe. This is particularly significant because these differences make it virtually impossible to come up with a universally accepted notion of human rights definition. As such, each state is compelled to say that under their cultural norms and ideals, an act viewed, as a violation of human rights or suppression of freedoms is perfectly normal and within their constitutional and sovereign right. In fact, some go as far as arguing that the whole notion of human rights protection lacks any international legal protection or basis.

It is important to note that many positive commendable strides have been made as a result of this new aggressive approach of pursuing and enforcing human rights abusers globally, however the seeming contradictions lead U.S. to the underlying question; is this issue of human rights intruding over old legal concerns a solvable issue? Due to the increased interdependences in today's globe and enormous advances in technology which allow for instant access of alleged human rights violations in our living rooms via satellite TV, internet etc, the prospects of this issue being solvable are very good because world perspectives are more in concert, for instance a perceived violation is beamed all over the globe and if this is a valid issue it becomes very difficult to deny the allegations against a global audience in the name of the states sovereign right.

Human rights can be accommodated within international law through the various bodies of the UN. The UN views severe human rights violations to be dealt with through international channels. The International Court of Justice is also obligated to take up matters concerning severe human rights violations. Recent examples where we have seen human rights violations channeled through international law include the violations in Rwanda and the Milosevic trial. Thus said, as complicated and difficult this subject matter of human rights and international law presents, the overall outlook seems positive however long the journey may take.

REFERENCE NOTES

1. Malanczuk, Peter, AKEHURST'S Modern Introduction To International Law, 2004.pg172.
2. Malanczuk, Peter, AKEHURST'S Modern Introduction To International Law, 2004. Pg17
3. Malanczuk, Peter, AKEHURST'S Modern Introduction To International Law, 2004. Pg 19
4. Malanczuk, Peter, AKEHURST'S Modern Introduction To International Law, 2004. Pg22
5. Malanczuk, Peter, AKEHURST'S Modern Introduction To International Law, 2004. Pg395
6. Malanczuk, Peter, AKEHURST'S Modern Introduction To International Law, 2004.pg402
7. Weiss, Forsythe, and Coate R., The United Nations and Changing World Politics, 2004. Pg129
8. Weiss, Forsythe, and Coate R., The United Nations and Changing World Politics, 2004. Pg153
9. United Nations. (2005) www.un.org
10. Weiss, Forsythe, and Coate R., The United Nations and Changing World Politics, 2004. Pg155
11. Weiss, Forsythe, and Coate R., The United Nations and Changing World Politics, 2004. Pg156
12. Weiss, Forsythe, and Coate R., The United Nations and Changing World Politics, 2004. Pg16
13. Weiss, Forsythe, and Coate R., The United Nations and Changing World Politics, 2004. Pg47
14. Weiss, Forsythe, and Coate R., The United Nations and Changing World Politics, 2004. Pg48
15. Weiss, Forsythe, and Coate R., The United Nations and Changing World Politics, 2004. Pg5

CHAPTER XI

THE INTERNATIONAL ECONOMY

11.0 ARGUMENTS FOR FREE TRADE

Proponents of free trade or open markets in the classical economist era argued that such a practice was a force in promoting the international division of labor since it allowed for nations to channel their competitive edges on goods they could produce at the cheapest cost thus resulting in specialization of production. The rationale for this thinking lays emphasis on the notion that each nation to a degree has inherent competitive advantages such as climate, mineral endowment, and skills. Utilizing such given natural competitive advantages thus fosters free trade. Early economists such as Adam Smith pointed out the principal of "labor theory of value" which implies labor as a homogeneous factor cost and thus the cost of goods being contingent on the labor pool required to produce a given good. Smith further argued using a simplistic 2 nation, 2-product ideal called the "principal of absolute advantage" that trade was most beneficial when one country has an absolute comparative advantage. Given all these arguments, the cumulative effect is said to be higher consumption and investment while consumers enjoy lower commodity prices.

Arguments against free trade

Adversaries of free trade point out that host nations tend to impose trade restrictions in the form of quotas and tariffs against foreign imports. In addition to protectionism, arguments against free trade imply that such trade promotes outsourcing and dumping of cheap products, which in turn can result in an imbalance of trade. Local jobs are also threatened as production facilities are relocated and thus could create unemployment.

Factors fostering growth after WWII.

After WWII holocaust nightmares, there was a renewed collective embrace by the international community to move forward and this in turn created a globalization wave from the mid 1940s to the early 1980s. The current ongoing surge in free trade began in the early 1980s in part due to some developing nations breaking the ranks of LDCs and becoming newly emerging economic forces, this was particularly evident with the far-east Asian "Tiger" nations. Countries such as Malaysia, Thailand, China and so forth were a big driving force in this trend. Other factors can be attributed to technological and information advances, ease of mobility, and a more liberalized environment (NAFTA, GATT).

Impact of changing supply-and-demand conditions on international terms of trade

Shifting supply and demand conditions creates an interesting dilemma on traditional international terms of trade in the sense that enforcement of such terms is almost impossible and the propensity to violate labor practices is very likely. Trying to police unfair trade and labor practices globally is a very challenging proposition.

11.1 ALTERNATIVE TRADE THEORIES

Leontief Paradox challenge toward the overall applicability of the Factor Endowment Model

The Leontief Paradox undermined the conclusions drawn in the factor endowment model by using empirical studies in 1947 and 1954. Wassily Leontief's investigation followed the assumption that since the United States was recognized as having abundant capital and relatively scarce labor, it should follow according to the factor endowment theory that the United States would export capital intensive goods and import labor intensive goods. Given this premise, Leontief analyzed over 200 capital and labor ratios of export/import competing industries, his findings in contrast to the factor endowment model found that the capital/labor ratio for U.S. exports was lower than that of competing import industries.

Differences between the Heckscher-Ohlin theory & Ricardian theory in explaining international trade patterns.

The Heckscher-Oblin theory implies that factor endowments are the source of comparative advantage among nations where as the Ricardian theory states that the source of comparative advantage is contingent on relative costs.

Theory of overlapping demands.

Staffan Linder's theory of overlapping demands contends that factor-endowments play a pivotal role in world trade that involves primary products, natural resources & agriculture goods but has no implication in the global trade of manufactured goods. The theory uses the rationale that the main driving force in the trade of manufactured goods is domestic demand since manufacturers will tend to manufacture goods which have a large domestic market, and the overflow of such goods are exported to nations with similar consumer tastes. In essence, the theory implies the export or trade of manufactured goods an extension or function of domestic production.

11.2 TRADE BARRIERS AND NON TRADE BARRIERS

Specif Tariff

Expressed in fixed monetary terms per physical product imported without regard to value or quantity of imported item. Advantages of such a tariff include its simplicity and relative ease in application, its ability to shield domestic producers in times of a recession when consumers buy cheaper domestic products than more expensive exports. Main disadvantage lies in the fact that protection of local producers has an inverse relationship with import prices.

Ad Valorem (of value) tariff

Expressed as a fixed percentage of the value of imported good.

Advantage: tariff inherently distinguishes product quality assuming there is a correlation between price and quality. This type of tariff also offers consistent protection to local producers, as price fluctuations do not affect its effectiveness. The tariff also offers revenues that are proportionate to the value of goods.

Disadvantage: determing value (customs valuation) of imported good can be cumbersome. Variations in methods used to determine a goods value, e.g. U.S. uses free on board (FOB) while Europe follows the cost-insurance-freight (CIF).

Compound Tariff

Applied to manufactured products that contain raw materials subject to tariffs.

Advantage: protects local suppliers of raw materials and consequently promotes manufactures use of local materials.

11.3 Trade blocs and Trade policies for Developing countries

Trade liberalization existing on a non-discriminatory basis versus a discriminatory basis

Non-discriminatory form: relationship involves a mutual agreement by parties involved to have a reduction of trade barriers on a nondiscriminatory form. A good example is the World Trade Organization

Discriminatory form: this relates a group of nations forming regional trading arrangements among themselves e.g. NAFTA, COMESA, EU

Common Agriculture Policy as a controversial issue for the EU

This policy created a problem for the EU because of the differences in production efficiencies amongst the farmers within the union, for instance, German grain farmers had higher production costs than French farmers, therefore under the EU's price-support program, countries with lower efficiency costs have lobbied for high support costs even though not necessary, but rather as a free benefit. This as such has created inefficient farm production.

Generalized system of preferences

This initiative is intended to help developing nations gain access to world markets by offering non reciprocal tariff relief or preferences to exports from developing countries in order to allow such countries an opportunity to enter the global trading market while strengthening their manufacturing base.

11.4 ADAM SMITH'S VIEW ON INTERNATIONAL TRADE & THAT OF THE MERCANTILISTS.

The center piece of Adam Smiths view of international trade was the notion of free trade (open markets) unlike the mercantilists view during the period of 1500-1800 which stipulated that in order for nations to obtain a positive trade balance, they had to put in place Tariffs, quotas and other prohibitive measures. Adam Smith called for free trade stating that such an approach would promote international specialization resulting in each nation producing goods they were most efficient at producing. Adam Smith justified his theory with the principal of cost differences being the driving force in production, therefore some nations may have natural advantages such as mineral wealth, special skills, labor supply and so forth. Smith's theory is founded on two principals; labor theory of value and absolute advantage. Therefore, the underlying difference between Smith and the Mercantilists is trade restrictions vs. free trade.

11.5 Conditions necessary for a developing country to establish a market economy

a). Market—determined prices/ Open economies

Prices are not controlled or manipulated by the government or a central body but rather are self determined with the forces of demand and supply. Price is the driving force and consumer's ability to purchase goods and services determine the price levels. No state planning and control of foreign and domestic trade. (open for debate.)

b). Independent Buyers and Sellers with property & legal rights

Buyers and sellers need to be able to operate in their own interest without any coercion or intimidation, these two entities are the driving force of the market economy. In essence, buyers and sellers need an environment where they can trade openly and have their vested property and legal rights.

c). Stable governments with limited role in economy

A developing country also needs a stable government with a laissez faire approach in order to foster an open market otherwise market failures arise under oppressive or intimidating conditions.

d). Good Fiscal and monetary policy

Developing countries need stabilized currencies and avoid erratic fluctuations, high inflation, and overall poor monetary/fiscal policies.

11.6 OUTSOURCING.

Outsourcing can take many forms, it could be a company delegating some of its functions to a subcontractor, it could also involve the transfer of jobs or certain function capabilities overseas or it could follow a company relocating part or the entire production process offshore. Outsourcing could also be domestic, an example could be a financial institution with its headquarters in Boston delegating the functions of collections on delinquent accounts to an outside unrelated collection company operating in Atlanta.

Benefits of Outsourcing

1. Promotes competition among global companies, as the cost margins of firms are reduced due to relatively low labor and factor costs associated with outsourcing.
2. Increased competition and reduced factor costs in turn translate to lower consumer prices, the consumer is therefore left with more disposable income which is reinvested back in the economy resulting in creation of more jobs and an overall expanded economy.
3. Outsourcing is a driving force for innovation; due to the increased competition, companies are forced to constantly develop new products in order to maintain or gain a competitive edge.
4. Outsourcing brings an opportunity for new exports because as income levels rise in host countries such as India and China, the consumers in those markets are able to afford new products that may not be readily available in their country therefore fostering exports.

Disadvantages of Outsourcing

1. Loss of jobs in communities where production facilities and functional units relocate from
2. Potential to drive wages down
3. Exploitation of laborers in developing nations as labor laws offshore may be difficult to enforce

11.7 STEPS TOWARD ECONOMIC INTEGRATION

Economic integration refers to the process of removing restrictions on international trade, payments and factor mobility. A classic example of integration is the European Union. Outlined below are the steps followed for integration.

1. Removal of tariffs and establishment of a free-trade area.
2. Customs uniformity
3. Elimination of non-tariff trade barriers such as border control and customs red tape.
4. Formation of common Central Bank, e.g. European Monetary Union (EMU). This is typically parallel with steps toward a new currency.
5. Convergence, i.e. the alignment of economic and monetary policies to bring involved countries on a similar economic performance threshold.
6. Full fledged economic integration.

World Trade Organization (WTO) rules for commercial conduct of trading nations

1. Membership provision required since the WTO is an international organization
2. Members still required to uphold GATT rules affecting trade pacts negotiated under GATT auspices
3. Members required to be committed to unified package of agreements administered by the WTO
4. WTO reserves the right to reverse policies of protection in critical areas such as agriculture and textiles
5. Member nations free to set their own environmental, labor, health and safety protections.
6. Disputes by member's states administered through numerous councils and committees of the WTO
7. Agreements by member nations pertaining to tariff cuts and reduction of non-tariff measures are implemented by the WTO.
8. Members trade practices are regularly examined by the WTO; member states are also required to update their trade statistics that are maintained by the WTO database.
9. Trade in services; intellectual property and investment are included in the multilateral trading system.

11.8 PAYMENTS AMONG NATIONS & THE FOREIGN EXCHANGE MARKET

Balance of international indebtness & balance of trade

Measures the level of international investment of the United States, essentially weighs the value of U.S. investments abroad versus foreign investments in the United States. This is a measure of both short and long term investment positions of the private and public sector of the economy. It is not however a measure of debt owed. Balance of international indebtness differs from balance of payments in that it compares levels of investment abroad vs. foreign investment in the United States where as the balance of payments is a record of a country's economic transactions with other countries in a given year.

Forward market & Spot Market

In a forward market, currency is bought and sold now for future delivery, with the delivery time typically being 1 month, 3 months or 6 months from the transaction date. In a spot market, currency is bought and sold for instant delivery usually two days after the transaction.

What factors underlie currency exchange values in a free market?

Market fundamentals, this includes economic variables such as productivity, inflation rates, real interests rates, consumer preferences and overall government trade policy. Market expectations also play a role in currency exchange values, by this we mean things such as news of future market fundamentals and general trader opinions or speculation about future exchange rates, essentially chatter among traders.

Factors that apply to short-run exchange rates (few days to weeks)

Dominant factors are transactions involving transfer of financial assets (bank deposits), these transfers respond to variations in real interest rates and future expectations of exchange rates. The medium-run (several months) is greatly driven by cyclical forces within the economy

Factors that apply to the long-run exchange rates (1-5 yrs)

Primarily determined by investment capital inputs & the flow of goods and services. These variables respond to forces such as inflation rates, investment returns, consumer preferences and government trade policies. Long-run value changes to the exchange essentially are a result of exchange trader responding to four factors:

A). Relative Price Levels
B). Relative Productivity Levels
C). Preference for Domestic or Foreign Goods
D). Trade Barriers

Monetary approach to exchange rate determination addresses the shortcoming presented by the two traditional approaches (elasticity's & absorption), which do not associate monetary consequences of balance of payments adjustments. The monetary approach contends currency depreciation can contribute to the balance of payments standing.

Factors affecting exchange rate movements:

- Employment levels
- GDP
- Level of business activity
- Deficits
- Other macroeconomic variables

Government's main role in rate determination:

The government's principal role essentially is to intervene in adverse periods when the foreign exchange markets show a great deal of volatility which could hurt the economy in the long-run, whether this is a good practice or not is debatable, my view is that government intervention in rate exchange markets if used only in dire situations serves the populous a greater benefit.

Managed Floating Exchange

Managed floating exchange rates are determined by forces at play within the free-market, essentially demand and supply forces with occasional minimal government intervention through the Central Bank. Managed floating rates are governed by informal guidelines established by the IMF, these guidelines are used for coordination of national exchange rate policies. The guidelines also address two major concerns, the first involving nations intervening in exchange markets in order to circumvent exchange rate movements that might weaken their currency position. The second concern relates to disorderly or erratic market fluctuations, therefore member states can intervene on the exchange markets to prevent sharp erratic exchange rate movements from day to day and month to month.

Managed floating exchange rates were adopted by industrialized nations in 1973 following the breakdown of the international monetary system, which was based on fixed rates. Managed floats operate under the underlying concept of a "clean float" which translates to a market rate determination as opposed to a "dirty float" which refers to the practice of not letting the free-market forces of supply and demand achieve their equilibrium role.

Perfect capital mobility and the effectiveness of monetary and fiscal policies under fixed exchange rate.

Under a fixed exchange rate system, perfect capital mobility means having a measure of controls on capital movements, such controls are also referred to as exchange controls. These controls are government imposed in order to support fixed exchange rates and prevent speculative attacks on currencies.

Fixed exchange rates and developing countries

Fixed exchange rates are good for developing countries because it provides for a stabilizing effect since currency markets in most developing countries are still a work in progress and thus can be very volatile. Fixed rates also present an opportunity for the government to somewhat control capital flows, this is important for developing countries in that the government can influence its payments position. Developing nations government's can therefore encourage or discourage certain transactions by offering different rates for foreign currency for different purposes which can be of critical importance for developing country.

11.9 ZAMBIA'S TRANSITION TOWARD AN OPEN MARKET ECONOMY.

Zambia is a landlocked nation located in central southern Africa, eight countries namely, Tanzania, DRC, Malawi, Namibia, Angola, Mozambique, Botswana and Zimbabwe border it. The land area covers 752,614 square kilometers. The most recent census figures put the population figures at 10 million. The country's GDP was listed at $4.1 billion according to figures from 2003. Zambia has one of the highest urbanized population rates in the Sub-Saharan region with the figure estimated to be at 46% [1]. The principal city and commercial capital is Lusaka (pop 1.5 million). Other major cities include, Ndola, Kitwe and Livingstone. Copper and Cobalt exports account for 77% of export earnings and the remaining primarily agriculture and tourism. Average daytime temperatures are 15-27 Celsius. Zambia is a country with an enormous amount of mineral resources with copper dominating, other minerals include, zinc, lead nickel, uranium, coal, gemstones, gold, etc. Zambia is however internationally recognized as a major copper and cobalt producer. Since the 1920s when copper production began, the social and economic fabric has heavily relied on this industry.

The primary purpose of this analytical review is to explore and examine the steps Zambia has embarked towards becoming an open market economy. The review will address some of the strategies employed by the Zambian government and point to some successes as well as failures.

Dawn of open market forces

The early 1990s in Zambia were dominated with a hive of activity centering on the dawn of democracy, for the first time since the country's independence in 1964, multi-party elections were in full swing. The country had been governed by the strong hand of its founding president, Dr. Kenneth Kaunda since independence under a one party state, and for the first time the prospect of a new government regime was not just a buzz but seemed rather an eminent reality to come. A new government would in fact be elected into power bringing the principles of democracy to this nation, underlying this democracy movement were sweeping economic implementations intended to move Zambia into a free enterprise open market.

Mission

"Successfully transition Zambia from a government owned parastatal economic structure to a fully fledged open market economy with underpinnings of capitalism."

TABLE 11

Objectives and Strategies Matrix

Objectives	Strategies
1. Increase Investment Activity	Liquidate government parastatals into private holdings
2. Increase productivity and job opportunities	Sell Mining Assets, the backbone of Zambia's economy, over 80% foreign revenues
3. Reduce Inflation Rate to less than 18.5%	Sound monetary policy compounded by cumulative effect from above mentioned strategies
4. Stabilize exchange rate (Market Determined)	Improved foreign reserves as a result of favorable export earnings due to high metal prices
5. Boost tourism	Advertising campaign through Visit Zambia awareness drive to attract western tourists
6. Increase Real GDP	Agriculture, mining, tourism and manufacturing
7. Poverty Reduction	Agriculture, mining, tourism and manufacturing as driving forces

Implementation of strategies & objectives

Mining and Manufacturing strategies:

Declining world copper prices, inefficiencies and the ailing mining infrastructure had taken its toll on the entire industry with production numbers at their lowest output. In the mid 1990s, the Zambian government began a full-scale drive to privatize the Zambian Copper mining industry. Bids and tenders were formally put out to the public and major mining companies began to line up and submit bids, the process as one might expect was long and drawn out with a lot of red tape and bureaucracy. In 2000, the Zambian government had completed the comprehensive privatization of the Zambian copper industry. After dismantling the massive Zambia Consolidated Copper Mines Company, which was the ninth largest copper mining company in the world, the mining sector was completely privatized with foreign companies.

Tourism and Agriculture sector:

The strategy to boost the agriculture sector was to target Zambia as a potential major grower and exporter of agriculture and horticulture produce. The selling point to investors was the vast abundant quality arable land, very good climate and a relatively good transportation network. The Zambian authorities realized how much underutilized their land resource was, of the 60 million hectares of arable land, only 15% was being cultivated. [6]. The government strongly encouraged commercial farmers by offering them incentives that in some cases were tax induced to get these farmers to relocate to Zambia. The campaign attracted hundreds of commercial farmers from South Africa and Zimbabwe (many whose farms had been seized by the Mugabe regime).

In the tourism area, Zambia implemented an advertising initiative called the "visit Zambia campaign", this campaign was to showcase all of the abundant natural beauty and wildlife the country had to offer, the target market for this marketing campaign were Europe, U.S.A & the Far East. The pivotal aspect of the campaign was promoting the Victoria Falls, which is listed as the 7th wonder in the world, the campaign was also designed to coincide with the 100th (centennial) anniversary celebrations honoring David Livingstone who founded the Victoria Falls in the town of Livingstone, Zambia. The government also felt its 19 National Parks & 34 Game Management areas were untapped. [7].

Observations

Strengths:

- Mineral natural resource endowment & energy resource
- Vast arable unutilized land
- Relatively strong human capital resource
- Stable government
- Pleasant climate
- National park system & Victoria Falls (seventh wonder)
- Weaknesses
- Underutilized natural resources
- Underutilized tourism
- undiversified economy, too much reliance on copper reserves
- Unemployment too high & Poverty constraints
- Poor health system

Opportunities

- Capitalize on rising world copper prices
- Increased tourist visitation
- Commercial agriculture sector expansion
- Manufacturing sector virtually non existent

Threats

- AIDS epidemic
- Erratic world copper prices & subsequent copper substitution
- Shaky democracy
- Unpredictable exchange currency rate
- High urbanization, poverty and unemployment
- Brain drain, too many professionals relocating to the Western countries and neighboring southern African countries such as Botswana & South Africa where better wages and opportunities present themselves.

Concluding Remarks

The trade liberalization moves undertaking in Zambia towards its quest to be a full fledged open market economy have had mixed results. The single most important strategy naturally involved the privatization of the mining industry. The new multinational companies that now run these mines for their part have pumped in millions upon millions of dollars in infrastructure enhancements, which have resulted in efficiencies and production being boosted. World copper prices have also appreciated on the commodities market in the last few years. On balance this objective has been a plus for the Zambian nation even though it needs to pay attention to employee union issues regarding wage compensation. Recent employee strikes could be a concern, however to their credit, the multinational companies responded swiftly with a 30% wage increase to mine workers which settled things down. Another worrying issue with the multinational mining companies has been the spate of mine accidents where mine workers were killed underground in failed shafts and explosions, such incidents caused alarm in the mining region because they had not occurred at such a frequency with the government owned mining companies.

Macroeconomic objectives have been very positive, GDP has continued to grow the last four years largely attributed to favorable world copper prices and improved efficiencies and production levels. Inflation levels have also shown marginal declines but have rather been offset by food price inflation increases, so while this objective has been somewhat met, a lot of work needs to implemented in the area of food prices, this was also largely impacted with low maize (corn) yields due to droughts. It is imperative that the government also redirect their focus on commercial farmers to encourage them in producing consumer crops such as grain rather just paying to the higher paying cash crops such as tobacco. Other potential underutilized sectors are manufacturing and tourism, these areas offer vast foreign exchange potential. The AIDS pandemic is very worrisome, perhaps the biggest constraint Zambia faces, and all resources need to be allocated in order to overcome this threat. It's a good start for Zambia in its journey to a free-market economy, however, the journey is also proving to be long and bumpy.

REFERENCE NOTES

1. http://usembassy.state.gov/zambia/cguide.html
2. *www.glencore.com*
3. Anglo American Fact Sheet
4. US Geological Society
5. *www.mining.co.za/copperbelt*
6. http://www.boz.zm/Economics/economics_main.htm
7. http://www.boz.zm/Economics/economics_main.htm

CHAPTER XII

FINANCIAL ANALYSIS

12.1 OBJECTIVES AND COMPETANCES

1.) The section presents an overview of financial decision-making. Some key specific objectives are outlined below.
2.) Know function and structure of financial markets
3.) Demonstrate competence in financial ratio analysis
4.) Have an understanding of applying discounting methods for present & future value calculations
5.) Apply valuation models to bonds, preferred stocks and common stocks.
6.) Understand the different types of risk and relationship to rate of returns.
7.) Understand the concept of weighted average cost of capital
8.) Utilize capital budgeting methods such as net present & internal rate of return
9.) Utilize financial forecasting and planning techniques
10.) Incorporate working capital management to cash management, credit management, inventory management and short-term financing.

12.2 OVERVIEW OF FINANCIAL MANAGEMENT

The field of financial management is essentially comprised of three areas. The first area relates to **money and capital markets**. In this concentration an analyst will primarily deal with the securities market and financial institutions.

The second area lays emphasis on **investments,** the stem of this area deals with making investment decisions both on an individual basis and organizational level. The investment manager through his or her expertise makes the tough decisions on which securities would best suite the respective investment portfolio. The third and final area is **financial management**, which involves business decisions within firms and other business entities. As one can see, all three fields are closely intertwined thus it is very important that successful financial managers have a good understanding of each area.

12.3 CREDIT POLICY

An effective company credit policy usually will have the following staples Solid Credit standards

- Clear credit terms emphasizing the credit period & terms of cash discounts
- A detailed Collection policy
- Five "C's of Credit: Character, Capacity, Capital, Collateral & Conditions
- Monitoring Accounts Receivable
- Average Collection Period(ACP) or Days of Sales Outstanding (DSO)
- Aging Schedules, Analyzing Changes in Credit Policy.

TABLE 12: CREDIT POLICY VARIABLES: Effects & Changes

VARIABLE and CHANGE	Effect on DSO (Days sales outstanding)	Effect on Sales	Effect on BAD DEBT EXPENSE
Credit Period Shortened	Decreases	May Decrease	Indeterminate effects
Cash Discount Increased	Decreases	May Increase	Indeterminate effects
Credit Standards Tightened	Decreases	May Decrease	Decreases
Collection Policy Tightened	Decreases	May Decrease	Decreases

* DSO (Days sales outstanding)

INVENTORY AND THE ECONOMIC ORDERING QUANTITY (EOQ)

Assume that you are examining the Inventory practices of your firm. You believe that order sizes may be larger than necessary. You decide to look at one key product. For this product, you have been placing orders for 5,000 units. Each unit costs $3.20 and there is a fixed cost of $100 per order. Sales for this product are 25,000 units per year, and are uniform throughout the year. Annual carrying cost is 20% of Inventory value.

a). What is the current cost of inventory?
   Carrying or Holding cost:
   Step 1. Determine average cost = 5,000/2 = 2,500 units
   Step 2. Carrying cost = 2,500 x $3.20 x .20 = $1,600
   Step 3. Ordering cost = orders per year = 25,000/5,000 = 5
           Ordering cost = 5 x 100 = $500
   Step 4. Total cost = 1,600 + 500 = 2,100
b). Now use the EOQ model to determine the optimal ordering quantity; and calculate the new cost of inventory based on this ordering quantity.

   EOQ = square root of $[(2xFxS)/ (CxP)]$ where:
   F is the fixed cost per order
   S is the annual sales per order
   C is the annual carrying cost expressed as a% of inventory value
   P is the purchase price per unit of inventory

   For this example, = square root of $[(2x100x25,000)/(.20 x 3.2)$ = 2,795 order size
   Average inventory: 2,795 divided by 2 = 1,397.5
   Orders per year: 25,000 divided by 2,795 = 8.94454 times per year
   Costs: carrying cost: 1,397.5 x 3.20 x .20 = $894
   Ordering cost: 8.94 x 100 = $894
   Total cost: $1,788

Notes:
.   Mathematically, if we use the exact average inventory and the exact orders per year, then the carrying cost and the ordering cost will be equal.
.   If we make small adjustments to the number of orders per year and the size of the orders, then the carrying cost & ordering cost will be close, but not equal.
.   Note this model can be modified to include safety stocks.

12.4 CASH CONVERSION CYCLE

ILLUSTRATION

40 DAYS (Timeframe between point A & B)

35 DAYS (From B to C)

A). BUY
B). SELL GOODS & SERVICES
C). COLLECT

Inventory Conversion period: 40days (A to B)

Receivables Collection Period (DSO/ACP): 35 days (B to C)

Cash conversion cycle: 40 + 35 - 15 = 60 days.

12.5 PRACTICAL DEFINATIONS

Working Capital:

This refers to current assets used in operations.

Net working capital:

The difference between current assets and current liabilities (current assets - current liabilities.)

Net operating working capital:

(Cash + A/R + Inventory) - (A/P + Accruals)

Working Capital and the Cash Conversion Cycle

Firm X has annual sales of $720,000 and cost of goods sold is $288,000

Therefore: Sales per Day = 720,000/360 = $2000
Cost of goods sold per day = 288,000/360 = $800

Given this information from the balance sheet:
Account Receivables: $70,000
Inventory: $50,000
Payables: $12,000

Inventory Conversion Period:

Inventory/(daily sales) = 50,000/2,000 = 25 days [implies 25 days worth of inventory]

Receivables Collection Period (or DSO) :

Receivables/(daily sales) = 70,000/2000 = 35 days

Payables Deferral Period:

Payables/(cost of goods sold per day) = 12,000/800 = 15 days

Cash Conversion Cycle:

[implies from the time you pay for something and get back return$$$]
(25 days + 35 days - 15 days) = 45 days

Determining the amount of working capital the firm must finance:

Multiply the Length of Cash Conversion Cycle by the Cost of Goods sold
That is:
Length of Cash Conversion Cycle X Cost of Goods Sold per Day
(45 days x 800 = $36,000)

12.6 COST OF TRADE CREDIT

Credit Terms: 3/10, net 60

Implies if cash discount is accepted, then purchase price is reduced by 3%, and payment must be made in 10 days, If cash discount is not taken, then the whole amount must be paid in 60 days. Given this circumstance, if a $100.00 purchase is made with the 3% cash discount (derived from the 3/10 terms), total amount paid within 10 days is $97.00 However, if cash discount is not taken, then the $100.00 would be due in 60 days. This translates into $3 in interest for a 50-day period (60 - 10 days).

$3 in interest on a $97 purchase, which is 3/97 =   3.09%

However this only covers a 50-day (60 - 10) period, to get an annual figure [assuming a 360 day year] 360/50 = 7.2

Therefore,   3.09% x 7.2 =   22.3% annual interest

% Cost of trade credit formula (general terms) =

Discount %/(1 - Discount %)   x   360/ (total credit period- discount period).

12.7 IMPORTANT FINANCIAL RATIOS

LIQUIDITY RATIOS

1. **Current Ratio:**
   Current assets /current liabilities (measures ability to meet short term debts/obligations)

2. **Quick Ratio or (Acid Test):**
   Current assets - inventory /current liabilities (measure of meeting short term debts w/out relying on sell of inventory)

ASSET MANAGEMENT RATIOS

1. **Inventory Turnover Ratio:**
   Sales / Inventories (how well is firm managing inventories)

2. **Days Sales Outstanding (DSO),** also called **"average collection period"** (ACP), used to appraise accounts receivable. (Receivables/ Average sales per day = Receivables/Annual sales/360)

3. **Fixed Asset Turnover ratio:**
   Sales/ Net Fixed Assets (how well is company uses its plant & equipment

4. **Total Asset Turnover Ratio:**
   Sales/Total Assets (measures turnover of all assets or capital intensity)

5. **Operating Capital Requirement Ratio::**
   Operating Capital/ Sales (relationship between Sales & operating. capital.)

DEBT MANAGEMENT (LEVERAGE) RATIOS

1. **Debt Ratio:**
    Total Debt/ Total Assets (percentage of funds from creditors how heavily financed is firm)

2. **Debt to Equity Ratio:**
    Total Debt/Total Equity (compares borrowed funds to stockholder funds)

3. **Times Interest Earned (TIE) ratio:**
    EBIT/Interest Charges (where EBIT is earnings before interest & taxes, this ratio measures the level to which operating income can decline before firm is unable to meet it's annual interest cost

4. **Fixed Charge Coverage Ratio:**
    Similar to above ratio but goes on to include lease payments as well as sinking fund payments. (EBIT + Lease Payments/ Interest charges + Lease payments) + (Sinking Fund Payments)/(1-Tax Rate)

PROFITABILITY RATIOS

1. **Profit Margin on Sales:**
    Net income available to common stockholders divided by sales

2. **Basic earning ratio (BEP):**
    EBIT / Total Assets (shows raw earning power before taxes and leverage)

3. **Operating profit margin after taxes:**
    NOPAT (net opt. profit after taxes) divided by sales (shows how profitable operations are after tax obligations)

4. **Return on Total Assets:**
    Net Income available to common stockholders divided by total assets (shows return on total assets after interest and taxes)

5. **Return on common Equity:**
    Net income available to common stockholders (Measures rate of return on stockholders' investment)

MARKET VALUE RATIOS

1. **Price/Earnings (P/E) ratio:**
   Price per share/Earnings per share (how much investors are willing to pay per $ of reported earnings how market values stock)

2. *Earnings per Share:*
   Net Profit After tax - Preferred stock Dividends/Average number of shares outstanding. (how much profit each share of common stock earns).

3. **Book Value per share:**
   Common equity / Shares Outstanding (how investors regard company)

4. **Market/Book ratio:**
   Market price per share/Book Value per share

When dealing with ratios, it is important to place numbers being utilized in comparable terms so as to get accurate measures. To do this , the consumer price index or CPI as it is commonly referred to is normally utilized. This typically gives a base year as a point of reference for inflation. This is illustrated below:

Current dollars x = CPI base year/CPI current year Base year dollars

FINANCIAL AND BUSINESS STATEMENTS SNAPSHOT

A critical tool in assessing and analyzing a company's financial wellbeing lies in the organizations books or financial statements as formally known. Financial statements are what an x-ray or c-scan are to a medical doctor. Prior to proclaiming a diagnosis, the physician carefully looks at the charts to get a clear road map and pinpoint the state of the patient. In similar fashion, the corporation in our illustration takes the role of a patient and the financial statements are the analysts charts. Thus said, under public disclosure laws, companies in many jurisdictions report the financial state of their organizations via an Annual report. The annual report contains three key statements: the balance sheet, the income statement and the statement of cash flows.

THE BALANCE SHEET

The balance sheet effectively is a frozen snapshot of what assets the company owns and what debt is owed at a specific point in time. Listed in the balance sheet will be the company's assets, liabilities and owners equity. In very simplistic terms, assets represent things of value a company owns. Liabilities represent debt obligations the company owes to non owners. Owners equity also kwon as Stakeholders/Shareholders equity is the difference between assets and liabilities.

THE INCOME STATEMENT

The income statement is a comprehensive report of the company's operational activities over a given period of time, typically for a fiscal year. Reports in some cases may be based on semi-annual or quarterly periods. The income statement is also referred to as the profit and loss statement (P&L). The statement reports on revenues (how much money the company brought in from its operations) and expenses (how much money the company paid out. It's a very useful tool because one can see a company's track record in making or losing money

THE STATEMENT OF CASH FLOWS (SCF)

The statement of cash flows or cash flow statement details a company's flow of cash receipts and cash payments over a period of time. Cash inflows represent money coming into business while cash outflows represent cash paid out by company. The statement offers a cumulative effect of relationships in the balance sheet and income statement as relates to a company's liquidity management. The statement of cash flows is a useful tool when looking at a company's ability to meet short-term obligations, i.e.: pay its bills.

CHAPTER XIII

ETHICS IN BUSINESS

13.1 OVERALL OBJECTIVES

This chapter offers an examination of common ethical issues and conflicts managers often encounter within their organizations and how to best deal with such issues utilizing logical ethical thinking. As such codes of ethics, international ethics, moral issues, environmental ethics and various other concepts are analyzed. The global era today is a constant changing and often complicated dynamic, thus this section attempts to offer the reader a broad overview to help them become better managers and leaders. The section opens with an overview of the United States Constitution given this is a section dealing with ethics, it is imperative that students always have an understanding of their constitutional rights.

Why have a Code of Ethics?

- to define accepted/acceptable behaviors;
- to promote high standards of practice;
- to provide a benchmark for members to use for self evaluation;
- to establish a framework for professional behavior and responsibilities;
- as a vehicle for occupational identity;
- as a mark of occupational maturity;"

Source: website of http://www.calsca.com/ethics_lscabc.htm)

IMC USA Code of Ethics

All IMC USA members pledge in writing to abide by the Institute's Code of Ethics. Their adherence to the Code signifies voluntary assumption of self-discipline above and beyond the requirements of law. Key provisions of the Code specify:

Clients

- Members will serve their clients with integrity, competence, and objectivity, using a professional approach at all times, and placing the best interests of the client above all others.
- Members will establish realistic expectations of the benefits and results of their services.
- Members will treat all client information that is not public knowledge as confidential, will prevent it from access by unauthorized people, and will not take advantage of proprietary or privileged information, either for use by them, their firm or another client, without the client's permission.
- Members will avoid conflicts of interest, or the appearance of such, and will disclose to a client any circumstances or interests that might influence their judgment and objectivity.
- Members will refrain from inviting an employee of an active or inactive client to consider alternative employment without prior discussion with the client.

Engagements

- Members will only accept assignments which they possess the expertise to perform, and will only assign staff with the requisite expertise.
- Members will ensure that before accepting any engagement, a mutual understanding of the objectives, scope, work plan, and fee arrangements has been established.
- Members will offer to withdraw from a consulting engagement when their objectivity or integrity may be impaired.

Fees

- Members will agree in advance with a client on the basis for fees and expenses, and will charge fees and expenses that are reasonable, legitimate and commensurate with the services delivered and the responsibility accepted.

- Members will disclose to their clients in advance any fees or commissions that they receive for equipment, supplies or services they could recommend to their clients.

Profession

- Members will respect the individual and corporate rights of clients and consulting colleagues, and will not use proprietary information or methodologies without permission.
- Members will represent the profession with integrity and professionalism in their relations with their clients, colleagues and the general public.
- Members will report violations of this Code to the Institute, and will ensure that other consultants working on behalf of the member abide by this Code.

The Institute of Management Consultants USA, Inc. (IMC USA) adopted its first Code of Ethics in 1968. Since that time IMC USA has modified the wording of the Code for additional clarity and relevance to clients. The current Code was approved February 22, 2002. It is consistent with the International Code of Professional Conduct published by the International Council of Management Consulting Institutes (ICMCI) of which IMC USA is a founding member.

Members who apply for the CMC (Certified Management Consultant) designation must pass a written examination on the application of the IMC USA Code of Ethics to client service. The CMC mark is awarded to consultants who have met high standards of education, experience, competence and professionalism.

ETHICAL ISSUES & BUSINESS:

13.2 ENVIRONMENTAL PHILOSOPHY

Latest thinking in environmental philosophy seems to have taken a non-exploitive ethic. The latest thinking follows the premise that human beings must not take on the environment as dominators, but rather as generic participants in the whole dynamic. Following such thoughts, new ideas which somewhat take an eccentric view have evolved the notion of deep ecology which essentially proclaims the immediate halt of domination of human beings on the environment. Some of the more radical concepts have gone as far as promoting drastic measures including indulging in lawlessness in order to save the environment.

Such views challenge the older views, which basically considered the environment as a means to wealth, which was to be exploited without consequence in order to attain as much wealth as possible. As such, these new views are drastically at odds with the older views which centered on utilitarian doctrines that professed, that despite the effects of pollution being harmful, the social costs passed on to society were more beneficial therefore validating pollution.

13.3 Risk Analysis

Risk analysis pertaining to human risks typically is a function of two processes. The first process involves the collective factors of risk assessment, which heavily relies upon scientific and technical inputs. Harmful effects are identified through collection of quantitative and objective data. Having identified the associated dangers, a series of tests on laboratory animals are conducted in order to quantify the risks. The second part of risk analysis is characterized as risk management. Essentially this is a non-scientific process based on the law, politics, economics and ethics. Proponents of risk analysis regard its heavy use of scientific and technical tools as a major strength. By the same token, some disadvantages of this method are the physiological differences presented by lab animals to humans, as such critics argue that relying on animal tests may lead to unreliable conclusions

Cost benefit analysis is the tail end of the risk analysis process where associated costs and benefits of a proposed action are compared. Typically, such analysis involves assigning monetary coefficients in order to facilitate comparisons. If it is determined that the benefits exceed the costs, then the proposed action is deemed favorably and vice-versa.

Advantages of cost benefit analysis

- Methodical
- Optimal alternatives in terms of economic inputs
- Acts as rational measure to emotional arguments
- Helpful to regulators in determining the most efficient policy

Disadvantages:

- Determining cost/benefit values difficult & controversial
- Valuation of human life complex/controversial
- May result in trade-offs of environmental quality
- Subjects of regulation may pass costs to innocent parties by raising prices of their end products in order to cover their costs.

13.4 Global Competition

U.S. Global competition strengths:

- world leader in super-computers
- software engineering
- artificial intelligence
- computer-aided design
- engineering, telecommunications, genetic engineering & rocket propulsion

Weaknesses:

- consumer products
- semiconductors

One strategy that proved successful and effective was reduction in costs. This included lateral moves where partnerships with suppliers were embraced in creating long-term relationships, which subsequently created greater efficiency, lower costs, greater profit margins and a competitive edge. Similarly, integration of departments within the organization resulted in lower costs and allowed emphasis on product quality control and development. Outsourcing is another strategy that was effective. In this instance, the organization is able to utilize cheap labor in certain locales particularly third-world countries thereby drastically reducing their costs and thus enhancing their competitiveness. Other cost cutting strategies include direct foreign investments.

The second area of success pertains to improvements in productivity through mergers and alliances with the assumption that such actions foster efficiency by sharing risks.

Host country Fears:

a). Human rights abuses - governments fear that multinational companies have a tendency of disregarding such rights. Common abuses cited include those pertaining to, child labor abuses, and exploitation of local workers by paying low wages.
b). Environmental concerns - multinationals assume less social responsibility and in turn pollute the host nations environment without regard to the consequences.
c). Protectionism issues - host governments fear multinationals present unfair competition to local industries and eventually may drive them out of business.
d). Cultural & Ethical differences.

To counter these and other fears, governments impose measures such as restrictions in the form of trade barriers, outright trade bans, and institute quotas on imports. Despite these underlying conflicts, some notable benefits result from such partnerships as summarized below:

- provide local employment
- transfer of technology
- boosts standard of living
- enhances foreign exchange reserves
- opens foreign markets

13.5 PAC's, NAFTA, WORKER & CONSUMER RIGHTS, TITLE VII

Business interests attempt to influence the political environment by utilizing political action committees, commonly called PAC's. They take advantage of a legislative loophole that allows for organizations to set-up PACs. In this manner , they are able to solicit contributions. Business interests also employ brokering and bundling techniques to facilitate contributions to candidates. Another common avenue used involves donations by means of soft money. Finally, donations into the political arena are made through unlimited independent expenditures such as campaign advertisements.

Current campaign laws call for full public disclosure of contributions and expenditures. In addition, restricted contributions by individuals and PACs to candidates are allowed. These limits are guided by an assortment of spelled-out legal limits.

By making contributions, business organizations hope to gain access, influence and receive favors to promote their corporate interests. I believe these are dangerous trends in view of current practices, which need to be reformed. It seems current legislation is ineffective as business interests always find loopholes to side step the law. The greatest danger I see is a situation where the fine line is crossed and politicians become pawns of business.

NAFTA

1). NAFTA is a treaty embarked by the United States, Canada, and Mexico which created the largest trading bloc in the world with over 400 million customers. The primary objective of this agreement was to promote trade by lifting certain barriers such as tariffs, duties and so forth. The treaty was to benefit all parties involved by expanding GDP and creating jobs.

2). NAFTA Skeptics

- US will loose jobs to Mexico due to cheap labor.
- Will result in lower wages for low-wage jobs in the U.S.
- Prone to worker rights violations
- Environmental degradation in places like Mexico lacking strict standards.

3). NAFTA Proponents argue that free trade is necessary for economic growth.

- Goods exported to member countries will in turn support jobs in home country.
- Increases GDP

4). The numbers suggest NAFTA is proportionately a minor factor in the American economy and likely more significant for the Mexican economy.
5). The political & social arguments seem more exaggerated than the implicit economic impact.
6). Time needs to be allowed to see what direction the current NAFTA arrangement takes before considering expansion.

Consumer Rights

The consumer movement has been very instrumental in making business more conscious and cognitive to consumer views in general. Due to various concerns by consumers and advocates, the business community to some degree acknowledges these groups as major stakeholders. As such, many corporations in their corporate statements specifically make it a point to address customer satisfaction as a primary goal. Some of the major landmarks of this movement can be traced to the early 1960s by pioneers such as Rachel Carson. Other early notable figures in this movement include, Ralph Nader, John F. Kennedy, and Peter Drucker. In the 1980s, Peters and Waterman in their book, "In Search of Excellence" reinforced commitment to this movement. Ralph Nader's influence over the years has pressured congress to respond by stepping up efforts of regulatory agencies protecting consumer rights. Ralph Nader's influence though has diminished as corporations and the republican congress found ways of slowing this movement. Many other significant advocate groups exist and are always keeping a keen eye.

Important authorities and legislation today are in place to protect consumers. These include groups such as "The Consumer Product Safety Commission", which was created in 1972 to protect consumers in terms of safety and so on. This agency regulates a wide assortment of consumer products. The National Highway Traffic Safety Administration, created in 1966 is concerned with automobile & truck safety. Several other such agencies exist acting as shields to consumer rights.

Worker Rights

Workers today are still demanding the traditional concerns such as safety at work, medical benefits, equal treatment, better wages and so forth. The movement today is not as passionate as was the case in earlier years. The nature of today's workers demands has drastically changed, where as in the past workers were typically concerned about stability and loyalty from employers in terms of job security, recent trends fostering global economies wiped out that philosophy. Today, employers are accustomed to downsizing and turbulent forces at the work place. As such, today's employees have become savvy and less concerned about job security and company loyalty, instead they focus on improving their marketability through on-going training. Workers like employers have also developed less loyal to organizations, and are quick to move to another job offering more rewards. Recognizing this dynamic, companies routinely encourage self-improvement and will offer sponsorship toward training as they constantly seek a highly skilled streamlined workforce. These new rights have been fostered due to competitive and global forces where companies have to keep reorganizing their structures to stay afloat.

Title VII

Title VII has been interpreted as requiring preferential treatment through its underlying theme, which prohibits discrimination in any aspect of employment. The Supreme Court has struggled with the issue surrounding the interpretation of Title VII mainly from a philosophical and constitutional right standpoint. The philosophical argument implies Title VII goes against the ideal of equal opportunity in essence. Another source of conflict is those who contend that Title VII undermines the principle of achievement based on merit and as such constitutes a violation of individual rights. The Supreme Court finds itself entangled with arguments of people who feel their rewards have been taken away from them despite not practicing any discrimination behavior.

On the other hand, the Supreme Court is confronted with an alternate set of arguments centering on utilitarian considerations, which advocate that title VII benefits everyone by fully utilizing all available talent and thus creating political stability. Other arguments include those relating to the ethical theories of justice and ethical theories of rights. In the end, no easy answer exists with this issue, on balance I think Title VII is required and essential for utilitarian reasons as well as for ensuring everyone has equal access and opportunity.

13.6 CORPORATE GOVERNANCE

Critics of corporate governance feel that the performance of board members in boosting equity investment is inadequate and in many instances these board members do not take into consideration the views of employees, stakeholders, society, etc in their decisions. In fact critics feel most such decisions are made contrary to the stakeholders concerns. Critics also point out that board members are grossly over paid relative to the functions they perform, many feel the board members do not spend enough time on company matters but merely act as rubber stamps of the company's executive staff.

Some of the suggested reforms include calls to evaluate the performance of the board of directors. This suggestion stipulates that while some boards engage in some sought of evaluation, usually such evaluations are not objective and refrain from negative feedback but rather are simply self-serving. Another suggested reform calls for the separation of the CEO and the Board Chairman. Advocates of this suggestion believe this would be an effective way of diluting the power base. However, I feel even if these suggested measures were to be adopted, their impact would be minimal as these boards exert a lot of power and influence to circumvent the effects.

13.7 INTERNATIONAL MONETARY FUND& AFRICA: ETHICS EXAMINED

The African continent is one graced with abundant natural wealth but is always seemingly at crossroads with its quest to rise from the grips of poverty and human catastrophes. The last decade has been particularly brutal and with devastation of epic proportions. The continent is at a critical desperate point. To understand and shed some light into how and why the continent is in this position and continues to struggle, this review examines the relationship between Africa and the International Monetary Fund. The review further addresses the issue in terms of the underlying ethical practices employed by the IMF in its lending and general practices. The review takes a look at the nature and consequence of this relationship keeping the ethical concerns at the forefront. In part, the analysis focuses on four ethical questions relating to:

- Structural Adjustments
- IMF as a driving force for debt
- Exploitation
- IMF interests and motivations.

The relationship between Africa and the IMF has never been at the center stage of controversy more so than now. At the forefront of this ensuing outrage are the practices the IMF is being accused of employing toward these poverty stricken nations. The main issue echoed by activist groups and the African leadership being that pertaining to conditions IMF imposes to these nations in order for them to attain loans. Many have argued that so often these conditions are not only unfair but, also amount to ineffective policy. Furthermore, African nations insist these imposed structural adjustments are harmful and counteractive. These nations further contend that these same imposed policies are driving them into more debt and at a local level responsible for social unrest, unemployment and economic degradation.

IMF sees the situation differently and stands by its policies and practices. As opposed to the critics views, IMF sees the problem as a function of host countries engaged in mismanagement and bad policy selection. As one may expect, this is clearly a complex subject matter with so many variables. However, this paper will primarily look at the ethical issues as relates to policy. As we explore this sometimes fascinating, sometimes troubling dilemma, the author employs all available resources and heavily relies on factual secondary sources in addition to his firsthand personal experiences.

Literature Review

This subject matter has received extensive attention from researchers of all backgrounds. Most of the material uncovered was from the 1990s onward with the vast majority conducted by non-governmental organizations. The IMF itself was a great resource especially with statistical information. Equally resourceful was material from activist groups and vigilante watch groups. It seems most of the material outside of the IMF and World Bank took an anti-IMF position. For the most part, most resources presented an objective point of view.

Tale of the IMF & African courtship

The ethical question that arises is a derivative of increasing inequalities primarily between the developed and least developed nations. According to the United Nations Development Program [1], global inequality is worse now than ever before. In 1950 the gap between the richest and the poorest country was about 35 to one, while by 1992 it had widened to 72 to one. As such per capita incomes in these poor countries has continued to decline in the last decade, particularly in sub-Saharan Africa. This is a very disturbing trend and sadly, the disparity continues to widen.

As a youngster growing up in Zambia in the 70s and 80s, I remember a very different Africa than what we have seen in the last decade. Indeed poverty and other associated social ills were apparent then, but the comparison to today is inconceivable and simply pales to the present sub-Saharan Africa. I can recall then president, Dr Kenneth Kaunda vehemently opposed to the IMF programs. What was in place then was more of a socialist approach where government was essentially central in providing all social services such as education, health-care, and so forth. Generally people were significantly better off in many aspects. Government agencies may not have been run as efficiently as those in the developed nations, but nonetheless were able to provide basic needs such as medical treatment, elementary & higher education, social security and various other such services at no cost. People for all intensive purposes had a sense of empowerment and hope.

However, under growing pressures to secure vital foreign exchange, which is a lifeline for many of these African countries, desperation and necessity would call for drastic measures. A vast majority of these countries had been able to cope well and manage to sustain a reasonable marginal self-sustaining existence, however a host of factors including the continued decline in commodity prices (which accounted for almost all foreign exchange revenues) left the African leadership scratching their heads. Whether coincidentally or a case of doomed destiny, the IMF was suddenly in the picture, thus a beginning of an intricate courtship. This courtship would eventually transcend all odds and end up in matrimony. This was no marriage that called for a honeymoon, time was of the essence, and so it was, a union was matriculated. From the get go, this relationship was rocky and as intense as a championship chase match. One might in fact describe it similar to a dysfunctional marriage scripted out of Hollywood and conceived in a Las Vegas drive-through establishment by two intoxicated partners.

Under its articles for lending funds,[2] the IMF was quick and swift to spell out an assortment of conditions that had to be met in order to process and facilitate the release of funds. This is one area where some ethical questions on the part of the IMF come into play, which will be further examined in the latter part of the paper. However questionable the motives and intentions of the IMF, indeed they could have very well been well meant, however what is evident are the harmful implications such tactics have had. Over the years most of the African leadership relented to the spelled out terms, therefore going about implementing a series of economic and monetary changes such as, deregulation, opening up markets to foreign firms, constant devaluation of currencies, etc. All said, these adjustments would have devastating consequences of catastrophic proportions, basically causing many of the economies to self-implode.

The IMF on the hand in its defense of its policies contends the catastrophic turn of events are not a result of their policies but rather a function of bad governance at the local level and gross mismanagement at the local administrative level. The argument is a two-fold argument with each side engaged in finger pointing much like a squabbling couple. Revisiting the subject of initial intentions of the IMF in my estimation presents U.S. with an unquestionable ethical dilemma. One indeed might ask, *did the IMF engage in unethical behavior by imposing these structural adjustments?* This is a question among others we shall address and continue to revisit in this review in trying to ascertain reasonable answers. As with many ethical questions, one might contend that the answer is only as good as the bearer, in other words, reflects the bearers inclinations. Thus said, let me assure the readers that as the surrogate conduit, my assertions and opinions are simply a derivative of facts examined and from personal experiences. (income disparities and poverty concentrations).[3]

Imposed Structural Adjustments

The subject relating to IMF sanctioned structural adjustments has caused the greatest uproar by far. Non-so evident is the escalating disdain for these adjustments than the recent influx of protests mounted by activist groups at scheduled IMF global meeting locations. The outrage in many instances has strayed from peaceful protests to violent clashes, in fact some extremist groups have gone as far as staging intricate planned sabotage activities. Recent clashes at the WTO, IMF and World Bank summit[4] seemed to have set a wave of defiance directed toward these groups. Following are some examples of scores of protests that have ensued: The IMF & World Bank summit in Prague drew large crowds in arms[5,]. At a Washington, D.C. summit, protesters exceeded 30,000.[6]. In Lusaka, Zambia where officials from the IMF and Zambian parliament members were meeting to address poverty reduction, the scenes and drama that followed are narrated in the excepts below from the Times of Zambia.[7]

LUSAKA, April 26 (Oneworld.Net)—Scores of anti-International Monetary Fund (IMF) protestors were dispersed by armed riot police in Zambia's capital Lusaka yesterday after they attempted to picket outside a hotel where IMF and Zambian officials were meeting. Protestors, brought together by leading women's rights groups opposed to IMF and World Bank policies which attempt to price open markets—accused the Fund of bringing misery to poor countries by imposing strict conditions on their economies, which benefit only the rich.

"IMF policies are killing us, especially women and children," said Emily Sikazwe of Women for Change shortly after the aborted demonstration.

Officials from the IMF and the Zambian parliament were meeting to discuss their partnership for growth and poverty reduction. Speaker of the National Assembly, Amussa Mwanamwambwa, told IMF representatives that Zambia's continued indebtedness to the IMF had resulted in a perception that multilateral creditors were obstacles to the attainment of domestic socio-economic needs.

"It is important for the IMF to use this [visit as an] opportunity to explain before the people's elected representatives the IMF s difficulties and objections to the worldwide call for total debt cancellation," Mwamamwambwa said.

The IMF says its lending schemes were broadened recently through the establishment of the Poverty Reduction and Growth Facility. The scheme to cut poverty would be planned by government with input from civil society, said IMF Assistant Director for Africa Reinold Van Til.

Why all this outrage one might wonder? To get a firm understanding of the underlying issue, it is important to go back and examine the pertaining institutional functions of the IMF.[8,pg. 3&4 IMF supplement] In its provisions, the IMF gives itself a broad jurisdiction over nations requiring loans. For instance, the IMF can demand and monitor exchange arrangements. This broad mandate over policy is what Sub-Saharan nations resent in that they feel they are not able to institute their own policies better suited to their agendas, but instead continuously being forced into harmful structural adjustments. Their debt on the other hand keeps growing by leaps and bounds, what they call the debt trap. Due to their need for foreign exchange, they find themselves in an uncompromising situation where they keep borrowing at inflated interest rates while their cumulative debt balloons. This leads to the 2nd ethical question I present. "Recognizing the vulnerable position of these nations, how can the IMF justify keep driving them deeper into debt while subjecting them to outrageous interest rates, even in cases where the principle owed has been paid over and over in interest charges". A recent World Bank Report on Global debt revealed the following disturbing points.[8]

1. The IMF extracted a net $1 billion from Africa in 1997 and 1998, reversing the trend of the last five years. At the same time, it spent billions bailing out bankers in East Asian crisis economies.
2. Developing countries paid back $13 for every $1 they received in grants in 1998, up from $9 in 1996.
3. Commodity prices have plunged, crippling the poorest countries ability to repay foreign debt.
4. Despite borrowing less than they paid back in 1998, total debt in developing countries rose again by $150 billion to a new total of almost $2.5 trillion.

Structural adjustments cause an even greater ill in terms of social and human costs. The human tales at face value present a very disturbing picture, indeed I have experienced firsthand on a personal level the human impact and ultimate cost. Some of the most commonly employed structural adjustments include:

a): Privatization

This occurs when governments are required to sell government owned entities to the private market, sometimes referred to as privatization. Such measures usually lead to mass unemployment in the long run, substantial pay reductions by private companies, degradation of services previously offered at subsidized or for the most part at no cost by the government, particularly social services such as health and education. These policies also thwart local enterprises that are not able to compete with foreign companies.

b): User Fees

These policies call for charging for services such as medical care, education and social security. While they may be better suited for developed nations, such programs are ineffective and very harmful in poor countries as illustrated by some testimonials presented in the paper later. This particular policy unlike others has caused the greatest human impact.

c): Promotion of exports

While it may seem like a good policy on paper, when put in practice this practice can be destructive particularly to domestic traditional subsistence farmers who are forced to farm more export oriented crops. In many cases, they end up being driven off their lands to make room for large commercial farmers. In addition to displacing rural farmers, it promotes hunger and destitution because consumer crops which fed local populations are replaced by commercial crops that yield high margins such as tobacco.

d): Devaluation of Currency

Countries are constantly requested to devalue their currencies as a condition for receiving loans. Naturally, this drives cost of imports high by lowering the purchasing power, which eventually leads to lower standards of living, social unrest, inflation, unemployment and a host of other ills. These are just a few of the controversial restructuring policies. The following exhibit presents some testimonials echoed by common folks.[9]

Globalization

This follows our third ethical dilemma, which contends *that western countries gain at the expense of developing countries.* The share of income of global transactions is less than 2% accounting for African markets and continues to decline.[10] The polarization of views on globalization couldn't be better illustrated by the opinions of the Indian Finance minister and the World Bank chief executive both commenting on the same subject.[11] Jashwan Sinha, Indian finance minister had this to say, globalization must be managed in the best interests of everyone in the world, especially the poorer countries. James Wolfensohn, the head of the World Bank echoed these sentiment, globalization was probably inevitable and protestors were wrong to think that it was a process, which was under the control of international institutions. Such contrasting views simply further illustrate the complexity of such matters. Basically, two schools of thought almost always at odds with each other comprise the main players.

Third World leadership usually asserts that the IMF and its likes are institutions controlled by a few wealthy countries with destructive intentions designed to further enrich these already wealthy countries while destroying third world nations. The IMF however sees the situation in a different light and offers the explanation that they are simply lending money at cost with the interest of African nations at the centerpiece. The ethical dilemma here in part is :*whose interest is the IMF concerned with and at what cost?* I raise this question in part because it is at the cornerstone of the globalization issue. As pointed out earlier, the IMF through its statements and press releases contends that globalization is an inevitable function of the market forces, therefore distancing itself from the conflict. However, one would wonder whether past actions support this notion. Similarly, the IMF discredits accusations by African leadership that the IMF is essentially a loan-shark entity exploiting and crippling them. Its assertion remains firm stating that it views itself as an organization strongly committed to assisting these poor countries in their plight to end their social ills and rise from poverty.

As we draw to the end of our quest in our exploration of the troubled marriage between the IMF and Africa, indeed one can agree that this union is a complex one with so many variables. It is ironic that as I was conducting research on this subject, all my emotions were evoked, whether through laughter, saddens, contempt, intrigue, etc. such was the tale of this compilation. However, one thing that cannot be overlooked is that there are some troubling transgressions involved, particularly the human costs. Throughout the paper we raised some ethical questions and now we try to conceptualize some answers. The object of the paper was not point fingers or pick sides, but rather point out some questionable ethical practices. On the first issue which centers on structural adjustments, I think it is clear some of the practices employed particularly the four we focused on earlier, under the key adjustments constitute unethical practices on the part of the IMF. Similarly, on the second question raised regarding debt, I thought for the most part the IMF acted irresponsibly with unethical persuasions. On the third question dealing with exploitation by western countries, I failed to see any ethical malpractice. Likewise on the question of whose interest the IMF was acting on and at what cost, I found it difficult to raise any ethical concerns even if one was to assume IMF was acting on behalf of other interests, if anything what can be said is that this is a case of profit with hints of greed but isolated from ethical concerns. I should note the IMF should be commended on some recent steps taken in instituting debt relief to various African countries, that in itself is a big step.[12]

Recommendation & Implications

The IMF clearly has work to do given all the issues raised, most critical in need would be the revision and overhaul of loan conditions, however one group that cannot be left out of this equation are some of the corrupt African Leadership who perpetuate some of these sad manifestations to continue. This analytical review did not indulge on the subject of the rampant corruption on the continent, but clearly that has a large role into the problems, thus deserving a special mention. The implications are grave naturally with sad human impacts that will affect many generations to come.

REFERENCE NOTES

[1]. United Nations Global Program. (2001).
Retrieved from group data base
www.un.org

[2]. International Monetary Fund Report. (2001)
Retrieved from group data base
www.imf.org

[3]. World Bank(2001)
Retrieved from group data base
www.worldbank.org

[4]. World Development Movement Report. (2001). *States of Unrest.*
Retrieved from group data base
www.pages.hotbot.com

[5]. *Denouncing Global Capitalism.* (2001)
Retrieved from group data base
www.news.bbc.co.uk

[6]. *Denouncing Global Capitalism.* (2001)
Retrieved from group data base
news.bbc.co.uk

[7]. Times of Zambia. (April, 26, 2000)
Retrieved from:
www.oneworld.com

[8]. International Monetary Fund Report (2001).
Retrieved from group data base
www.imf.org

[9]. Jubilee 2000 Coalition (2001). *IMF takes $1 billion from Africa*
Retrieved from group data base www.jubilie2000uk.org

[10 & 11]. BBC News online(2000) *World Bank Development Committee.*
Retrieved from group database
www.news,bbc.co.uk

[12]. BBC News online(2000) *World Bank Development Committee.*
Retrieved from group database
www.news,bbc.co.uk

CHAPTER XIV

ORGANIZATIONAL BEHAVIOR

14.1 OVERVIEW

Management thought is an ever-evolving field of study as organizations at all levels seek to find the right balance between theory and functionality in enhancing maximum returns. Indeed it can be quite said that management thought as a concept is a true mosaic. Four distinct areas encompass management thought transition. The first era is what is referred to as the **classical or scientific** era. This era can be credited for such prolific theorists such as Henri Fayol, Frederick Taylor and Max Weber. The contribution of these three men is daunting, today Frederick Taylor is commonly referred to as the "father of scientific management". Max Weber is called the "father of organizational theory". Last but not least by any means is Henry Favol who many through his prolific studies on increasing productivity is credited as the father of modern day chain factories and large complex organizations. Fayol is well known for his definition of management as a derivative of five functions:

1.) Planning.
2.) Organizing.
3.) Commanding.
4.) Coordinating.
5.) Controlling.

The second era of management thought was the **behavioral era**, this period saw emphasis being placed on the human aspect being incorporated into management which to a larger extent explains the household names to come out of this era. The three main players were Abraham Maslow, Fredrick Herzberg and Clayton Alderfer. Abraham Maslow is today widely known for his "Hierarchy of needs theory". Frederick Herberg is known for his "Two-Factor Theory also referred to as the motivation hygiene theory. Clayton Alderfer tweaked Maslow's Hierarchy theory and came up with the ERG theory. The third era known as the **contemporary era has** the likes of Douglas Mcgregor, Victor Vroom and so forth. Mcgregor of course, is widely known for his Leadership theory which was coined as "Theory X and Theory Y" and was somewhat controversial particularly the notion concerning the theory that implied that employees inherently did not like work and thus must be forced or coerced. Vroom's "expectancy theory" on the other hand stated that employees were motivated to work as a function or probability of reward. The fourth and final era is the **modern era**. In this period we find theorists combining today's challenging global business decisions with past theories. Peter Drucker and Edward Deming are notable theorists of this period, as will be illustrated in the latter part of this section where I present an exploratory analysis into Mr. Edward Deming emphasizing his famous Total Quality Management theory he exported to Japan in the 1950's.

14.2 OVERALL OBJECTIVES AND COMPETENCES

1.) Understanding the fundamentals of Organizational Behavior.
2.) Group dynamics
3.) Organizational structure.
4,) Managing & Communication
5.) Cross cultural dimensions
6.) Leadership Qualities
7.) Time Management
8.) Dealing with and overcoming stressful situations
9.) Conceptualizing management theories to practical situations.

These are some of the few specific objectives.

14.3 OVERVIEW OF SELECTED THEORISTS:

Clayton Alderfer: Research Interests

Human needs: Focused on Existence, Relatedness and Growth.

Organizational Diagnosis: Various articles such as *The invisible director on corporate boards* published in the Harvard Business Review, Nov-Dec 1986 and *Directorship*, which raised questions about how well corporate directors assess the performance of chief executives. Gives reasons for concern and addresses evaluation avoidance. Jun 96, Business Source Elite.

Race Relations: article titled field experiment for studying race relations embedded in organizations. Research study on the psychological effect of data gathering methods in studies on race relations showed that better relationships were established between researchers and respondents if they had the same race, sex and social background. Also found that responsiveness of respondents failed to alter the results of race relations studies. Jan 96, Journal of Organizational Behavior. *{member of race and gender balanced consulting teams; very active in trying to change race relations in organizations.}*

Group & Inter group Dynamics: article titled, Understanding embedded inter group relations: a comment on Yammarino and Jung. Points at lack of research to supporting link between leadership and level of analysis, also examines findings about individualism vs. collectivism. March, 1998 Journal of Applied Behavioral Science.

Personality Leadership & Educational Leadership

Courses Taught:

- Group psychology of organizations
- Interview and observation in organizations
- Group relations and organizational diagnosis
- Experimental group dynamics

Supervision in organizational psychology

- Prominent Theories:
- Alderfers Motivational Theory

Illustration of diverse works:

- Examination of article on Asian American and Leadership.
- Questions raised about corporate directors assessment of chief executives.
- Field experiments conducted examining race relations embedded in organizations.

- Biography of Henry (Hank) W. Riecken, a prominent applied behavioral scientist.

Maslow's Hierarchy of Needs

Maslow's hypothesis follows that every human being has a hierarchy of five needs.

1.) Physiological - associated with shelter, food, sex & other bodily needs.
2.) Safety - Protection from physical and emotional harm.
3.) Social - affection, friendships, relationships, belonging . . .
4.) Esteem - self respect, status, achievement and so forth.
5.) Self Actualization - drive to strive to reach ones potential. Relating to self-fulfillment. Maslow further separated these needs into lower & higher order needs. Lower order needs are those satisfied externally (physiology & safety).
   Higher order needs are satisfied internally (social, esteem & self actualization).

Herzberg's Two-Factor Theory

Also referred to as the motivation - hygiene theory. Emphasizes the individuals attitude toward work as playing a critical role in determining success or failure of the task at hand.
Key question of theory:
What do people want from their jobs?
Herzberg concluded that results were significantly different when people felt good about their jobs as opposed to negative perceptions.

1.) Proposed notion of "satisfaction vs. No satisfaction".
2.) Pointed out importance of conditions surrounding the job, e.g. work relations, job security, compensation etc. Herzberg called these factors Hygiene Factors.

McGregor's Theory X and Theory Y

Present's two distinct views of human beings.
Theory X (Negative) - implies managers hold four assumptions

1.) Employees inherently dislike work, will avoid work whenever possible.

2.) Following assumption 1, employees must therefore be forced, threatened in order to achieve goals.

3.) Employees will avoid responsibilities and seek formal direction.

4.) Employees place security over factors associated with work. (show little ambition.)

Theory Y (Positive)

1.) Work viewed as natural as rest or play

2.) Self-direction and control utilized by employees when committed to objective.

3.) Average person capable of learning and seeking/accepting responsibility.

4.) Decision making widespread within population, not just function of managers.

Vroom's Expectancy Theory

States that "the strength of a tendency to act in a certain way depends on the strength of an expectation that the act will be followed by a given outcome and on the attractiveness of that outcome to the individual".

Employee standpoint: He or She will be motivated to give their best effort toward a specific task when they believe their efforts will be rewarded with the greatest recognition whether through a bonus or other recognition by the organization.

Three main areas of focus:

1. Effort-performance relationship which deals with individual perception.

2. Performance-reward relationship relates to the extent of individuals belief that they will be rewarded.

3. Rewards-personal goals relationship pertains to the attractiveness of rewards to individuals.

Paul Hersey and Ken Blanchard's Situational Theory (SLT)

Description: A contingency theory that focuses on the followers readiness.

Main Points:

1. Successful leadership is achieved by selecting the right leadership style.

2. Theorists argue that this successful leadership is contingent on the level of the followers readiness.

Why focus on the *followers*?

Emphasis on the followers in leadership effectiveness reflects reality in that it is the followers who accept or reject the leader. Regardless of what the leader does, the end result depends on the actions of his or her followers.

Readiness defined: Extent to which people have ability and willingness to accomplish a specific task.

Leader—Follower relationship: SLT views this relationship similar to a parent/child relationship. As the child becomes more mature and responsible, the parent needs to relinquish control of the child to a degree.

Four key behaviors of SLT:

1.) Followers Unable and Unwilling: Leader needs to give clear and specific directions.
2.) Unable and Willing: Leader displays high task orientation to compensate for followers lack of ability, also has to get followers to buy into his/her desires.
3.) Able and Unwilling: Leader employs supportive and participative style.
4.) Able and Willing: Leader does not do much.

Concluding Remarks:

* Theory has wide appeal with management specialists, used at over 400 of the Fortune 500 companies.
* Builds on logic that leaders can compensate for ability and motivation limitations in their followers.
* Research efforts to test and support theory generally disappointing, some argue due to scientific inconsistencies in methodologies.
* Even though theory is widely popular, complete endorsement of this theory is cautioned against.

Ohio State Studies

Most comprehensive of behavioral theories from Ohio State University research that began in the late 1940s. Study identified two categories:

1.) Initiating Structure: extent to which a leader is likely to define and structure his or her role and those of subordinates in the search for goal attainment. It points to behavior such as assigning group members to particular tasks, expectations of workers to abide outlined standards and the critical role of deadlines.

2.) Consideration: Leader exhibits job relationships by showing concern for followers comfort, well being, status and satisfaction. Such a leader helps employees with personal issues, is friendly, personable, and approachable and treats employees equally.

Research Findings:

- Leaders high on initiating structure and consideration tend to achieve high employee performance and satisfaction.
- Leaders behavior focusing on initiating structure led to greater grievances, absenteeism, etc.
- High consideration negatively related to performance ratings of leader by his/her superiors.

University of Michigan Studies

Leadership studies conducted by U. of Michigan survey research center.
Objective: Locate behavioral characteristics of leaders that appeared to be related to measures of performance effectiveness.
Two main dimensions of leadership behavior:

1.) Employee Oriented: Leader emphasizes on interpersonal relationships.
2.) Production Oriented: Leader emphasizes on technical or task aspects of the job. Main concern is accomplishing group tasks.

Conclusion: Employee oriented leaders associated with higher group productivity and higher job satisfaction.

Edwin Locke's Goal Setting Theory

1.) Emphasizes the importance of outlining specific goals to shoot for vs. generalized notions such as "do your best". Clear goals in turn will yield better results and performance.
2.) Intentions to work toward a goal are a major source of work motivation.
3.) Difficult goals if accepted result in higher performance than easier goals. (ability & acceptance being held constant). Acceptance of a

difficult goal means an employee will do their best until the goal is achieved, lowered or abandoned.

4.) Feedback leads to higher performance than non-feedback. People will do better when they get feedback on how well they are performing. Feedback also helps point out what needs to be worked on.

5.) The more specific a goal, the more it triggers the internal mechanism.

Other factors influencing the goal setting theory:

A). Goal commitment: level of individuals commitment toward goal.

B). Adequate self-efficacy: individuals belief that he/she is capable of performing task. Individuals with high self-efficacy will try harder in difficult situations than those with low self-efficacy. Similarly, individuals with high self-efficacy will respond better to negative feedback.

C). Task characteristics: goals more attainable when simple rather than complicated.

D). National culture: better suited cultures than others.

Remarks:

Intentions through hard and specific goals are a great motivating force that could lead to higher performance under ideal conditions, however, no evidence exists associating this notion with higher job satisfaction. Issues pertaining to participatory set goals have mixed results.

Non-charismatic Theories

Theory has three main components:

1.) Stresses symbolic and emotionally appealing leader behaviors.

2.) Explains how certain leaders are able to achieve exceptional levels of follower's commitment.

3.) De-emphasizes theoretical complexities and looks at leadership from the "average person" point of view.

Description: states that followers make attributions of heroic or extraordinary leadership abilities when observing certain behaviors. This is primary in distinguishing charismatic vs. un-charismatic leaders.

Related Studies: identifies five main characteristics of such leadership.

A.) Vision
B.) Willingness to undertake risks.
C.) Sensitivity to environmental constraints
D.) Sensitivity to follower needs
E.) Show behaviors that are out of ordinary

How do charismatic leaders influence followers?

Leader's articulate appealing vision, this vision then provides a sense of community for the followers by empowering them with better expectations with the organization. Leader follows up by communicating high performance expectations and reinforces confidence that followers can achieve these goals, which in turn builds follower self-confidence & esteem. Finally, the charismatic leader undertakes self sacrifices and engages in unconventional behavior.

Research Opinions:
Shows impressive correlation between charismatic leadership and performance levels. Most experts also contend that charismatic leadership can be a learned trait through training. Experts also conclude that charismatic leadership is not a pre-requisite in achieving high performance levels.

Organizational Behavior Concepts:

14.4 SELF-MANAGED VS. CROSS-FUNCTIONAL TEAMS

Self-managed teams typically consist of 10-15 members who perform interdependent jobs/tasks. Such teams also assume the responsibility of their former supervisors such as planning, scheduling, operating decisions, and so forth. Self-managed teams also select their own members and evaluate each others performance, therefore reducing or eliminating the role supervisory positions. Some of the drawbacks to such teams include negative results associated with the independent nature, high levels of turnover and high absenteeism levels.

Cross-functional teams on the other hand are made up of employees drawn from similar hierarchal levels but from different work groups, departments, zones, etc. Task force groups and committees are some examples of cross-functional teams. Drawbacks of such teams include, the difficulty to manage, the length of time it takes to build trust and how time consuming they can be due to the diversity of group members.

14.5 "INEFFECTIVE COMMUNICATION IS THE FAULT OF THE SENDER." DO YOU AGREE OR DISAGREE?

I am of the opinion that ineffective communication can be a function of both the sender and the recipient depending on the situation. While the sender can cause ineffective communication in some cases, the recipient may be at fault as well in some cases, for instance receivers may engage in selective perception where they choose to hear or see what they want hear/see based upon their needs, motivations, self-interests, background, and so forth therefore resulting in ineffective communication. Different interpretations of language on the part of both the sender or recipient can result in ineffective communication as well. A recipient overwhelmed with information overload may also cause ineffective communication by ignoring or overlooking certain information. Defensiveness on either the sender or receivers part can also result in ineffective communication. Finally, the sender can cause ineffective communication by filtering information to make it more favorable to their motives or goals. So essentially, ineffective communication can be the fault of the sender or the receiver depending on the situation.

14.6 HOW CAN AN OUTSIDER ASSESS AN ORGANIZATION'S CULTURE?

- Extensive homework and research on organization by talking with former employees, friends, and other associates.
- Consulting with professional groups is also critical as is obtaining as much information about the organization through article and media.
- Researching articles about organization in publications and online sources
- Physical surroundings offer significant clues of overall organization.
- Observing and paying attention to dress codes, office furnishings, personal behaviors, is also helpful. etc.
- Observing general outlook of employees, i.e. casual, serious, sad, and so forth
- Observing and asking what formal rules are in place within the organization.
- Not to be overlooked is the importance asking a variety of questions such as the organizational background, job descriptions, etc.

Four cultural types and the characteristics of employees who fit best with each

A). Networked culture:

In this type of organization, members are viewed as family and friends. Strong bonds exist, people know each other well and like each other as well. There is greater willingness to help those in need and communication of information is very open. A major drawback with this type of culture lies in the fact that the focus on friendships can lead to poor performance and creation of cliques. Employees better suited to this culture tend to be very sociable and have low solidarity qualities.

B). Mercenary culture:

Such organizations are extremely goal oriented/focused. People within the organization are very intense and determined to meet goals. Getting things done quickly is a top priority, people also have strong sense of purpose. Winning is critical even if it takes destroying those deemed as enemies. Little socialization occurs within such organizations and tolerance for low performers is very thin. This type of organization is better suited for individuals who are low on sociability and high on solidarity

C). Fragmented culture:

This is an organization comprised of individualists. Commitment to the individual and his/her job tasks is the first priority. Little or no identification with the organization exists. Employees are judged purely on their individual productivity and quality. A drawback with such a culture is the level of excessive critiquing of other members and the absence of camaraderie. This organization is better suited for individuals low on sociability and low on solidarity.

D). Communal culture:

This type of culture has a high regard for friendship and performance. A high sense of belonging and togetherness exists, however, there is also intense focus on goal achievement. The leadership of such groups typically is inspirational and charismatic while maintaining a clear vision of the organizational direction and future. This culture has a tendency of following a cult like structure as the followers take on the role of disciples to the leader. This culture is ideal for those high on sociability and high on solidarity.

14.7 DR. EDWARD W. DEMING1900-1993): ICON OF MANAGEMENT THOUGHT.

In today's global economy, survival of business entities is contingent upon maintaining a competitive edge , constantly reconfiguring the organizational structure, goals, positioning , strategy, and philosophy. Non-so evident is the rise of the Asian markets as a force to be reckoned with in global economics. Prior to the 1950's, the aforementioned Asian markets were merely a laughable joke in the world of global economics. The Asian markets, in particular Japan owes its economic success to a relatively mildly known scholar by the name of Edward Deming. One could have posed the question, who is Edward Deming?, and without doubt many would have drawn a blank response. Such is the tale of Dr Edward W. Deming. Obscure outside the world of management thought and yet incredibly so instrumental to the field as a whole. For a vast majority, the name would be no different from just another John Doe, however reality presents a more intriguing perspective to this man so often referred to as The Man of contemporary management thought. To quote a famous phrase, there is more than meets the eye, with regard to this man and his contributions to management theory and global economics. Thus said, this review attempts to present an objective look and overview of Dr Edward W. Deming, I will outline his background and explore his contributions to the field of Organizational Behavior and Management.

Historical Background

Dr Edward W. Deming was born, on October 14, 1900 in Sioux City, Iowa.(1900-1993) His early life was consumed by poverty and an underprivileged upbringing.[1] The setting of his family structure was a four-room tar paper shack where worry about their next meal was a constant part of their daily regime. Under such uncompromising confines, it was perhaps what shaped Deming to an icon he would later prove to be.[2] At the tender age of 8, Deming embarked on menial jobs out of necessity to help out the family financial woes and by age 17 having gathered up some savings, he enrolled at the University of Wyoming studying engineering, he would later progress to Yale University where he earned a Ph.D. in mathematical physics in 1927. [3] Despite being offered several offers in the private sector, Deming opted to take up a position with the Department of Agriculture in Washington D.C. where he would eventually meet his future wife. The real story of Deming however begins in the 1950s when he is introduced to Japanese officials. Prior to meeting with the Japanese, Deming had proposed his TQM theory but all his efforts were to no avail at home, his theory was widely rejected. During this period, Japan was just emerging from World War II and was in the mist of exploring all options of rebuilding, the Japanese took notice of Demings theory and the two parties met. This meeting of Deming and the Japanese would have unimaginable consequences.[4] It is important to point out that at this time, Deming was virtually an unknown.

An important factor to the success of this partnership was the Japanese willingness to listen, learn and make adjustments to their existing management styles to accommodate the teachings of Deming. As one source would put it, [5] The Union of Japanese Scientists which had sought out Deming listened as he taught them, and transformed their reputation for manufacturing from laughable to laudable. [6] For the next thirty years, Deming would devote his time working with the Japanese, it wasn't until the 1980's that the NBC network brought him to light in America through a documentary. The thirty relationship between the parties would forever transform the Japanese business sector and transform it to a premier force.

Prominent Theories & Contributions to the field.

a) Total Quality Management

Without any dispute, this is the theory that put Deming on the map of global economics. Today the theory is a buzzword and mainstay in the business circles, business curricular, and the global economy. Taken at face value, the theory seems bland and everyday commonsense, in fact some critics have gone as far as arguing that this theory has long being a part of the business world and Deming merely exported it to Japan and is unduly credited. However persuasive the argument, what cannot be disputed is the critical role Deming played in bringing the theory to prominence and staking its place as a mainstay. The contemporary management thought defines Total Quality Management (TQM) as, [6] A philosophy of management that is driven by the constant attainment of customer satisfaction through the continuous improvement of all organizational processes. This definition is in constant conflict with the notion of re-engineering, however the two concepts have distinctive differences despite having striking similarities. The concept of Total Quality Management can be summed up in seven steps outlined below, [7]:

1. Intense focus on the customer
2. Concern for continuous improvement
3. Improvement in quality of everything the organization does
4. Accurate measurement
5. Empowerment of employees

The notion of continuous improvement is the cornerstone of the TQM theory and is synonymous with all its elements. The theory contends that, [8] good is not good enough and criticizes managers who accept levels of performance below perfection. One of the key elements of TQM as earlier stated lies in achieving continuous improvement whilst constantly seeking to reduce or eliminate variability. Through the reduction or elimination of these inconsistencies, the theory seeks to achieve higher yields and higher quality. TQM is also critical of managers setting short-term goals, instead it encourages managers to perpetually strive for non-stop improvement and avoid being satisfied with short-term achievements. Another key element to the success of the theory was the incorporation of statistical data tools to precisely measure and project the life cycle of a particular production cycle. By employing such statistical projections, Deming was able to follow the flow of production and constantly enhance it in order to achieve the highest yields, quality and efficiency. In addition, Deming felt by using statistical data, he was able to pinpoint errors in the production cycle and promptly fine-tune such glitches, therefore allowing him to keep a competitive age.

The constant pressure of continuous improvement would shift the focus of TQM from quality to producing large volumes of quantity at rapid speeds using specialization techniques. [9] Due to this change of direction, TQM saw a rise and prominence of quality inspectors as a direct consequence of the rapid production process. The process of TQM follows these guidelines [10]:

- Quality is to satisfy agreed customer requirements continuously
- Total quality is to achieve quality at a low cost
- TQM is to obtain total quality by involving everyone's daily commitment

Successful implementation of the TQM process is contingent on following these steps outlined by Deming consisting of four principles and eight concepts.[11]

Principles

1. Delight Customer
2. Management by fact
3. People based management
4. Continuous improvement

Concepts

1. Customer satisfaction
2. Internal customers are real
3. All work is a process
4. Measurement
5. Teamwork
6. People make quality
7. Preventions
8. Continuous improvement cycle

The stages implementing successful TQM are outlined in four steps below[12]

1. Identification and preparation
2. Management understanding and commitment
3. Scheme for improvement
4. New initiative, new target and critical thinking

The techniques for suggested for successful TQM achievement are as follows[13]

1. Customer perception surveys
2. Cost of quality statement
3. Steering group
4. Quality coordinator
5. Top team workshops
6. Total quality seminars
7. Departmental purpose analysis
8. Quality training
9. Communication technique
10. Improvement action team
11. Task force
12. Quality circles
13. Suggestion schemes
14. Help calls
15. Visible data
16. Process management
17. Statistical process control
18. Process capability

19. Fool proofing
20. Just in time

b) The Fourteen Points condensed [14]

1. Adopt a new philosophy
2. Stop practice of buying at lowest prices
3. Institute leadership
4. Eliminate empty slogans
5. Eliminate numerical quotas
6. Institute on the job training
7. Drive out fear
8. Eliminate barriers between departments
9. Take action to accomplish change
10. Constant improvement
11. Cease dependency on mass production
12. Create Purpose
13. Allow workmanship
14. Constant Retraining.

c). The Seven Deadly Sins [15]

1. Lack of consistency
2. Emphasis on short-term goals
3. Evaluations
4. Mobility of top mgt
5. Depending solely on numbers to run organization
6. Excessive medical costs
7. Excessive costs of warranty

Literary Contributions: [16 & 17]]

Books:

- The New Economist (his final book)
- Out of Crisis

Articles:

- Over 171 articles and papers

Books about Dr Deming:

- Various books detailing his teachings as well as biographical books, a few include,
- Deming: The way we new him
- Deming Management at work
- Demings profound changes: when will the sleeping giant awake
- The Keys to excellence: The Story of Deming

Other Contributions and Influences:

- The W, Edwards Deming Institute (WEDI)

a non-profit organization founded by Dr Edward Deming in 1993. Its main purpose was to share and teach the Deming concepts.

- The Deming Cooperative

Provides information, programs, conferences, seminars and so forth utilizing the Deming teachings.

- Hundreds of consulting groups utilizing his principles
- His concepts are widely use in everyday curriculums.

Conclusion

Edward Deming "The Man" as he is so widely referred to by management scholars clearly has had a huge impact on today's and future generations. Most notable is the recognition of him being the father of the Japanese economic machine, which is today envied by many nations. His TQM teachings clearly had a dramatic impact on the Japanese business structure and are very much a part of the U.S. business structure. The success of the TQM theory transforming a war torn country from ravages and as a mere laughing stoke in the business world speaks volumes for this theory. Its continued appeal and in some cases , over-commercialization just goes to illustrate the impact Dr. Deming created. However, it is important to point out that Dr Demings legacy stretches beyond the TQM theory. Prior to his passing, he was widely sought for consultations, was bestowed numerous awards, and his teachings continue to be a part of everyday business. Demings theories have virtually spurned a cottage industry based on his teachings.

It goes without saying that Demings theory has its share of negatives, The most troubling aspect I uncovered in my research was related to TQM in its quest of constantly pushing managers to the envelop and making them not satisfied, but to keep pushing the wheel constantly. A negative consequence of this behavior is, it could lead managers to be stressed out and burnt out, and it could also make managers have a sense of under appreciation for smaller daily accomplishments. I also find the theories total disregard for short-term goals misleading. The overall benefits however clearly outweigh the negatives

and Dr Demings contribution to the field can only be summed up as remarkable and his place in history is fittingly as an Icon to Management Thought.

REFERENCE NOTES

1. Dobyns, Lioyd. 1990. *Deming wants big changes and he wants them fast.* Smithsonian
2. Dobyns, Lioyd. 1990. *Deming wants big changes and he wants them fast.* Smithsonian
3. Dobyns, Lioyd. 1990. *Deming wants big changes and he wants them fast.* Smithsonian
4. Dobyns, Lioyd. 1990. *Deming wants big changes and he wants them fast.* Smithsonian
5. Dobyns, Lioyd. 1990. *Deming wants big changes and he wants them fast.* Smithsonian
6. Robbins, Stephen P. 2001. *Organizational Behavior*, 9th ed, pg 15 & 451-53
7. Robbins, Stephen P. 2001. A *Organizational Behavior*, 9th ed, pg 15 & 451-53
8. Robbins, Stephen P. 2001. A *Organizational Behavior*, 9th ed, pg 15 & 451-53
9. Kanji, Gopal K; Asher, Mike, Understanding *Total Quality Management*, Total Quality Management, 1993 Supplement Advances, Vol. 4 Issue
10. Kanji, Gopal K; Asher, Mike, Understanding *Total Quality Management*, Total Quality Management, 1993 Supplement Advances, Vol. 4 Issue
11. Kanji, Gopal K; Asher, Mike, Understanding *Total Quality Management*, Total Quality Management, 1993 Supplement Advances, Vol. 4 Issue
12. Deming, Edward, *Out of Crisis*, MIT/CAES, 1986
13. Kanji, Gopal K; Asher, Mike, *Understanding Total Quality Management Total Quality Management*, 1993 Supplement Advances, Vol. 4 Issue
14. Deming, Edward, *The New Economics* (2nd edition) MIT/CAES, 1994
15. Kanji, Gopal K; Asher, Mike, *Understanding Total Quality Management*, 1993 Supplement Advances, Vol. 4 Issue
16 & 17. The Deming Institute (WEDI) MIT Deming Institute.

CHAPTER XV

INTERCULTURAL COMMUNICATION

15.1 OVERVIEW AND OBJECTIVES

This final chapter outlines intercultural communication on a broader scale in context to how this plays in this new global environment. Readers will be introduced to issues relating to value differences, religious beliefs, verbal and non-verbal communication, language issues, enculturation and many more concepts. The key area of intercultural communication is gaining a firm understanding how different cultures factor into the communication process while at the same time having an awareness, respect of cultures, beliefs and attitudes different from what one is accustomed to. This is a fascinating area of study and much of what a reader makes of it is a learning curve, in studying intercultural communications they are no right or wrong answers but rather intellectual insights.

15.2 IMPORTANCE OF INTERCULTURAL COMMUNICATION IN THE 21ST CENTURY

The 21st century has brought U.S. many new ideas and transformations. Indeed in some cases this century has exposed U.S. to new worldviews that once were a world apart from what we were accustomed to, and as we take a closer look at these new dimensions it is clear that at times such changes can be overwhelming as much as they could be interesting as well. We find ourselves rejecting or embracing such changes or in some cases shell shocked and not knowing what to make of it all. Gone are the days where our confines were uniform and the one size fits all paradigm could be applied, indeed it is not uncommon to be immersed in cultures within cultures which as pointed out earlier sometimes leads to colliding worldviews. Avoiding the aforementioned collision of worldviews is the very core and essence of intercultural communication as we traverse this 21st century.

Perhaps the most intriguing and paramount of such changes in the 21st century as relates to intercultural communication can be attributed to the phenomenon we have come to know as globalization. This phenomenon created in part due to technological advances and ease of mobility essentially wiped out cultural boundaries as we knew them, the world through the global interconnectedness is literally a virtual global village of commerce and trade. It is not uncommon to find one in the work place sitting side by side with co-workers from Brazil, Sweden, India in an office tower in Atlanta with its headquarters in Hong Kong. Such is our world in this era of globalization.

Given our current global condition, success as measured through being a productive and active participant of this new global era requires a keen cultural awareness and a good measure of effective intercultural communication. In our current global condition intercultural communication is a bridge to many obstacles associated with understanding different cultures and dealing with worldviews that may be different from ours. Those participants that effectively utilize the tools afforded by intercultural studies will find the transition in this era fluid and are certain to rip the rewards of globalization while maintaining their own beliefs and value systems while commanding a great understanding and respect of other worldviews. As one author put it, the manifestations of globalization are here to stay and there is no undoing them, therefore each participant needs to strive a balance in dealing with this circumstance otherwise they risk developing "unicist" belief systems and harbor feelings of discontent and anger.

The changes in the 21st century , globalization included are very challenging and the solution is not simplistic as they involve cross cultural conflicts, worldview conflicts, civilization conflicts and so forth, however a good grasp of intercultural communication skills only enhances one being able to overcome such obstacles. The importance of intercultural communication is further evidenced by the trend of many companies today offering intercultural awareness and intercultural communication training to their employees in order to maintain and develop a more productive and effective employee in this 21st century.

15.3 INTERCULTURAL COMMUNICATION KEY IN INTERNATIONAL BUSINESS

Intercultural communication skills are now more than ever necessary for success in international business as trade and commerce is no longer confined within national borders. In today's world most companies operate as multinational corporations with operating units all across the globe, as such the workforce is equally mobile crossing geographic borders. Thus international transactions involve a diverse group of cultures converging and facilitating such transactions, therefore it follows that those individuals who are well vested in intercultural communication skills will make for better & more effective international business professionals. A lacking of essential intercultural communication skills is likely to increase apprehensive behaviors and foster cultural conflicts & clashes particularly in this era of globalization. A positive mindset is essential in developing effective intercultural skills, such a mindset involves keeping an open mind, having patience and most important having the willingness and commitment to obtain such skills.

15.4 POTENTIAL CONFLICTS IN CROSS CULTURAL DIALOGUE

As Americans engage in negotiations with other cultures, they will certainly have to deal with conflicting issues relating to different belief systems, values, religions, attitudes, gender roles, social concepts, time concepts and all attributes that make up a given culture overall. In some cases the American culture may possess similar belief norms, however in negotiating with different cultures, a difference in view with one of the above-mentioned traits is recipe for conflict to arise during the negotiation process. Americans may also run into ethnocentric elements with the respective culture engaged in negotiations, such ethnocentric elements may also raise problems during this process of negotiation. Similarly, varying degrees of respective worldviews may present a problem during negotiations. Use of language whether verbal or nonverbal is another source of potential conflict when dealing with a different culture, closely related to this concept are time and space concepts as well.

All the above-mentioned problems could take the form of direct confrontation or in some cases indirect confrontation through third parties. Direct confrontation may result from transactional negotiations as well as conflict/dispute resolution. Another area where problems could arise is associated with the identity of a culture. Americans may run into what is referred to as "individualism vs. collectivism", this in itself could hinder the negotiation process. Other potential sources of problems could be encountered when caught up in cultural conflict related to "egalitarianism vs. Hierarchy" and "High vs. low-context communication". As we have seen several potential red flags could present a problem when negotiating with other cultures. Many more areas for potential problems during negotiations exist, these are some of the more likely and common ones.

15.5 ARE PEOPLE IN GENERAL PREPARED FOR THE INCREASE IN INTERCULTURAL CONTACT?

Indeed it is quite true that the dynamic of intercultural communication is more prevalent now more than ever. Contributing factors toward this phenomenon are things such as globalization which by its very nature brings about mobility of workers across borders and cultures. Equally important are the technological advances that have been attained such as the World Wide Web, satellite TV, and a host of wireless communication. Naturally this technological leap has at the very least served as an education platform for cultures to learn about each other from a distance. Another attribute to the rise in intercultural communication are immigration trends, typically relating to groups from third world countries relocating to the more affluent developed nations as they strive to seek a better livelihood. The influx of such groups can be clearly seen in N. America particularly states such as California, Texas and Florida which boost large Latino Hispanic communities.

As pointed out earlier, the trend is undoubtedly widespread and on the rise, however despite this trend, it is my belief that most people on the contrary are not prepared for this trend particularly here in N. America where issues relating to culture and race have a rocky history and always dealt with delicately with innuendos of political correctness. Even though most people are clearly aware of this trend, they may choose to block it off and perceive it as being out of their realm and merely an infringement on their cultural values as evidenced by the large anti-immigration sentiment and more recent Islamic Christianity scrutiny as a result of ongoing conflicts. Thus said, as this dynamic continues to ensue and expound itself, one begins to see the rise of sub-cultures within greater culture. A good example of which I have firsthand experience can be observed in the Miami-Dade-West Palm Beach metropolitan area, by all accounts a diverse cultural hub. From the outside, all the various ethnicities that make up this large urban area appear as a mosaic, however upon a closer look, one finds that each ethnic group creates its own self-sustaining niche based on cultural values, religion and language. As such you have bedroom communities such as Little Cuba/Hialeah with predominentantly Cubans, Little Haiti (Haitians), Lauderdale/Lauderhill/Broward county(Jamaicans & Islanders), West Palm Beach (Jewish) and so forth. For the most part, intercultural communication is somewhat hampered as each ethnic group holds their binding common denominator dearly and weary of letting in what may be perceived as being outside the norm, thus you have a situation where communication outside the norm is out of practicality & necessity.

15.6 WORLDVIEW FORMATION & CULTURAL DIFFERENCES

Most author's and scholars are of the assumption that worldview is implicit, implied in non-verbal expression thus it's actual formation a matter of speculation. Thus said, the formative period of worldview goes back to early childhood, in fact as early as infancy. The infant through cognitive behaviors as well as parental assertions begins to form its notion of worldview. In addition to parenting, the child's immediate environmental confines also play a vital role in the formation of a particular worldview. The author's also point to other extenuating factors such as religion/faith, social groups/class, school influences, physical environment and so forth playing a vital role in shaping worldview. Greater emphasis is placed on religion as a driving force. The argument presented by Emerson follows the notion that since religion shapes reasoning and provides meaning, importance and properness, as such Emerson asserts that since religious beliefs vary globally, it is follows people develop different worldviews. Chamberlain and Zika(1992) counter this notion and present religion as just one of many contributing factors in the formation of a worldview.

I believe there are indeed cultural differences in the process by which worldview is formed. An example would be three distinct family units on three different continents, (assume three separate families, one in each of these countries; Zambia, Columbia & Canada), all with similar religious persuasions, class, and social status. As these families evolve, the assumption being the time period and all other factor are relatively similar, each family unit would take upon its own worldview with cultural differences playing its part. The wide array of cultural groups across the globe in it's self perhaps is a good indication of cultural differences engrained in the mechanisms of worldview formation.

15.7 GENDER DIFFERENCES IN DECODING NONVERBAL MESSAGES

The greater consensus seems to support the premise that woman are overwhelmingly better at decoding nonverbal messages. Several researchers such as Judith Hall (1984) through her review of numerous studies on sex differences related to nonverbal decoding skills points to the same conclusion. Similar studies by Robert Rosenthal and the likes of Knupp/Hall also point to the female gender as being the better-equipped group to decode nonverbal messages. The only exception to this inference seems to arise from recent studies conducted by Knupp and Hall(1997) where men were found to be more equipped at decoding anger cues from other men. Another point worth noting , also from the same study found no tangible differences when it came to the ability of determining whether an individual was lying simply by means of nonverbal cues.

Several theories and notions try to offer an explanation as to why women seem to have a comparative advantage as relates to decoding nonverbal signals. Rosenthal(1997) offers the reasoning that women exhibit better decoding skills than men because they tend to gaze longer at faces of those they are interacting with therefore are more adapt at picking up on nonverbal signals. The other assumption gives credit to women's experience with children particularly in motherly caregiver roles. As such, the reasoning follows; this close contact with children who for the most part communicate with nonverbal cues enhances ones capability of reading, detecting and decoding nonverbal signals. Hall(1994) on the other hand suggests that since women typically tend to be more sensitive than men, they are more likely to seek and look for nonverbal cues as a means of maintaining the harmony. Nancy Henley (1973, 1977) presents an interesting perspective centering on the theory of "oppression" which contends that since women over periods of time have been in positions that carry less power, they invariably must learn the skills to read nonverbal messages from those with power over them. I tend to agree with all the explanations presented, however I also have a theory I thought about. I think women have perhaps developed a genetic internal signal that gives them a comparative advantage developed over millions of years of evolution. The combination of all the above factors over a period of time essentially gave the female gender an advantage.

15.8 CULTURAL CONFLICT AS A RESULT OF DIFFERENCES IN HIGH & LOW CONTEXT CULTURES

Differences between High and low context cultures can contribute to intercultural conflict in a variety of ways. The first such possible source of conflict can be attributed to the communication patterns within each culture. In high context cultures, we find a culture where communication is transmitted via a spiral logical configuration & nonverbal hints as well as indirect means, which is contrary to the communication patterns in low context cultures. In such cultures, we find the communication patterns follow a more direct verbal interaction compounded with a linear logical platform. Given these contradictory approaches in communication patterns within the two cultures, it would be therefore clear to see how this dimension would be a potential source of intercultural conflict.

The second potential source of conflict within the cultures relates to the cultural make up, particularly of importance the traits indicating as to whether a culture follows an individualistic or collective approach in its day to day interactions. On the surface this seems like a narrow dimension, however when we further examine this issue we see that central to each cultural behaviors are two very divergent behaviors. In low context culture we find that this entails an individualistic ideal, which is contrary to the collectivist approach found in high context cultures, as can be seen, such a contrary view could possibly contribute to conflict. Also a difference in conflict trigger mechanisms could be a source of conflict within the two cultures, for instance the value placed on saving face in low culture is not of paramount importance in high context cultures.

15.9 NEGOTIATION STRATEGY & CULTURAL VALUES

Cultural values as we know entail a variety of components which may be unique from one culture to another, in addition the norms associated with each culture will vary from culture to culture thereby allowing for each culture to have its own distinctive characteristics and belief systems. Given such a backdrop, it clear to see how a negotiator's plan could be affected. In planning for negotiations, the planner has to compensate for potential forces that may arise due to differences between individualistic vs. collective cultures otherwise risk the plan being derailed. Since the focus in individualistic cultures tend to reward individual accomplishments and generally promote autonomy of the individual, it is important to keep this in mind when dealing with cultures outside this framework as the reward mechanisms and expectations may be very different. For instance, in collective cultures, the emphasis is placed on promotion of the individual through interdependence of individuals, the team/village concept as a result is more dominant. Therefore, a negotiation plan that lacks a clear understanding of which cultural values are being addressed could be adversely affected. Similarly other cultural value issues related to egalitarianism vs. hierarchy and notions of high context vs. low context will affect the negotiation plan, thus have to be planned for as well.

15.10 MESSAGES OF RECONCILIATION, ASSIMILATION AND PLURALISM

Messages of reconciliation are voices that reflect the center position. Such messages emphasize moderation, tolerance, accommodation, integration and balance. As such, these messages are more inclined to support notions of diversity, multiculturalism, equal rights, and so forth. The civil rights movement under Dr King portrays a good example of how a balancing act was employed to stay in the middle with non-violent protest calls. Similarly the struggles of Nelson Mandela would seem to suggest a centrist position. Proponents of this concept argue for ideological moderation and shy away from the extremities of the "left wing" and the conservative "right wing". Some go as far as to suggest that messages of reconciliation essentially represent Middle America.

Messages of reconciliation relate to messages of assimilation and messages of pluralism in the sense that the messages of reconciliation functions as a buffer between the two extreme concepts. On the one hand are your messages of assimilation closely tied to the political right and on the other hand are your messages of pluralism which are associated with the extreme left both been held in balance by messages of assimilation as a bridge.

15.11 ENHANCING ONE'S LEVEL OF INTERCULTURAL AWARENESS

In this era of globalization and an ever-increasing interconnectedness, intercultural awareness is of paramount importance to intercultural communication. As companies more than ever operate as multinational global conglomerates, employers find themselves working across borders with people of cultures different from theirs. In addition, the effects of globalization have resulted in the influx of cross-migration as new immigrants seek new opportunities. Given all these manifestations of globalization and the new global economy, it is apparent to see that those individuals who possess a full grasp of cultural awareness through comprehension and understanding of other cultures will have a comparative advantage in this new global economy. Essentially, people in this group will tend to be more effective in understanding and communicating with other cultural groups therefore being better and more effective in the workplace and their respective fields. In addition people who are more culturally aware will tend to be more respectful, tolerant and understanding of worldviews different from what they are accustomed to which is a critical and invaluable trait. The importance of intercultural awareness is further substantiated by the increased number of cultural awareness seminars & training programs offered by corporations today.

15.12 HAITIAN CULTURE ANALYSIS

This review looks at the Haitian culture as a whole by analyzing dynamics such as language, religion, gender roles and so forth. A brief narrative of the historical perspective opens up the case study pointing to the founding of the island, colonialism, post-independence to present day Haiti. As the review manifests, it becomes very evident that Haitian Culture is unlike any other in the western hemisphere, which makes it so fascinating as a case study.

One such interesting dynamic of this particular culture pertains to its location in the western hemisphere; here we find a cultural group with African root's via the slave trade that is clearly distinct from other such groups in North America, South America & the greater Caribbean Islands. The most perplexing of such contrasts one finds lies in the linguistic traits. Most descendants of this manifestation adopted the English, Spanish or Portuguese tongue as their primary means of verbal communication, however such is not the case with Haiti where the Creole language evolved, even though bearing a resemblance to the French language, it is still clearly not mutually tied to French and holds its own distinctive verbal and written characteristics. Another interesting perspective to this culture lies in its religious convictions, Catholicism and a segment of Protestant beliefs plays a major role, however we find another dynamic segment known as Voodoo which plays a major role as a faith in this culture. The close ties to Witch Craft and indigenous African Native faiths presents an interesting view. These are some of the few interesting perspectives this paper will examine as earlier pointed out.

Historical Overview

The Island of Haiti was discovered by the explorer Christopher Columbus during his voyages in the late 1400's. The Island also referred to as the Island of

Hispaniola, which encompasses Haiti and Dominican Republic, both sharing the geographic landmass as neighbors. The Island was initially inhabited by the Taiw Indian's who called their homeland as Ayti or Hayti which translates to "mountains" as is characterized by the topography of the Island.[1.] The Indian native population would be virtually eliminated by the mid 1500's by virtue of disease, abuse and forced labor.

The Haitian historical time lime would follow several paths since it's discovery by Columbus. First ensued the Spanish discovery and Colonialization followed by French colonialization. The Spanish era began with about 2000 Spaniards who had about 30,000 African Slaves who were brought in to replace the decimated Indians. The French era was established in 1659 primarily playing a greater part was the French West India company. [2.] This period was driven by the sugar and coffee interests on the Island. Essentially the slave trade as a labor source to the aforementioned trade of sugar & coffee fostered this period. The inhabitation of African Slaves on the Island grew to over 500,000 by 1681[3.]

Following this period came the Haitian revolution also called the Slave rebellion in 1791 culminating in the Haitian Independence. U.S. occupation occurred between 1915-1934. The state since followed a string of military governments during the Papa Doc and Baby Doc era's. The state has struggled to have any stable governing body and has been plagued by instability, human abuses and widespread poverty. Today the Island is inhabited by about 7 million people primarily black African slave descendants with a minority population of mixed raced descendant's(5%) also known as Mulattos. The Principal city is Port au Prince with close to 800,000 people representing over 61 percent of the total urban population. [4].

Language dynamics

Two primary languages are spoken in Haiti, the main language spoken by over ninety percent of the population is Creole and a smaller segment speaks French or both. This duality of languages has resulted in an interesting cultural dilemma. Typically all Haitians across the spectrum were proud to embrace Creole as the national language and the use of French was limited to the elite part of society. Thus said, even though French was designated as an official language, it is essentially limited to very few government and commerce leaders. Here we see our first level of intercultural conflict based on language, where one use of language is associated with elitism and limited to formal settings and the other language is viewed as a lower class language.

Today however, these attitudes are far less visible as Creole has gained widespread positive perception and has been embraced by all the population as the language of choice. In fact, a sense of nationalism and pride is now associated with Creole usage.[5] The origins of the Creole language is somewhat unclear, some contend it evolved as a pidgin exchange between French colonialists and African slaves, while others contend that it came to the island as a full scale language. The former would seem logical particularly as many words in the Creole language have a French origin even though the two languages are no mutually comprehensible. [6.] It is also important to point out that Creole is not a dialect of French. One text offers the following description of Haitian Creole as follows: "autonomous language based on 17th century lexical French and on syntax principles of west African languages." [7].

For a good period of time, the Creole language had no written form, the first attempts to put Creole in written form were first conceptualized and materialized in the 1940's by an Irish Methodist minister known as H. Ormond McConnell and his companion a renowned American literacy specialist known as Frank Laubach. The two developed a written version based on the international phonetic alphabet.[8]. A new dynamic is evolving in present day Haiti as a result of mass migration of Haitians to north America, particularly south Florida and New York. Many Haitians now are more inclined to learn the English language out of practicality as they hold on to dreams of making it to North America, as such the use of English is growing in Haiti.

Religion

Roman Catholicism today is the official religion of Haiti, this religion gained ground after the Haitian revolution. Prior to the revolution plantation owners did not want religious education to the slaves in fear of their control being compromised. In fact in 1764 the plantation owners expelled the Jesuits for trying to spread the gospel.[9]. Eventually the religious evangelists primarily from Europe would penetrate the island and continue to spread the gospel. This spread of Christianity also involved attempts to eliminate ritualistic practices such as the widely practiced voodoo. Today, people in Haiti devote a good portion of their life to practicing religion, indeed unlike most other groups, Haitian people seem very faithful and committed to their Christian faiths. In my interviews and testimonials with the Haitian community here in south Florida, one common denominator as I conducted interviews from one family to another was the unquestionable faith to Christ, in fact I found that most everyday life was centered on work, family and the church. A smaller segment of the Haitian people(15-25%) follow protestant, Baptist and Methodist denominations.

Perhaps the most intriguing facet of life associated with Haiti lies in the rituals of voodoo faith. A lot of misconceptions and equal fascination with voodoo has existed for a long time as seen in movie portrayals, everyday conversation and so forth. In fact, in one of my interviews and testimonial sessions with members of the Haitian community, one of the facets that was raised when I had inquired about what most people are inclined to know when the first meet someone of Haitian descent, the interviewees would give me a friendly laugh and the overwhelming consensus was people's intrigue with Haiti and voodoo, indeed I must admit, I while trying to maintain my research platform had the voodoo issue in the back of my mind. What with this voodoo question is the million-dollar question as the saying goes. Such was my quest to uncover and have a true understanding of this manifestation particularly with some of the similarities of the African cultural rituals I had witnessed as a young boy in Africa.

Voodoo has been characterized as the unofficial religion of Haiti, indeed the practice is widely engrained in the fabric of Haitian everyday society, however to garner a clear perspective of this practice, a brief look at it's origins is essential. One text describes the birth of voodoo through night ceremonies and dances by slaves. One such famous gathering occurred in the summer of 1791 led by Bois-Caymen a slave overseer and voodoo priest.[10.] Such gatherings entailed slaves from different plantations meeting at night in a secret location and proceeding in dance song and ritualistic sacrifices to the ancestors & gods, this off course unbenounced to the slave masters, anyone caught organizing or participating in such rituals was essentially risking their life. My observation of the ritualistic practices of this belief have an unparallel similarity to African rural practices with hints of witchcraft. Both ceremonies are closely tied to animal sacrificial rituals to the ancestors and spirits. The processional march to the sacrificial site filled with song and dance to fever pitch levels also draws a parallel between the two cultures. The basic assumption of this faith can be characterized as a derivative of African traditional song and dance ceremonies that placed emphasis on giving thanks to the ancestral spirits and cleansing those who were perceived to be under the spell of evil or demonic spirits. The ceremonial rituals were conducted by the "high priests" and issues pertaining to evil spirits were designated to "Witch Doctors". The central theme of this belief seems misunderstood, but at close view one can see close parallels to many religious practices just different approaches.

Gender Roles & Family Structures

The gender roles in mainstream Haiti revolve around marital relationships, typically men taking up the role of head of household and engaging in the perceived masculine chores. Women for the most part are key in domestic roles such as cooking, cleaning, etc and play a critical role in child rearing. This phenomenon is even greater in rural areas. In the urban areas men and women enter into Christian marriages with vows exchanged and so forth, however, an interesting practice occurs in rural areas where typical marital ties among the peasants follow a mutual agreement between the wife & husband to have an economic partnership, such unions are not formal recognized marriages under the Haitian law but for all practical purpose are essentially unions. Such arrangements are referred to as "Plasaj" [11]. This practice is not only isolated to rural peasants but is also practiced by the poor in urban areas who do not have the funds marriage licenses and a formal wedding ceremony. Haitian families are usually of a large size, it's not uncommon for a family unit to have five, six, seven or more children. Aside from the mother & father roles, an integral part of the family is the extended family, it is a widespread practice for a household to have parents, children, uncles, aunts and grandparents all living under one roof. Everyone shares in the roles of raising and parental roles to the young children. Haitian life is centered on family and visiting between friends and family is a part of life and also serves as a pastime, particularly since Haiti as a third world society lacks many recreational amenities found in developed societies. It customary to offer food to guests when they come for a visit and even if one is full, it is considered rude and offensive to say no to the offer. Haitian people like many African cultures use a lot of gestures and are animated when conversing, touching, hugging & embracing are a common part of conversations, it is normal to see men talking and holding hands, laughing , embracing without any phobia.[12]. Church worship also plays a big part in Haitian life and it is customary for the whole family to attend church on Sundays. The main sport in Haiti is soccer also known as football, this by far the biggest pastime young kids engage in. Song and dance are a way of life as well, some of the Haitian rhythms closely resemble African rhythms and so does the rhythmic movements and gyrations. The education system follows a form of primary school and secondary school where students choose a concentration of subjects to focus on, students can choose science, liberal arts, mathematics etc. The staple food consists of rice usually mixed with beans, or vegetables, on weekends the rice may be eaten with chicken or beef/pork as a special treat as many cannot afford to eat as such on a regular basis. Other common foods include fish, vegetables and fruits.

Intercultural Dynamics & Interethnic Conflict

Haiti is primarily composed of three classes of people like many societies. The upper class constitutes a very small segment of about 2 percent of the total population and control's over 40 percent of the national income.[13]. This group controls most of the business sector and hold key government positions, until recently most of this segment are members of a group referred to as Mulattos who had wealth passed from generation to generation and through marriages between elite families. The term Mulatto essentially relates to Haitian's of mixed race with a lighter skin complexion. To be part of this elite group usually entailed being able to speak French and living a lifestyle with French etiquette. Everything tied to being French epitomizes this group, from names, lifestyle, mannerisms etc.

The second group is the Middle Class, this group is slightly bigger in size compared to the upper class but still relatively small when compared to the total population. Figures from the last census data had this number at about 5 percent of total population, even though the number is a little larger today.[14]. This group is made up of a mixture of black Haitian's and Mulatto Haitian's, interestingly enough, this is where the vast majority of conflict between the blacks and Mulattos can be found as both strive to leap into the upper class. The same French aspects found with the elite upper class are also a part of the middle class. This group is made up of young professionals and government workers.

The largest segment of population falls into this final segment of lower class, over 70 percent of the total population make up this group. Rural peasants and the urban poor constitute Haiti's lower class. The rural Haitian's basically live of the land as subsistence farmers occasionally making some extra money by selling produce at the market or on roadsides. The urban poor usually do the menial work, typically involving hard labor, also in this group are beggars, vagrants and so forth.

Power Distance, Worldview & Politics

As one would expect, the Power Distance Index (PDI) in Haiti is very high as most of the power, prestige and wealth lies in very few elite hands. Haitian Culture seems to follow a religious worldview, as pointed out earlier in the paper Haitian society is closely tied to Catholicism and Voodoo beliefs. The Haitian Culture also seems to be aligned as a "Being Culture", where the pace of life is slower without a rush, the concept of time follows a polychronic (P-time) dimension with less emphasis on stringent deadlines and schedules. There is also a great respect for the elderly as they are viewed as wise and a fabric to society which can be also seen in the way grandparents live with their families rather than being placed in nursing homes. Enculturation process in Haitian culture follows typical human interactions & observations. We also find widespread use of Kinesis particularly with the tendency for Haitians to use gestures and animated facial expressions in conversations. Cultural distance is virtually non-existence as everyone practically employees Creole as the language of choice. Politics are at the center of Haitian life, from colonial periods to post independence the politics of Haiti have been complicated. Post independence saw a succession of military governments with brutal dictators that ruled by fear and brutality. Attempts for traditional democratic governments all but failed resulting in military coups, rigged elections, corruption etc. In fact today is under political m turmoil with demonstrations to out the current leadership. One could argue that a great deal of poverty and mismanagement in Haiti today is a consequence of bad incompetent governments.

Conclusion & Recommendations

As we draw to the close of this review, the Haitian Culture continues to fascinate and intrigue my curiosity. I must admit this research and my numerous dialogues and interactions with Haitian people has made me more enlightened and left me with a greater understanding of this often misunderstood culture. Haitian people are very warm and welcoming people. What I found most intriguing during the course of my research was how this culture is so similar to my own African culture. Take away the language aspect, the two cultures virtually mirror each other. The strong Christian beliefs, Voodoo (which in my culture is essentially witchcraft & traditional healers), high ethics and morality, extended family etc are facets that also play an integral part in African culture.

The research also help dispel some misconceptions I might have had of Haitian Culture. For someone contemplating a visit to Haiti from the western world, a few adjustments may be necessary but nothing extra-ordinary. Simple adjustments such as being prepared for the widespread poverty and dilapidated state of affairs, personal caution would be recommended, avoiding traveling at night as pick pockets take such opportunities to do their deeds. Also when visiting a Haitian family and you are offered food, agree to at least sample it even if full as this is expected in this culture. Space use in Haitian culture is also different than in western cultures, so one should expect a lot close proximity and a good amount of hugging, shaking hands during conversations. Other than that, the Haitian culture is very open and pleasant and will always treat a guest with utmost respect.

REFERENCE NOTES

1.) Haggerty, Richard A. (1989). *Dominican Republic and Haiti, country studies*. Pg 203
2.) Wilentz, Amy.(1989) *The RAINY SEASON, Haiti Since Duvalier*. Pg 74
3.) Wilentz, Amy.(1989) *The RAINY SEASON, Haiti Since Duvalier*. Pg 74
4.) United States Department of State Country Profile(2003). Retrieved from group data base
www.governermentguide.com <*http://www.governermentguide.com/*>
5.) Haggerty, Richard A. (1989). *Dominican Republic and Haiti, country studies* pg 258
6.) Haggerty, Richard A. (1989). *Dominican Republic and Haiti, country studies*. Pg 258
7.) Savain, Roger E. (1993) *Haitian-Kreol in Ten Steps*. Pg 11
8). Savain, Roger E. (1993) *Haitian-Kreol in Ten Steps*. Pg 3
9.) Haggerty, Richard A. (1989). *Dominican Republic and Haiti, country studies*. Pg 267
10.) Haggerty, Richard A. (1989). *Dominican Republic and Haiti, country studies*. Pg 268
11.) United States Department of State Country Profile(2003). Retrieved from group data base
www.governermentguide.com <*http://www.governermentguide.com/*>
12.) Testimonial Interview: Sam Joseph, Haitian Immigrant.
13.) United States Department of State Country Profile(2003). Retrieved from group data base
www.governermentguide.com <*http://www.governermentguide.com/*>
14.) United States Department of State Country Profile(2003).

Auxiliary Resources:

- United States Department of State Country Profile(2003). Retrieved from group data base
- www.governermentguide.com
- University of Texas, Lanic site (2003) Retrieved from group data base http://lanic.utexas.edu/lalcb/other/
- Global Warrior site
- Ferguson, James (1987) *Papa Doc, Baby Doc, Haiti and the Duvaliers*.
- Trouillot, Michel-Rolph (1990) *Haiti State Against Nation*.
- Leyburn, James G. (1980) *The Haitian People*.
- Savain, Roger E. (1993) *Haitian-Kreol in Ten Steps*.
- Ridgeway, James, (1994) *The Haiti Files, Decoding the Crisis*.

- Testimonial interviews from Haitians in Miami-Dade-Broward metro area.
- <*http://www.haiti.org/*>
- *www.cia.gov/* http://www.cia.gov/

INDEX